IMAGES
of America

SPANISH HARLEM'S MUSICAL LEGACY 1930–1980

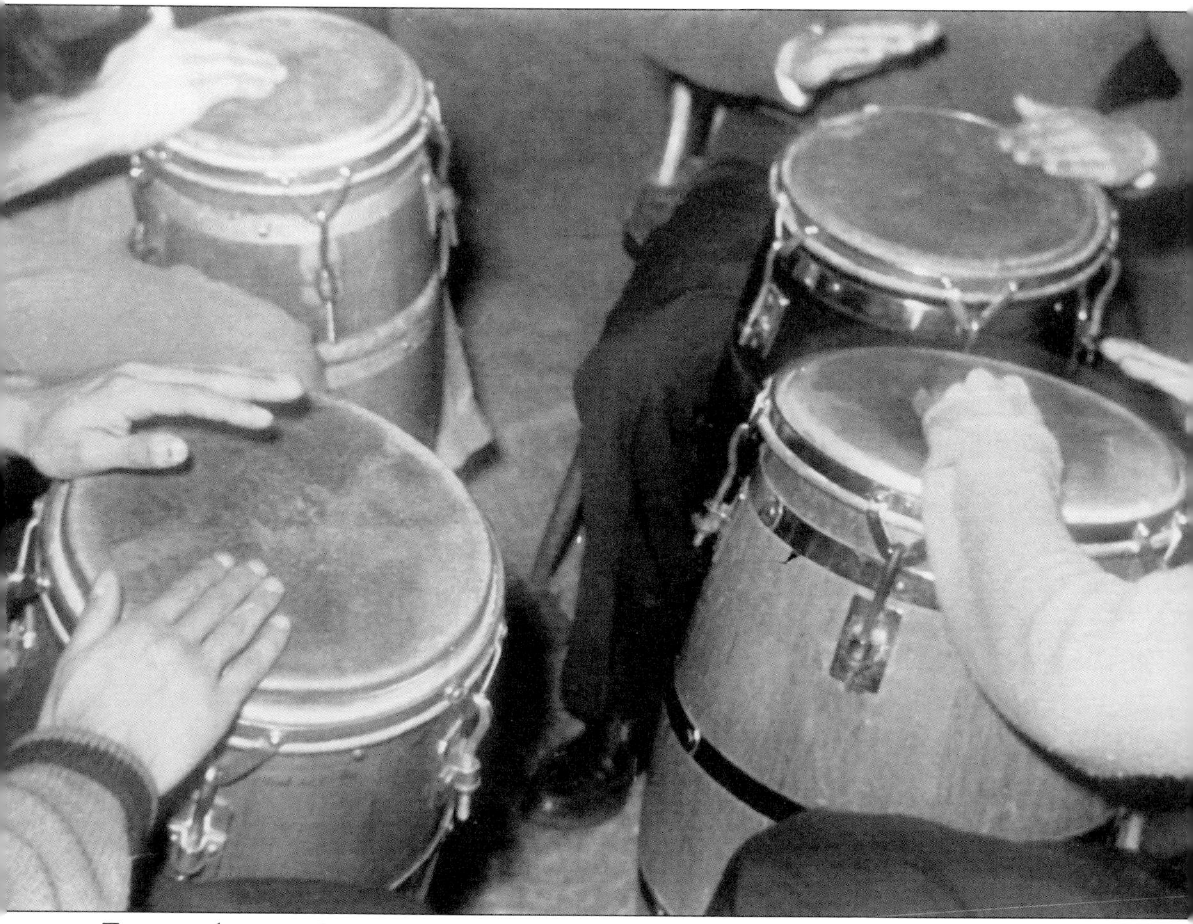

To some observers, Puerto Ricans and Cubans have a propensity for banging out rhythms on a kitchen table or on the side of an automobile. A percussionist can be found in almost every household, eager to bring out his conga drum at a party. This photograph was taken in 1956 in a loft on 19th Street and Sixth Avenue. The loft was rented by three artists who allowed a group of percussionists to use it every Monday evening as a gathering place for jam sessions. The percussionists who participated in these sessions were working musicians who played with many of the top bands of that era. The participants are, from left to right, (first row) John Palomo (Elmo Garcia and Johnny Pacheco Orchestras) and Ray "Little Ray" Romero (Tito Rodriguez and Ray Barretto Orchestras); (second row) Tommy Lopez (Eddie Palmieri and Vicentico Valdes Orchestras) and Papi Paganni (Tito Rodriguez Orchestra).

On the cover: Please see page 26. (Courtesy of author's collection.)

IMAGES
of America

SPANISH HARLEM'S MUSICAL LEGACY 1930–1980

Silvio H. Alava

ARCADIA PUBLISHING

Copyright © 2007 by Silvio H. Alava
ISBN 978-0-7385-5006-0

Published by Arcadia Publishing
Charleston, South Carolina

Printed in the United States of America

Library of Congress Catalog Card Number: 2006940153

For all general information contact Arcadia Publishing at:
Telephone 843-853-2070
Fax 843-853-0044
E-mail sales@arcadiapublishing.com
For customer service and orders:
Toll-Free 1-888-313-2665

Visit us on the Internet at www.arcadiapublishing.com

To my wife, Alicia, who insisted that I organize my large collection of photographs to leave for posterity.

Contents

Acknowledgments 6

Foreword 7

Introduction 9

1. The Immortals 11

2. The Big Three 21

3. The Successors 29

4. The Sidemen 57

ACKNOWLEDGMENTS

I do not think anyone writes a book or article by himself. Ideas are talked about with others, revised and altered many times before the writer feels comfortable in putting his or her name on the document.

I have managed to do this with the help of three important people in my life: my wife, Alicia, and my two daughters, Christina and Felicia. Without their editing and critique, I could not have put together this material with any degree of comprehension.

I also want to thank some individuals who have helped to shape my understanding of music in general and Afro-Caribbean music in particular. Very early in my life, I met George Russell while we were both hospitalized in a Bronx hospital. We were there a year, and George verbally tutored me on the essence of jazz and its language. A composer, arranger, and educator, he has been on the faculty of the New England Conservatory of Music for many years. Early in his career, he arranged music for the Dizzy Gillespie Orchestra before going on to record under his own name. John Palomo, a percussionist I met during my first years of marriage over 53 years ago, helped me get on the right track in understanding Latin music and introduced me to many excellent musicians who added to my knowledge. Rene Lopez, a musicologist, contributed to my knowledge of Cuban music.

And finally thanks to Danilo Lozano, flutist and educator currently on the faculty of Whittier College, whom I met when he was a teenager in California and while I was taking flute lessons from his father, the famous Cuban flutist Rolando Lozano. Rolando started his career playing for the famous Orquesta Aragon. Danilo furthered my technical understanding of Afro-Caribbean music and music in general.

Unless otherwise noted, all photographs used in this book are from the author's collection.

Foreword

I first met Silvio Alava about 20 years ago, when our paths crossed at a salsa music concert in the city of Los Angeles. I had seen this gentleman on previous occasions at various musical events throughout the city, always carrying a camera bag, ready to capture those great musical moments, and on a first name basis with the musicians. Our mutual interest in Latin music subsequently brought us together, forging a friendship that meant sharing information, nostalgia, and history, all related to a passion for everything musical and cultural. On weekends we would get together in our respective homes to discuss the latest records and view his most recent images. Eventually these gatherings led to something very special in our lives.

During the summer of 1990, Silvio, my wife, Yvette, and I began researching what would develop into *Latin Beat Magazine*, a music publication dedicated to the world of Latin music. On January 1, 1991, we launched the first issue of the magazine, which this year celebrates its 16th year as a publication.

A native of New York City's Spanish Harlem, Silvio lived and was a part of Spanish Harlem's musical legacy. From the legendary Palladium days of the 1940s and 1950s, which showcased the music of Machito and His Afro Cubans as well as the musical battles between the two Titos (Puente and Rodriguez), to the birth of Latin jazz, the early days of the Fania Records dynasty (with Johnny Pacheco, Willie Colon, and Hector Lavoe), and the percussive jam sessions of Tito Puente, Mongo Santamaria, Willie Bobo, and Ray Barretto, Silvio Alava has documented decades of Latin history through illuminating, distinctive images he has captured with a discerning eye.

Rudy Mangual
publisher/editor of *Latin Beat Magazine*

Introduction

Spanish Harlem's musical legacy started between the 1930s and 1980s, in an area the size of a village in New York City. This area was called "El Barrio" or "Spanish Harlem," where musicians from the Caribbean and their descendants began organizing musical groups, thereby adding to the diaspora that began in Africa and Spain. The music we now call salsa had its roots in Cuba, Puerto Rico, and Santo Domingo and continued developing on another island called Manhattan.

During the early 1930s, bands under the direction of Antonio Machin, Enrique Madriguera, and Xavier Cugat dominated the music scene principally because they were all white men. They played in segregated hotels frequented by the upper class. These talented men did not champion racism; they tried to make a living in the society around them. Cugat employed both Miguelito Valdes and Frank "Machito" Grillo during their early years in the United States. As I grew up in New York City, I began to attend dances and concerts throughout the city and learned about the early discrimination that occurred in places like the Taft Hotel and the Hotel Diplomat.

The images shown here are but a small portion of the musicians that shaped the music of this era with their unique styles and personalities. Many artists are omitted here either because I did not have my camera when I went to see them play or because I was too young to enter the venues where they appeared. I am not writing biographical notes on these individuals because the Internet and Google can do a better job than I. I am not writing from the viewpoint of a musicologist because I do not have the knowledge or musical training. I am writing from the viewpoint of an aficionado who followed some of these pioneers around in clubs and concerts with my camera because I loved, felt, and understood the language of the music. In the process, I got to know a few of them personally.

I purchased my first 35mm rangefinder camera in 1954 for about $50, paying for it $5 a week. A kind distributor in the building where I worked allowed me this privilege. Therefore, none of my images are before this date. I took all these early photographs without a flash using Kodak Tri-X 400 ASA film, hoping to capture a more realistic and moody feeling. I have since upgraded my camera and occasionally use a flash to fill in when I am photographing in low-light areas.

About that same time I met John Palomo, who became a lifelong friend. We were both recently married and starting to raise families. John was a young percussionist at that time, beginning to learn his craft and working with some of the lesser-known Latin bands in New York City. His wife and mine were related by marriage, thus giving me the opportunity to accompany him on many of his jobs. Because of this I was able to attend many dances and concerts "gratis" by just carrying his conga drum and, of course, my camera. Through John, I was able to socialize with many of the subjects in the photographs of this book and gain knowledge of the music through informal conversations between breaks or at social gatherings. I also learned that a young musician's life was full of hard work, disappointments, and meager pay.

Of special note is a year I spent with a group of percussionists. Together with two other painters, we rented a loft on Sixth Avenue (now known as Avenue of the Americas). On Monday nights, John Palomo, Ray "Little Ray" Romero, and I hosted jam sessions in the loft. These sessions served as an informal classroom for many of the participants, including this author. It was here that I learned the essence of the Cuban rumba and guaguanco rhythms and the importance of the clave, the very important pulse essential in this music.

During my lifetime I have lived on both coasts of the United States and have photographed many of these same artists when they appeared in Los Angeles. During the 1960s through the 1980s, Los Angeles became a logical visit for all the bands that went on tour. Many musicians who began their careers in New York moved to Los Angeles because of the abundance of work that became available due to the popularity of salsa music.

I hope this book will be a historical documentation of some of the musical figures who pioneered this music for the next generation of music lovers.

—Silvio H. Alava

One

The Immortals

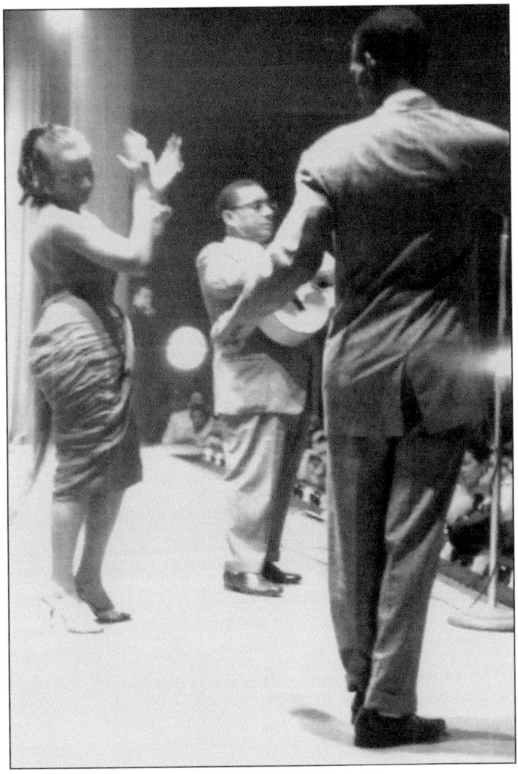

Celia Cruz is shown here at the Manhattan Center in 1959 with La Sonora Matancera. This was a reunion for them since their departure from Cuba earlier in the decade. Pictured with her are Rogelio Martinez on guitar and Carlos "Caito" Diaz with maracas.

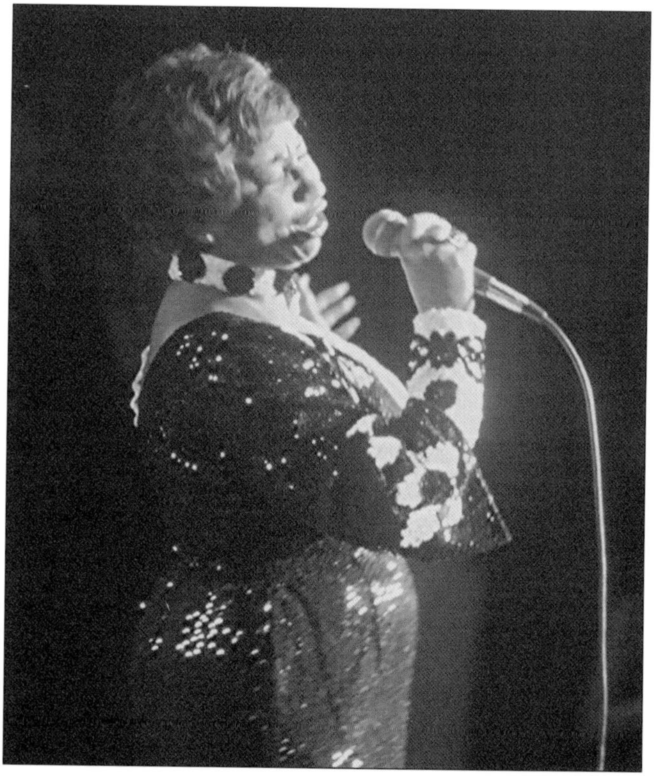

Celia Cruz visited Los Angeles frequently, appearing at the Hollywood Palladium, the Los Angeles Sports Arena, and other venues. She is shown here in 1979 at the sports arena, where she was accompanied by the Tito Puente Orchestra.

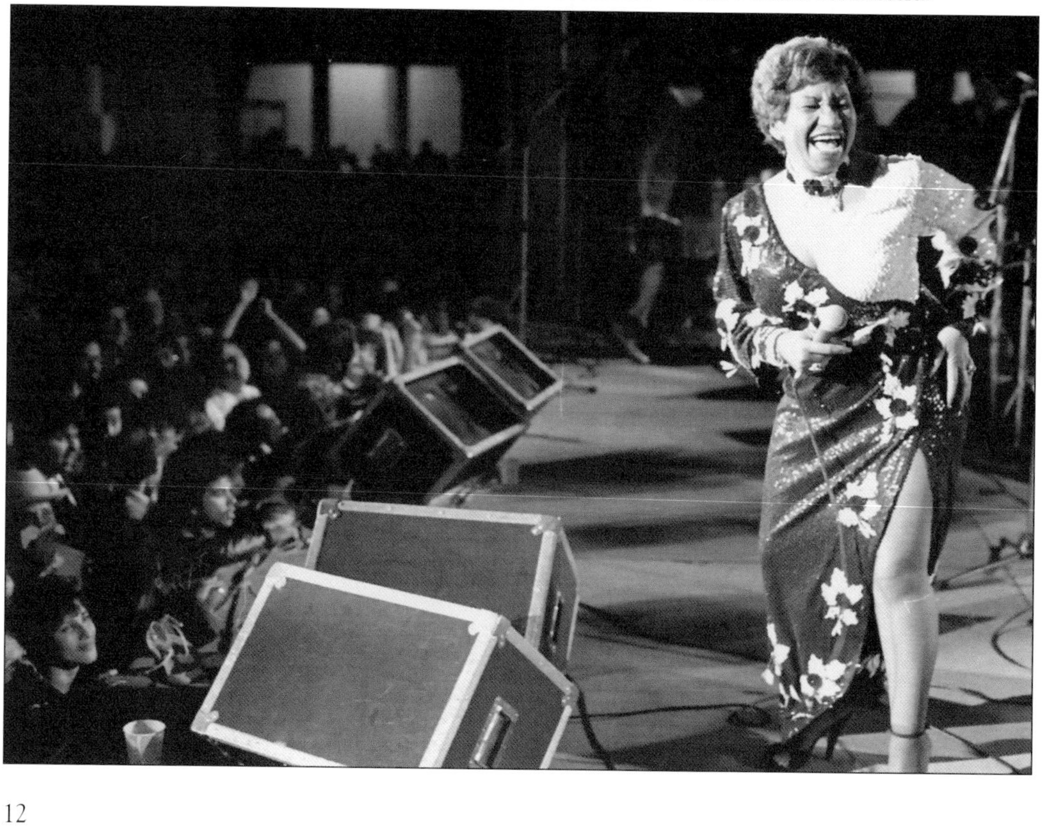

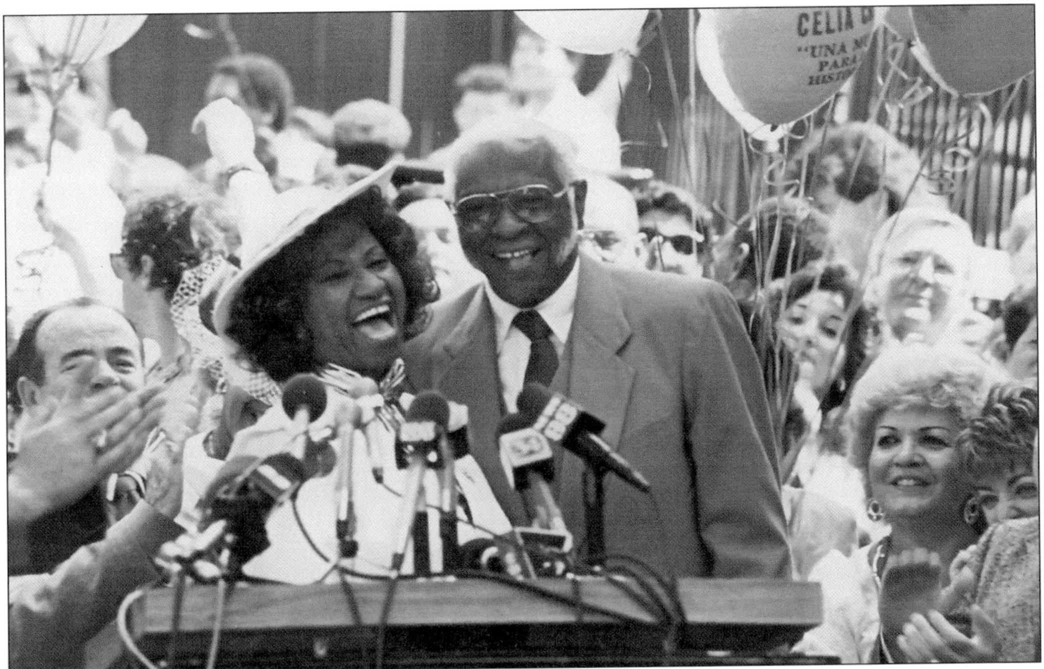

Cruz and her husband, Pedro Knight, are pictured here when she received her star in 1989 on the Hollywood Walk of Fame.

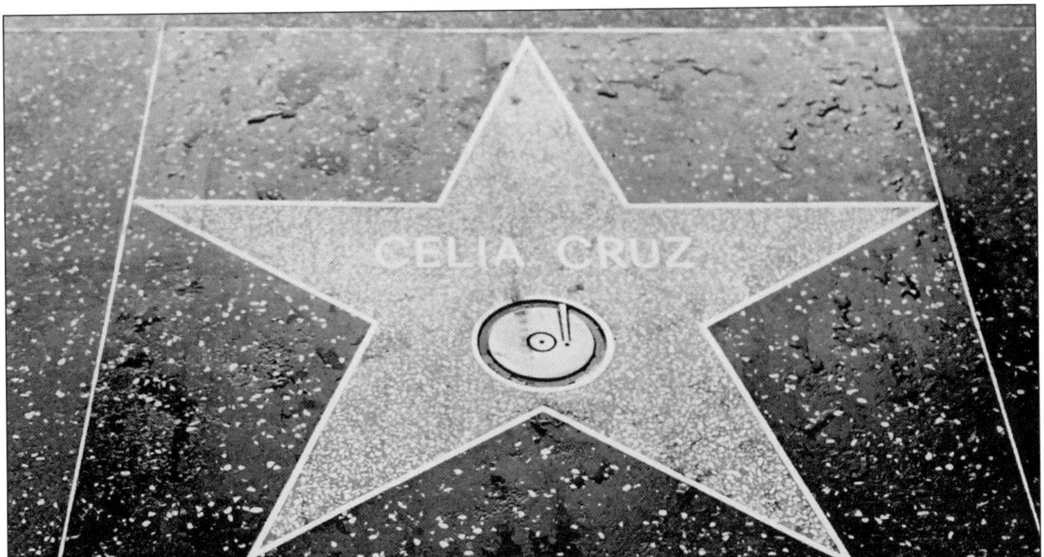

This is Cruz's star that appears on Hollywood Boulevard in Los Angeles.

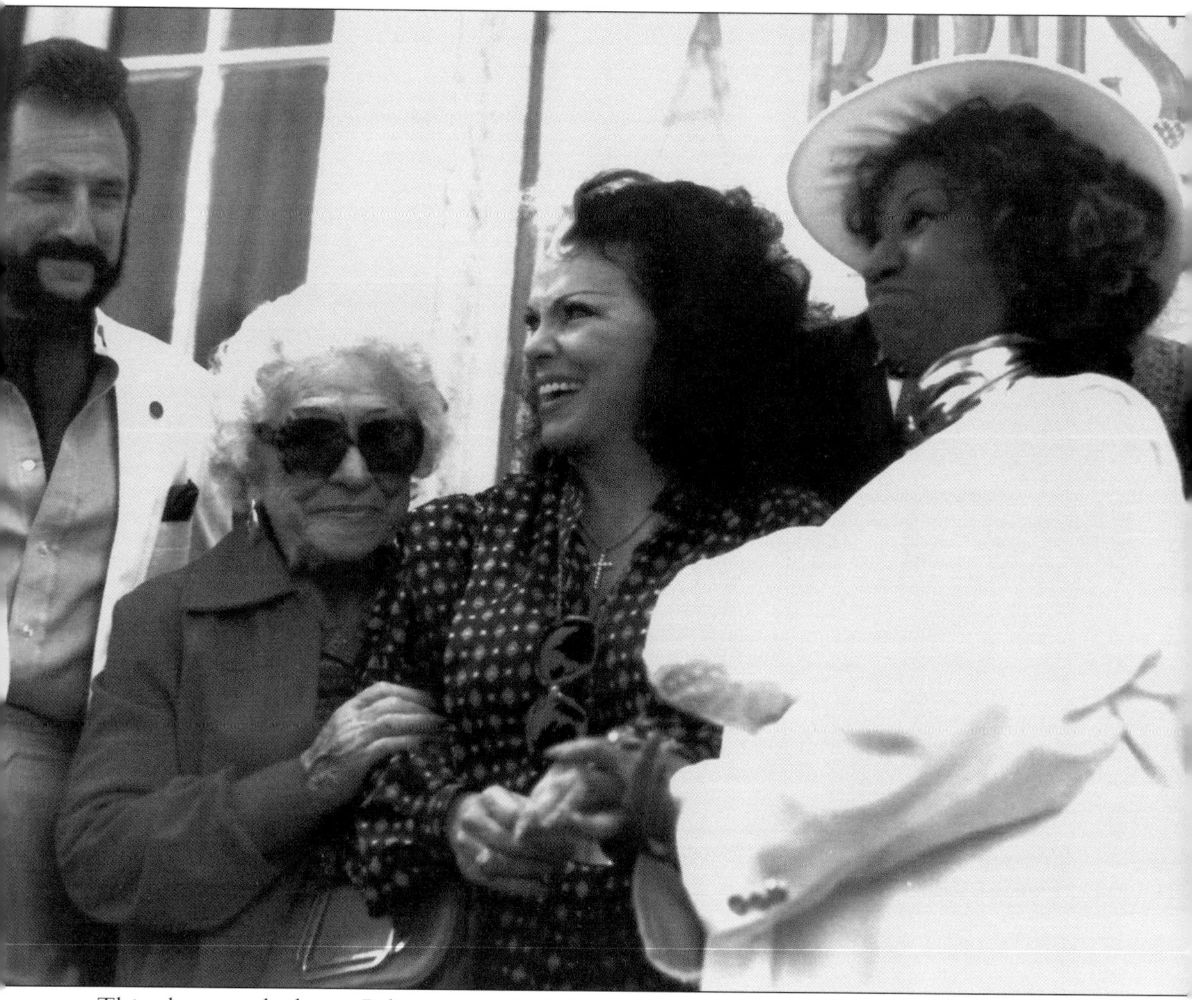

This photograph shows Celia Cruz with Yolanda Montes, known professionally as "Tongolele," when she attended Cruz's Hollywood star ceremony. Born in Spokane, Washington, of a Spanish/Swedish father and an English/French mother, Montes became a professional dancer at the age of 15 and worked in the Mexican film industry from the 1940s to the 1980s. She and Cruz were lifelong friends.

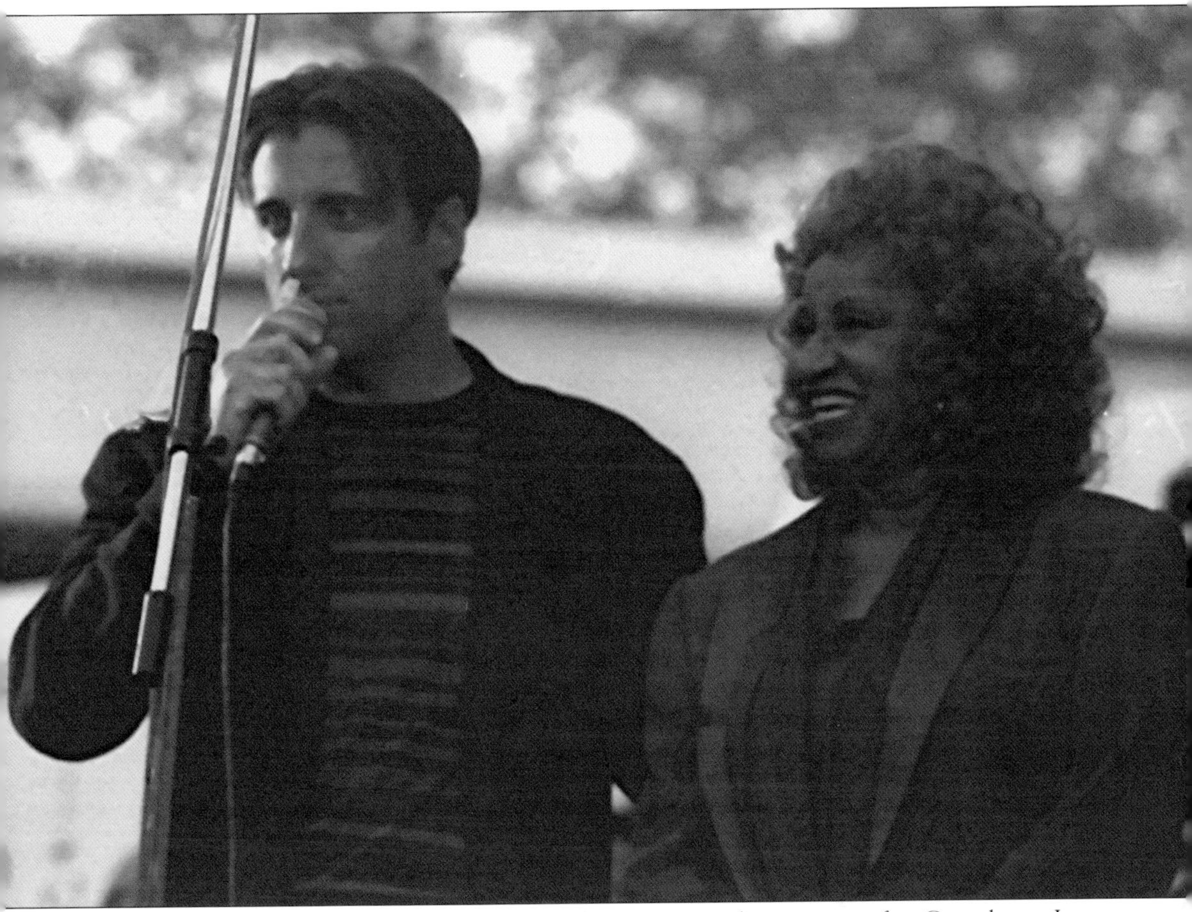

Film star Andy Garcia is seen here in 1986 at an award ceremony for Cruz by a Los Angeles–based Cuban social club.

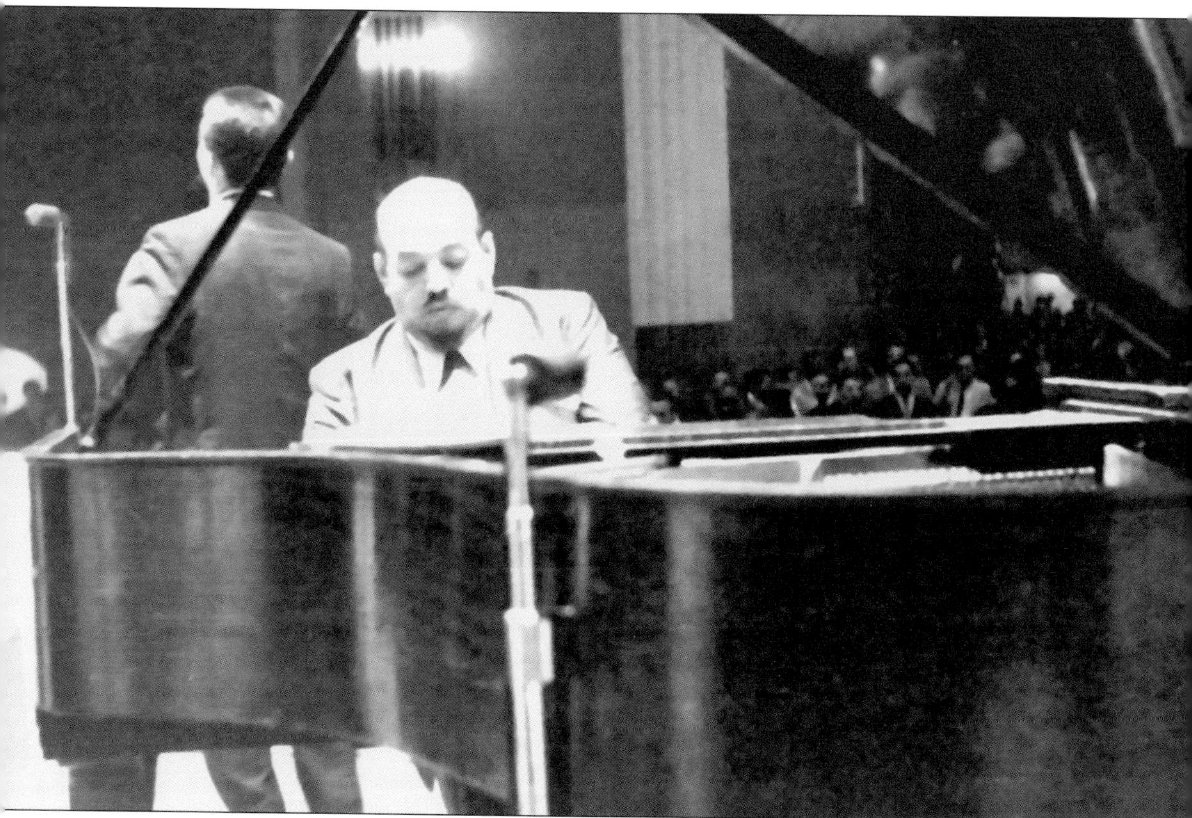

Pianist Noro Morales was one of the first Puerto Rican musicians to move to New York City. He arrived in 1935 and gained fame almost immediately playing with the top bands of the city. An accomplished pianist, Morales formed his own orchestra in the early 1940s and toured the United States as well as Latin America. He employed many prominent musicians and arrangers of that era. Morales moved back to Puerto Rico in 1960 due to ill health and for a few years lead a band and worked at La Concha Hotel. He died in San Juan in 1964. Morales influenced many of the pianists who followed him. Among them was Charlie Palmieri.

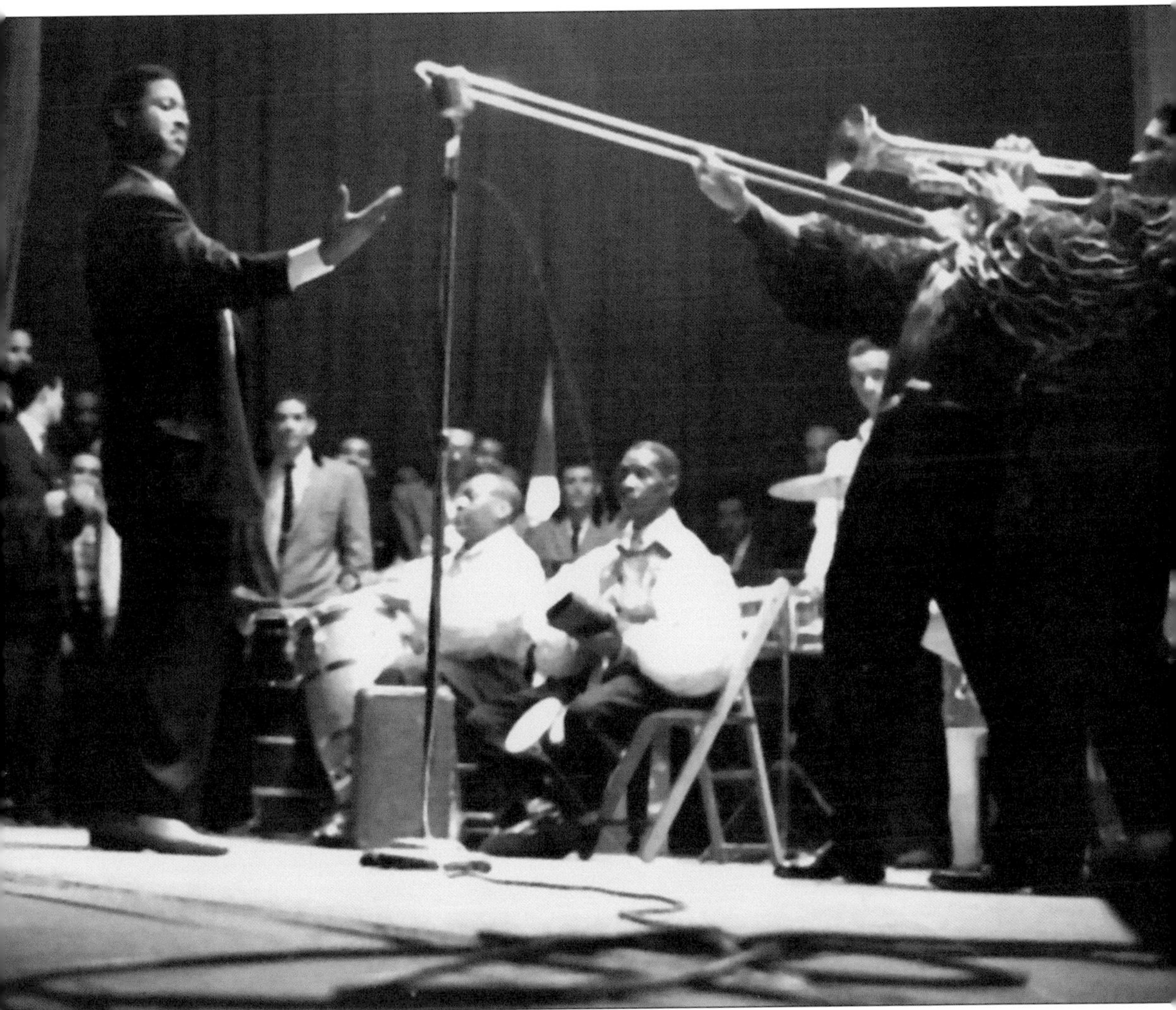

Beny Moré is leading his great orchestra. He danced in a unique style and led the band with his whole body, inventing riffs as he sang to the saxophone section, then another riff to the trombone section, and yet another riff for the trumpet section. The buildup of excitement was unbearable and caused the audience to scream in ecstasy.

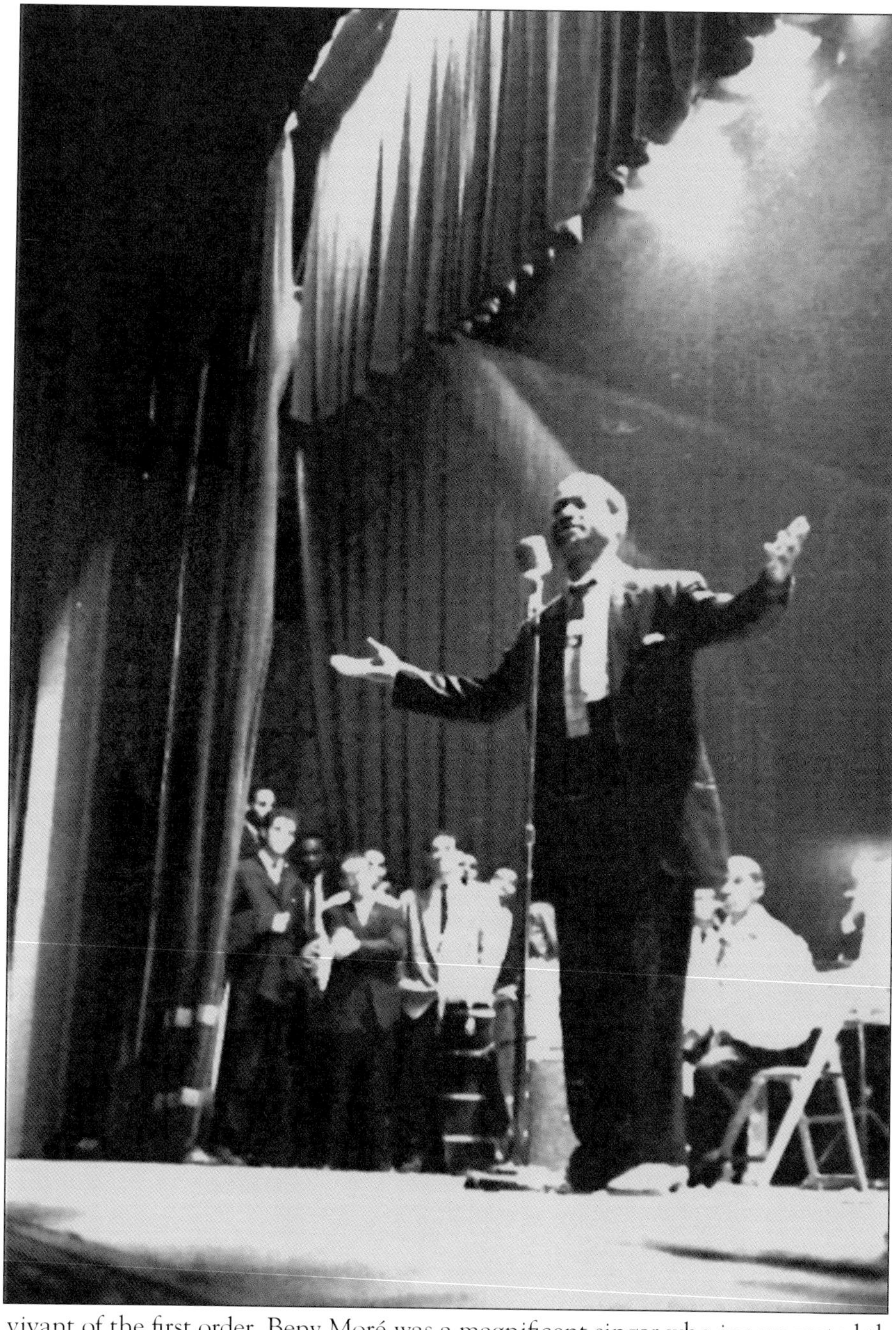

A bon vivant of the first order, Beny Moré was a magnificent singer who incorporated the Afro Cuban son and the guajira in his style to become one of Cuba's greatest singers. He started as a street singer until he was discovered by one of the singers of the Conjunto Matamoros. He was soon touring with them to Mexico and decided to stay there because of the abundance of work in the movie and recording industry. These photographs were all taken at the St. Nicholas Arena in New York City in 1959, the year Fidel Castro became prime minister of Cuba. Moré brought his whole band accompanied by bearded bodyguards in army fatigues to perform at a fund-raiser for the new Cuban government.

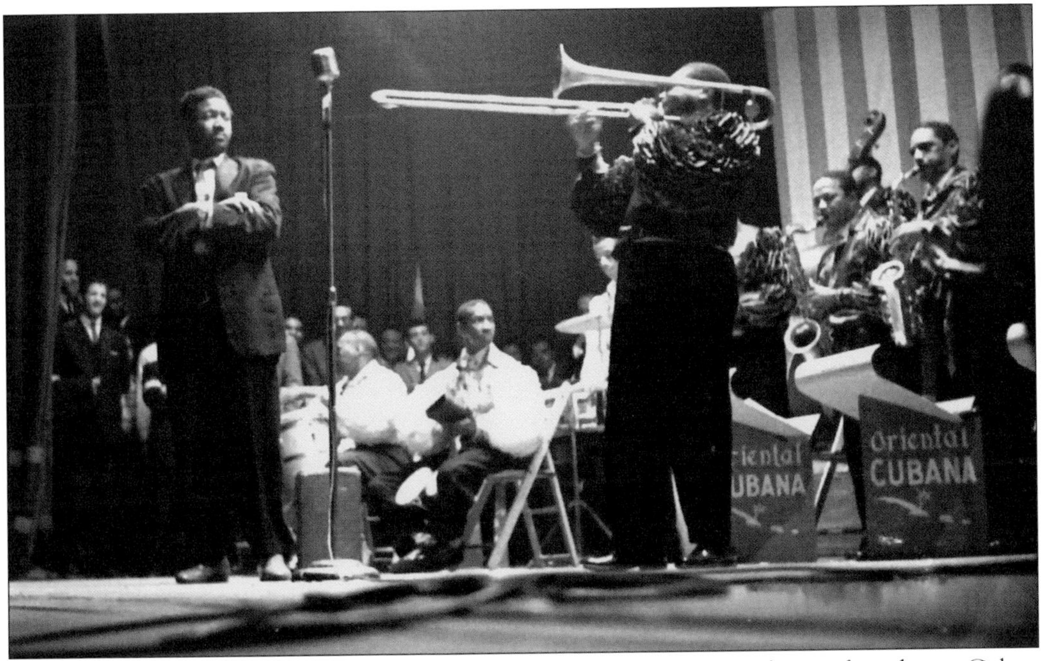

A notorious drinker of rum, Moré once serenaded the author's wife and some friends in a Cuban restaurant on 53rd Street and Ninth Avenue called El Liborio. She had gone to a dance earlier in the day to see Moré perform, but he never appeared for the performance. The group decided to go to this restaurant for a snack and there was Moré quite drunk, singing love songs for free to a group of teenagers. The author's wife said, "what came out of his mouth was pure joy." When Moré died in 1963 of cirrhosis, an estimated 100,000 fans attended his funeral in Cuba. He was only 46 years old.

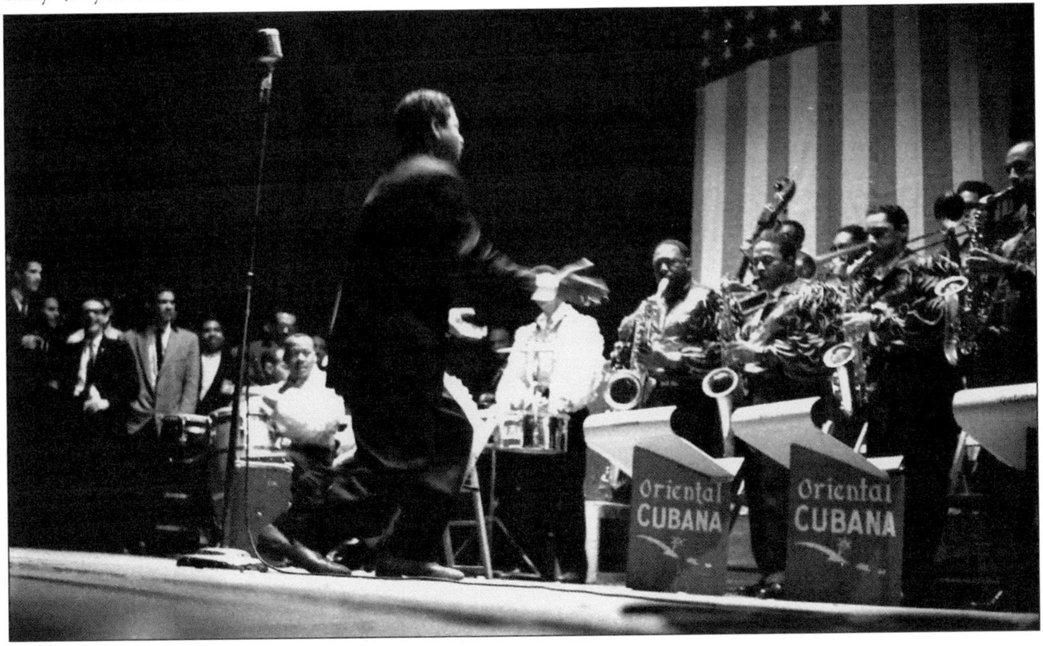

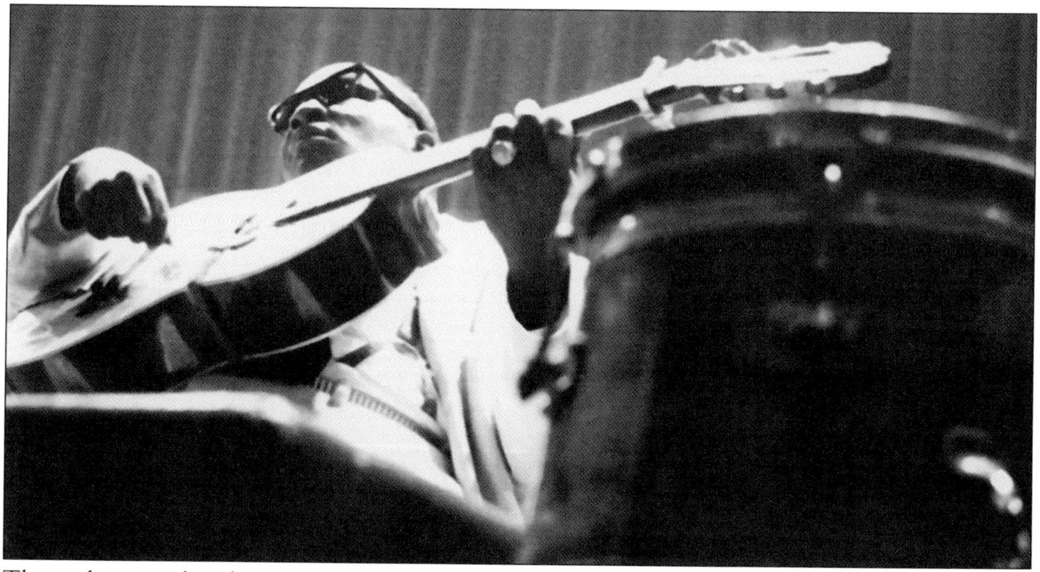

These photographs of Arsenio Rodriguez were taken in New York City in 1959 in a dance hall in midtown Manhattan. Many musicians who played this genre of music held this man from Cuba in high esteem for the important contributions he made to the development of the conjunto style. His compositions have become standard material in many bands. For a musician who had no musical training, his playing was rough but inventive and his solos dazzling. Arsenio is pictured here in his customary white suit with the wide pants he liked to wear. Arsenio and his brother Raul moved to Los Angeles in the early 1970s. He often spoke about the racial discrimination that black people had to endure in Cuba, but he also mentioned the close camaraderie he enjoyed with many of the well-known white musicians of that era. One of these gentlemen was the flutist Antonio Arcaño, who led the famous *charanga* "Arcaño y Sus Maravillas." According to Aresenio's brother Raul, Arcaño looked out for Arsenio by insisting that anyone who wanted his band had to hire Arsenio as well. It seems that Arcaño was way ahead of his time in the civil rights struggle. Arsenio died penniless in Los Angeles in 1971.

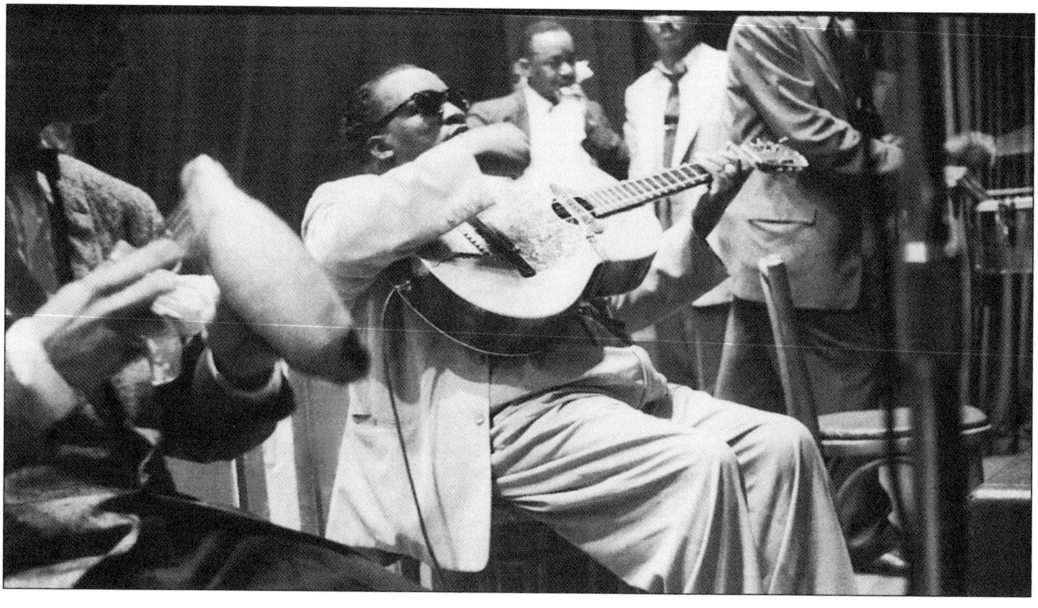

Two

THE BIG THREE

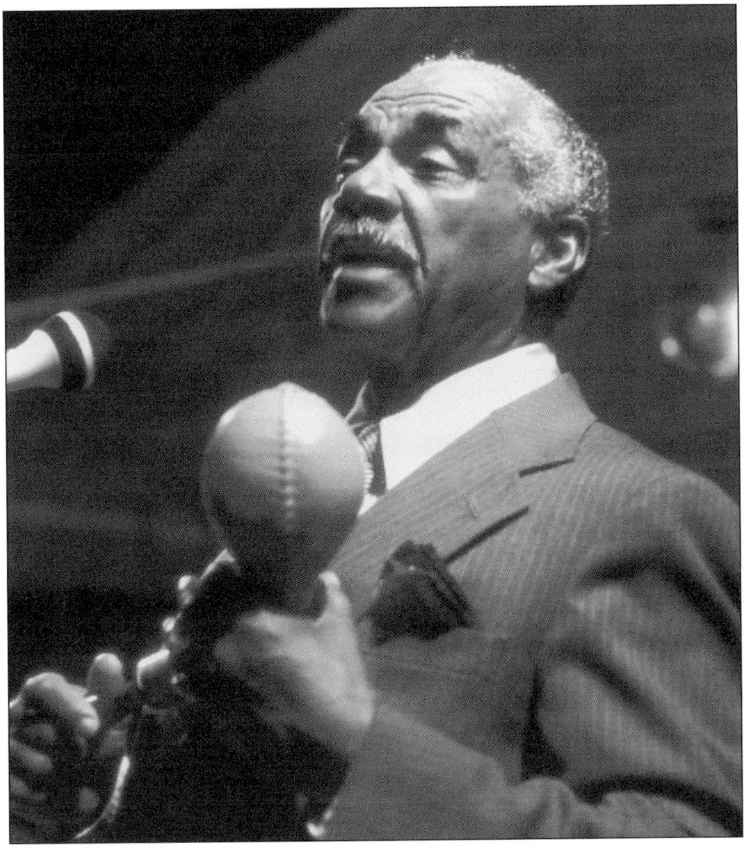

Frank "Machito" Grillo, the impeccable singer, maraca player, and gentleman, settled in New York City in the mid-1930s and became the quintessential bandleader of Machito and His Afro-Cubans, one of the best Latin orchestras ever assembled. He is shown here in the early 1980s at the Casablanca Ballroom in Los Angeles.

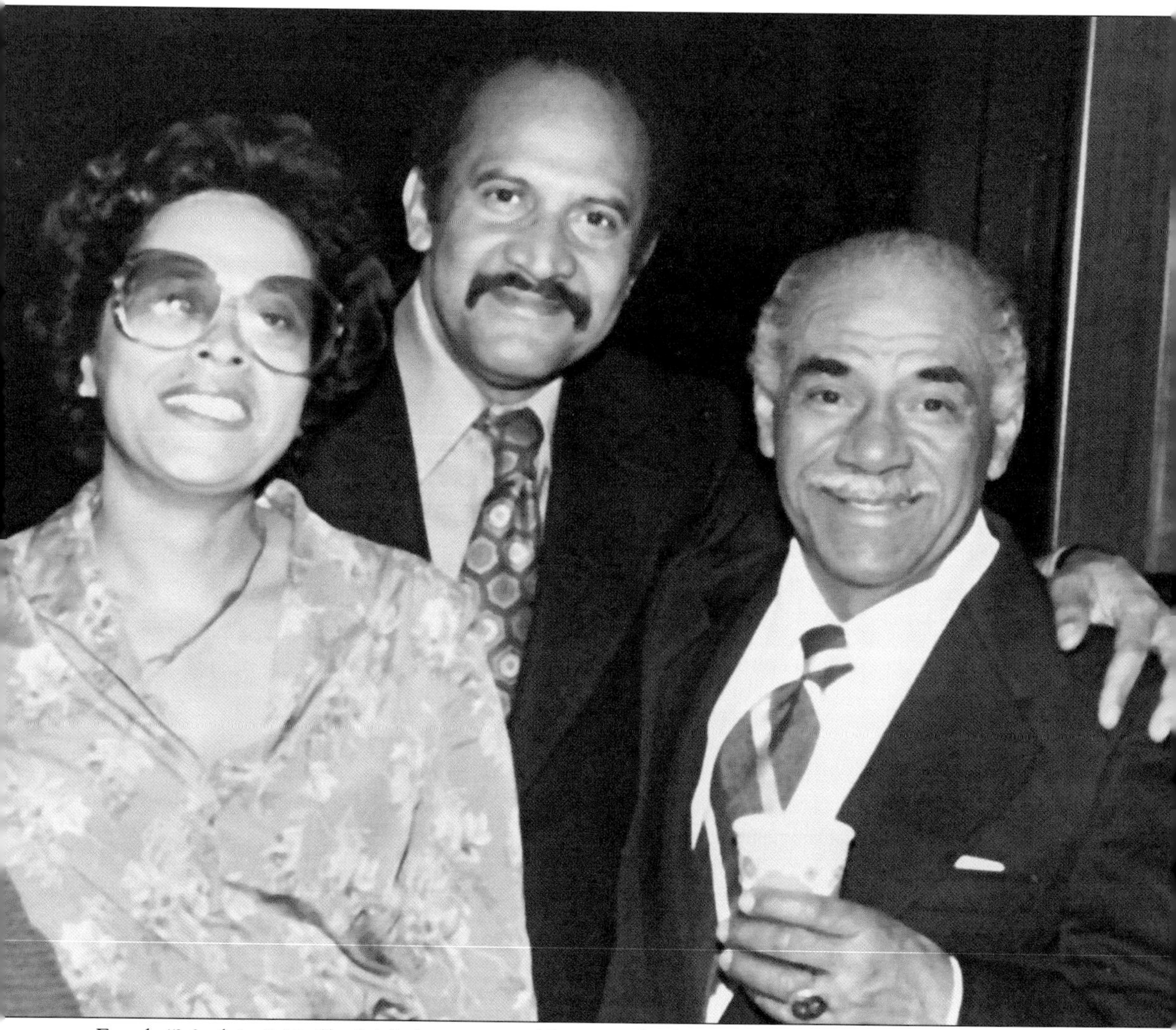

Frank "Machito" Grillo (right) is pictured here with the author and his wife, Alicia, backstage at the Casablanca Ballroom in 1983.

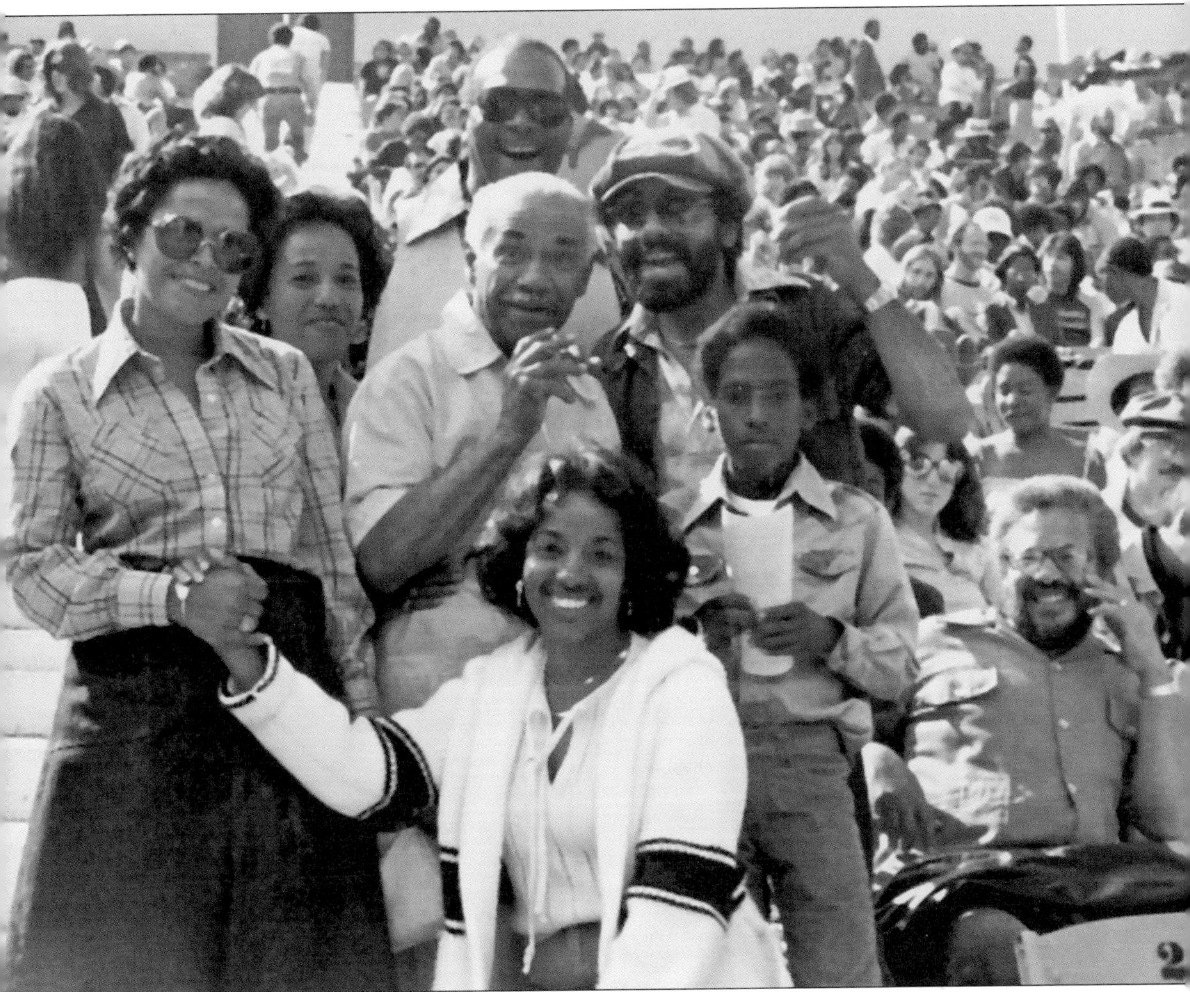

Machito greets old friends from Spanish Harlem at a concert in San Diego in 1987. Pictured here, from left to right, are the following: (first row) Anna Adorno, Dwayne Matos, and Bill Adorno (seated); (second row) Alicia Alava, Mary Matos, Machito, the late Tony Matos, and Tommy Martinez.

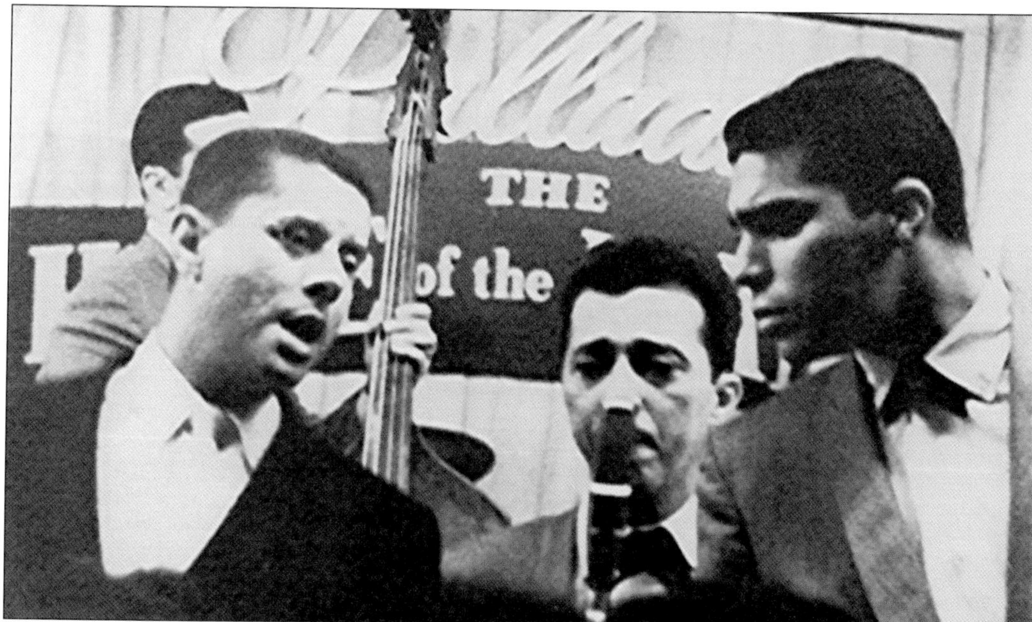

Taken in 1959 at the New York Palladium, this photograph shows, from left to right, Tito Puente, Bobby Rodriguez (on bass behind Puente), Santito Colon (vocalist), and Chickie Perez (percussion).

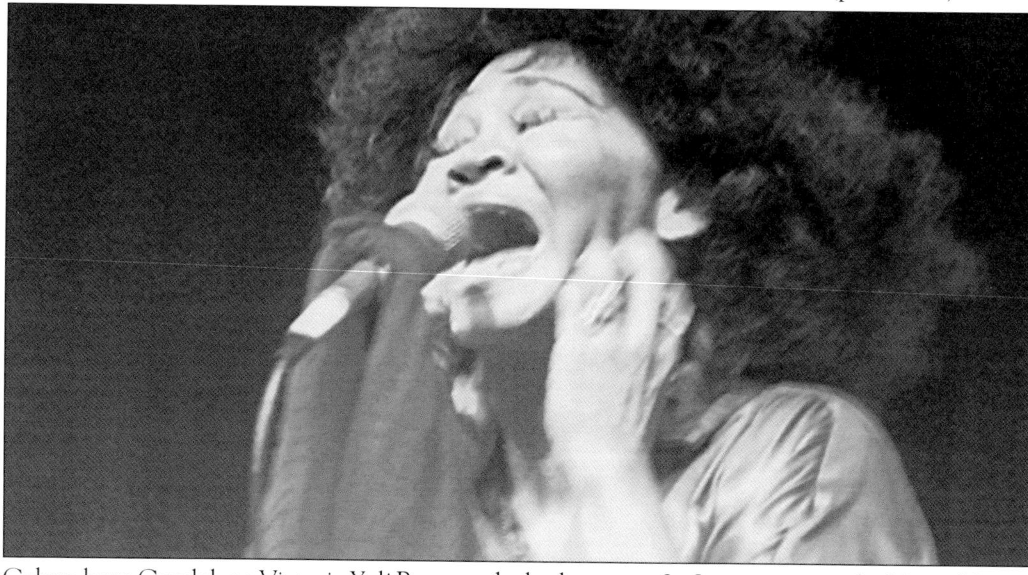

Cuban-born Guadalupe Victoria Yoli Raymond, also known as La Lupe, came to the United States in 1962. She had to leave Cuba because her expressive performances full of sexual suggestions embarrassed the revolutionary Castro government. Discovered by Mongo Santamaria in a small club in Manhattan, La Lupe went on to record many albums for the Tico and Fania labels. Her debut album was recorded in 1963 with Mongo Santamaria on the Milestone label with an all-star group of the best musicians in New York City. She became the reining queen of Latin singers of the late 1960s due to her recordings with Tito Puente. When her contract was terminated in the late 1970s, she became very ill and had difficulties getting employment. She died in 1992 and is interred in St. Raymond's Cemetery in the Bronx. This photograph was taken at the Hollywood Palladium, where she appeared with the Tito Puente Orchestra in 1975.

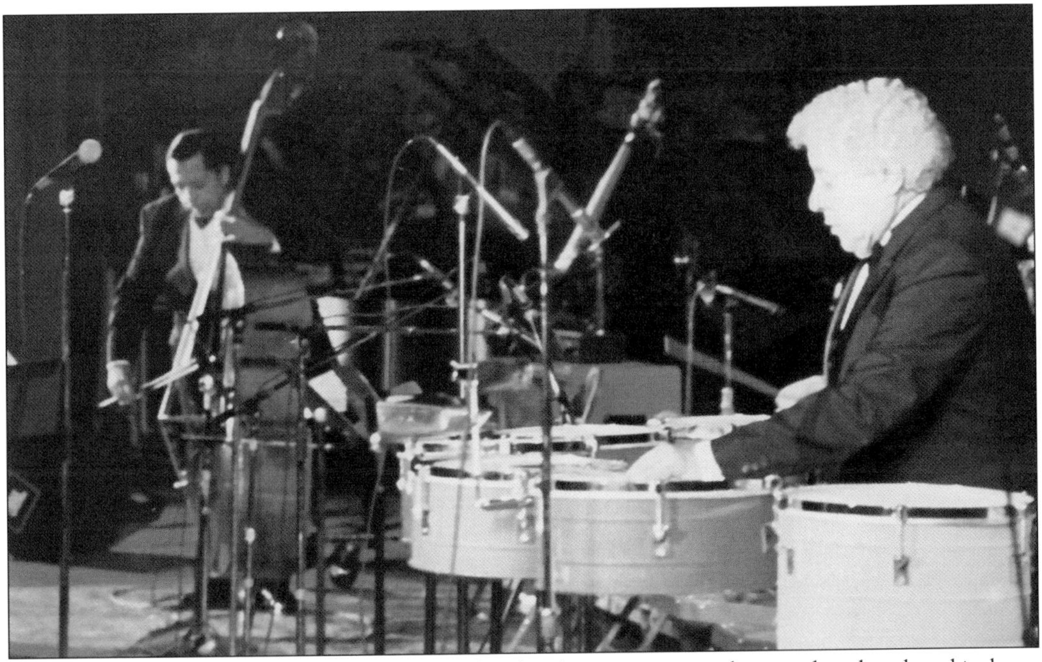

Puente was a phenomenal timbale player and utilized as many as six drums when he played in large shows. In this photograph, he is exhibiting his virtuosity at Hunter College in Manhattan during a 1985 concert in which he appeared with Israel "Cachao" Lopez, shown here playing bass.

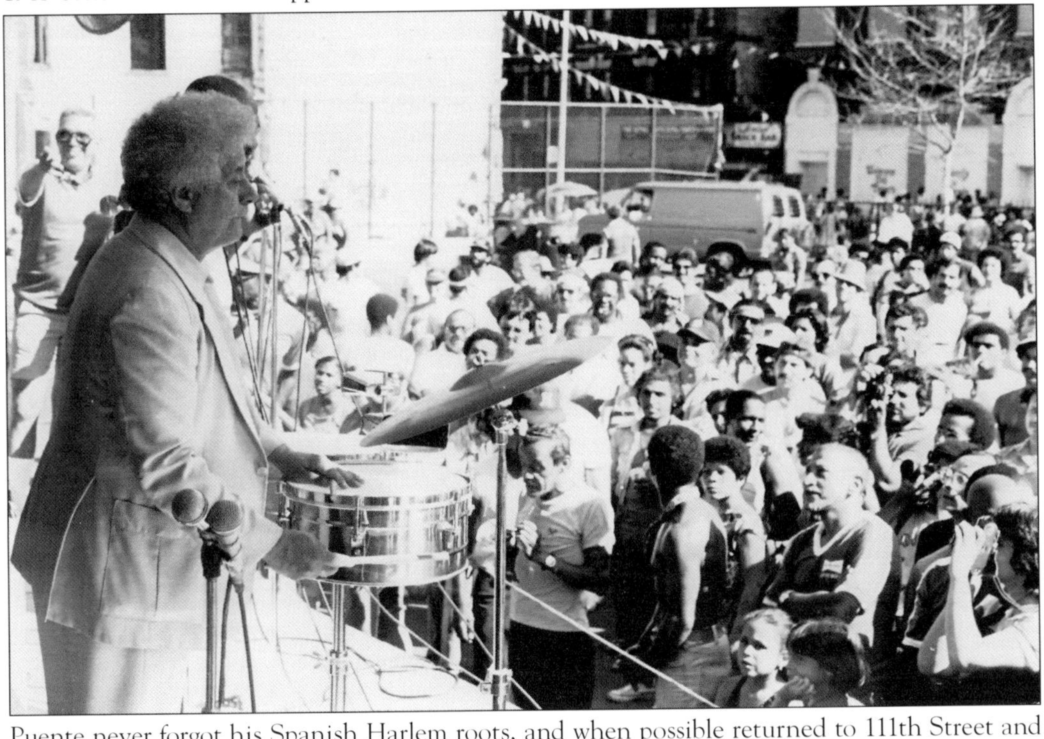

Puente never forgot his Spanish Harlem roots, and when possible returned to 111th Street and Fifth Avenue for the annual July Old-Timers Reunion celebration. Here he is in 1995, playing in the school courtyard.

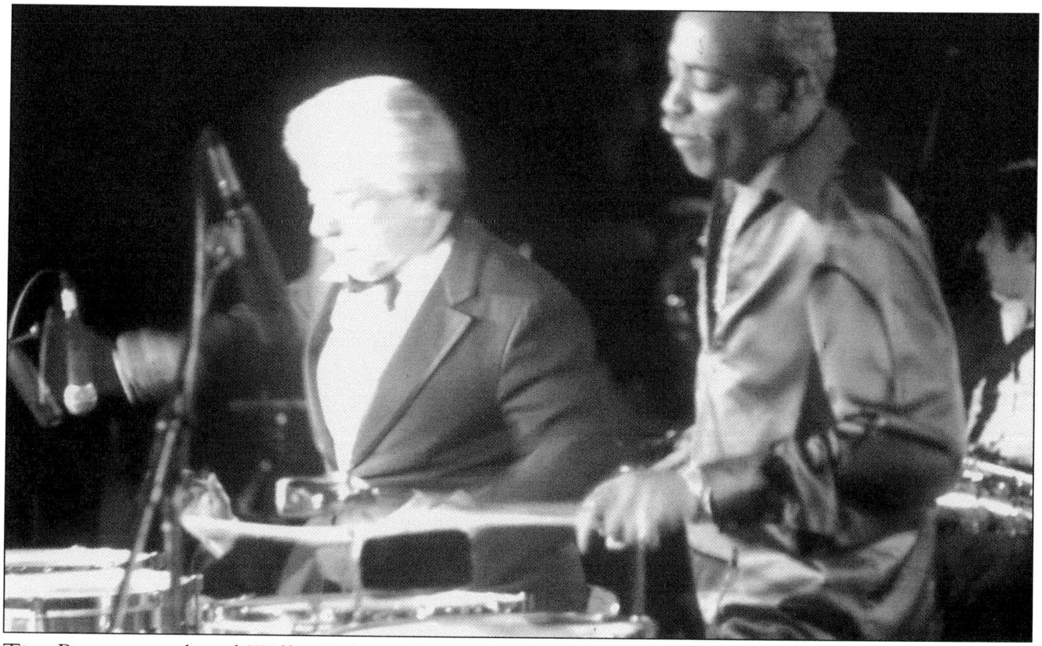

Tito Puente employed Willie Bobo in his orchestra in the mid-1950s. In three of Puente's most popular recordings, "Cuban Fantasy" (1955), "Top Percussion" (1957), and "Cuban Carnival" (1955), Bobo showed his exceptional talent. Puente always showcased new talent in his orchestra and used Francisco Aguabella, Candido Camero, Carlos "Patato" Valdez, and Mongo Santamaria in the aforementioned recordings. Bobo and Puente are dueling timbal solos in this photograph taken at a concert/dance in 1979 at the Los Angeles Sports Arena.

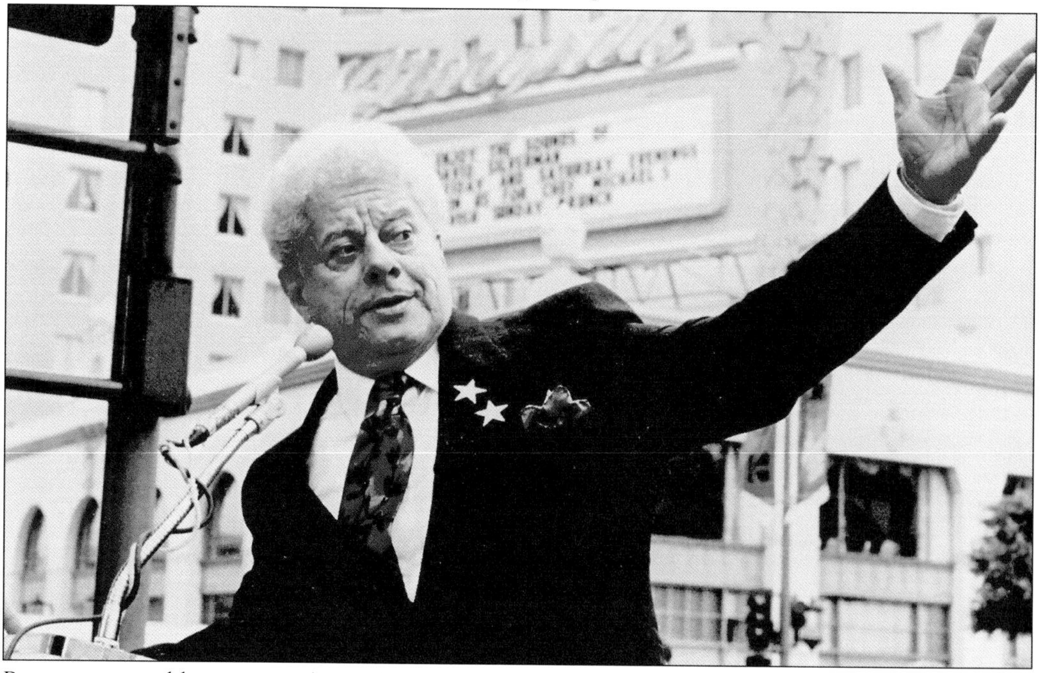

Puente received his star on the Hollywood Walk of Fame in 1990. He is shown here waving to his many fans.

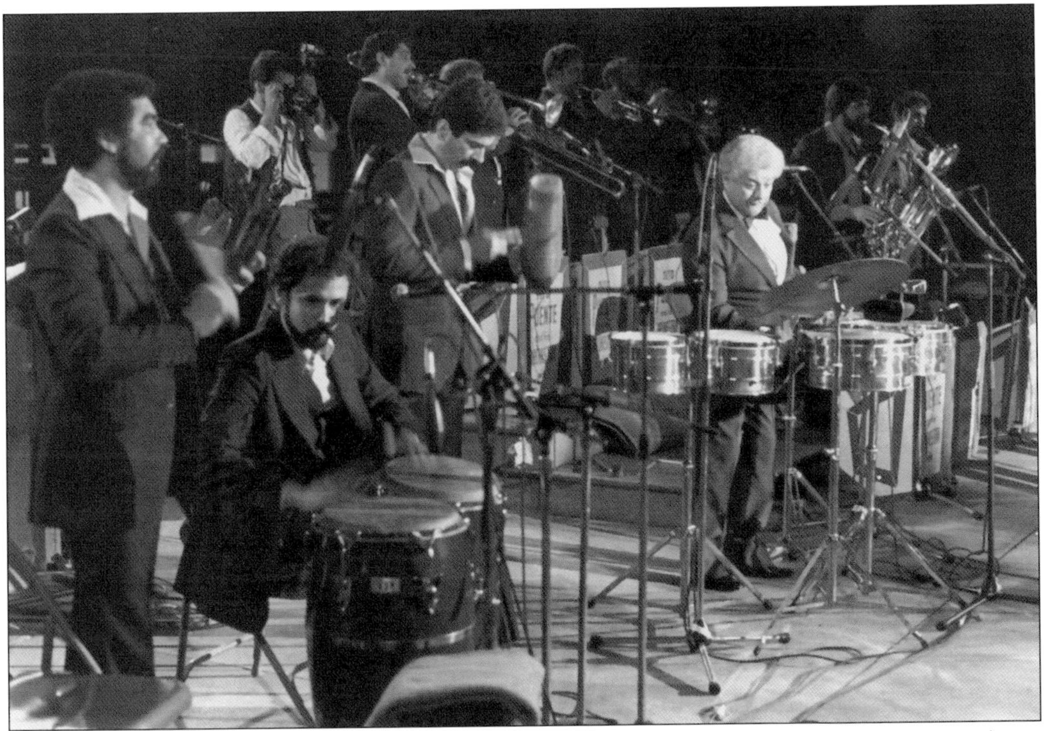

These two images were taken at the Los Angeles Sports Arena in 1979. Ernest Anthony Puente Jr. died in May 2000 in New York City.

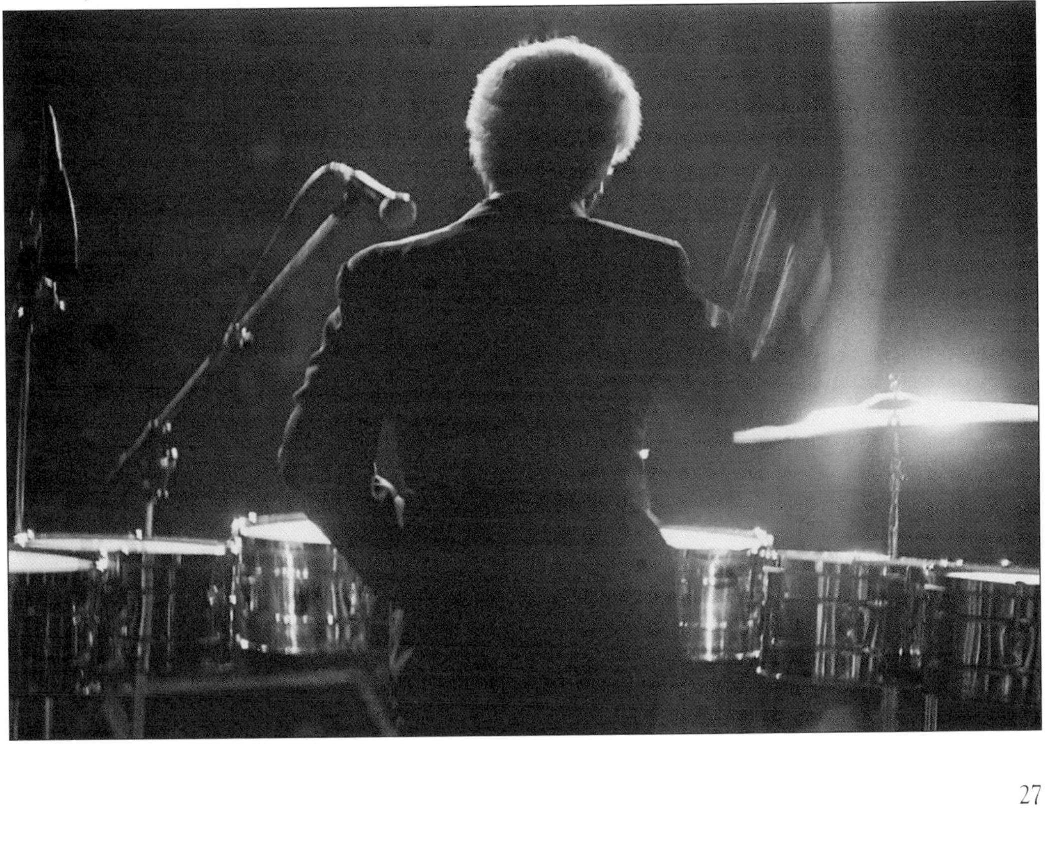

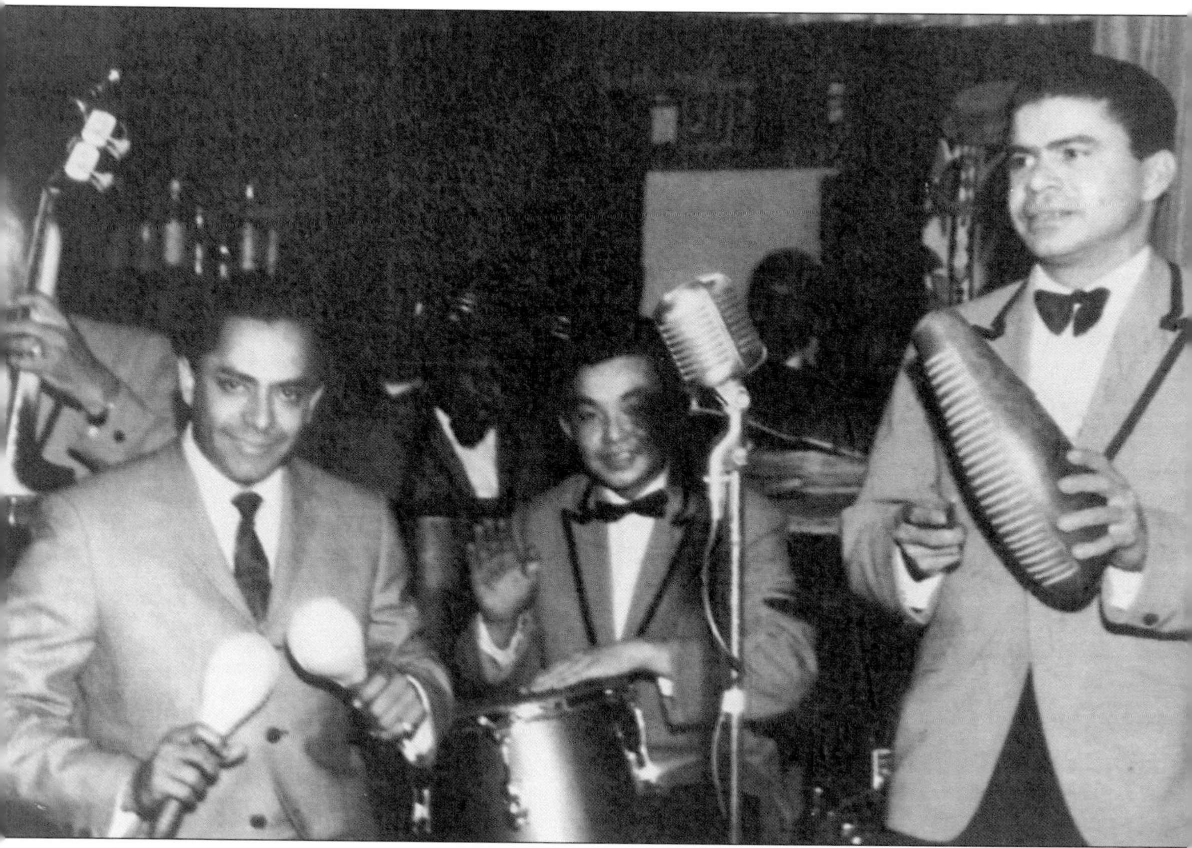

Shown from left to right are Julio Andino (bass), Tito Rodriguez (maracas), Tommy Saito (conga), and Vitin Gonzalez (quiro). This photograph is from the private collection of Saito. It was taken in October 1962 at the Boom Boom Club in Los Angeles. Some music fans are of the opinion that during the golden era of the Palladium in New York City, Rodriguez had the "swingiest" band of all. Perhaps this came from the love that Rodriguez had for Cuban music, especially the guaguanco form. Rodriguez's other great attraction was to the female audience. Blessed with exceedingly good looks, he had female admirers standing in front of the bandstand everywhere he played. Born in Santurce, Puerto Rico, into a musical family, Rodriguez left the island as a teenager to find his fortune in New York City. Talented both as a singer and percussionist, he quickly found work with Enrique Madriguera and Xavier Cugat. He formed his own band in the late 1940s and continued working until his death in February 1973. (Courtesy Tommy Saito photograph archives.)

Three

The Successors

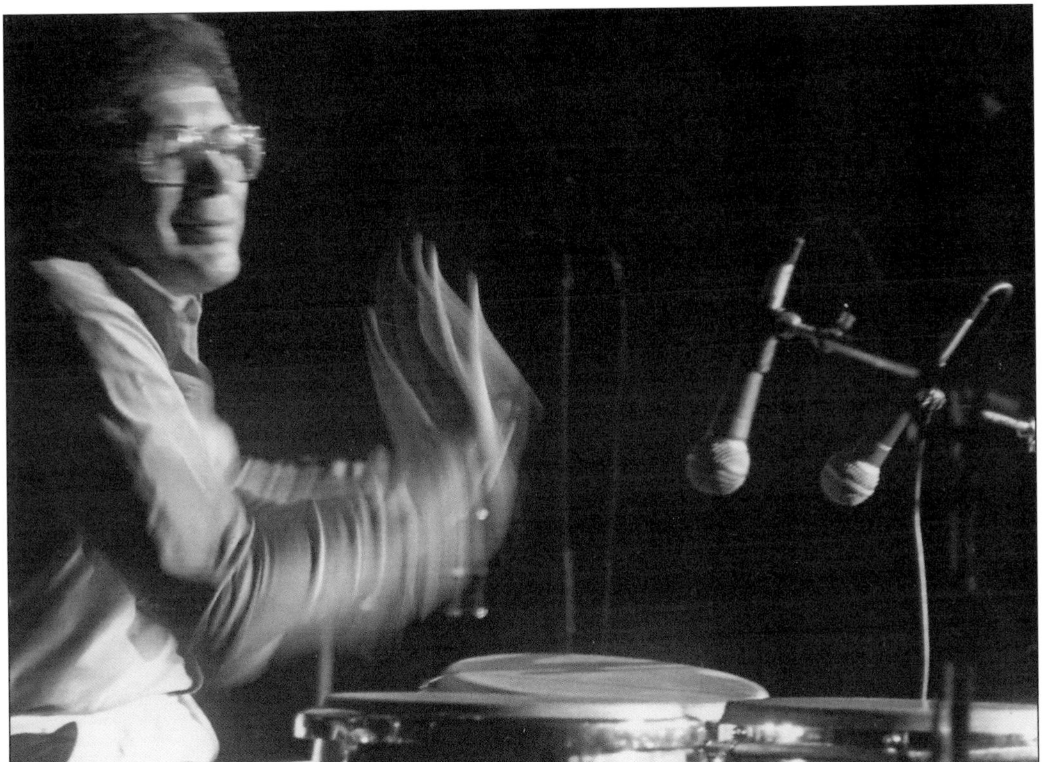

Besides the power he had on conga drums, Ray Barretto's ability to organize great orchestras was most evident. Since the early 1960s when he began playing with the Tito Puente organization, his strength was obvious, hence his nickname "Las Manos Duras" (hard hands). But his talent for employing talented musicians can be heard in albums like *Indestructible,* released in 1973, and *Rican/Struction*, released in 1979. The arrangements by Oscar Hernandez, Eddie Martinez, Gil Lopez, and Dick Meza are excellent examples of big band salsa music. His fast hands were captured at a concert at the Los Angeles Sports Arena in late 1979.

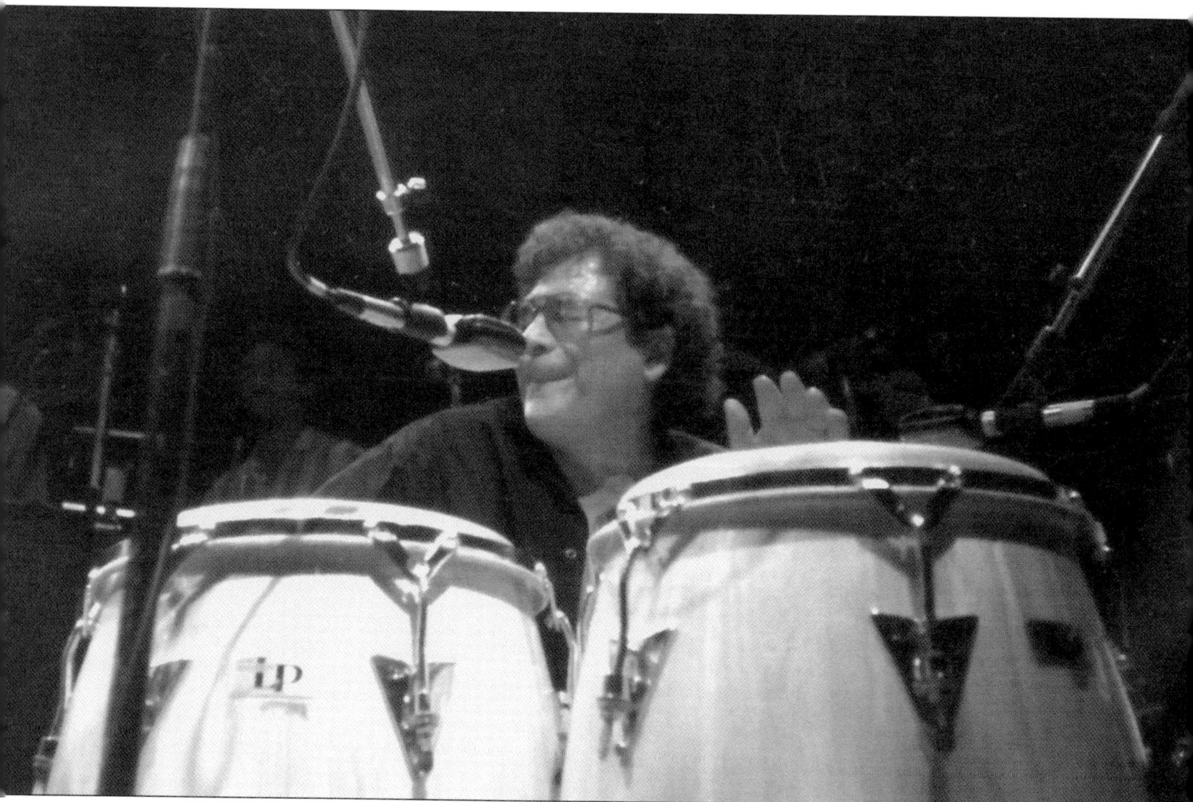

Ray Barretto has led many organizations for more than three decades. He employed some of the best musicians of his era and recorded memorable music to leave as a legacy. His last decade was mostly dedicated to playing Latin jazz with a small ensemble. Barretto died in February 2006.

Born in Puerto Rico, Francisco "Kako" Bastar came to New York City as a teenager and quickly became one of the most sought-after percussionists. Able to play bongos, congas, and timbales, he eventually formed his own group playing timbales exclusively. He is shown here in a recording studio in midtown Manhattan in 1957.

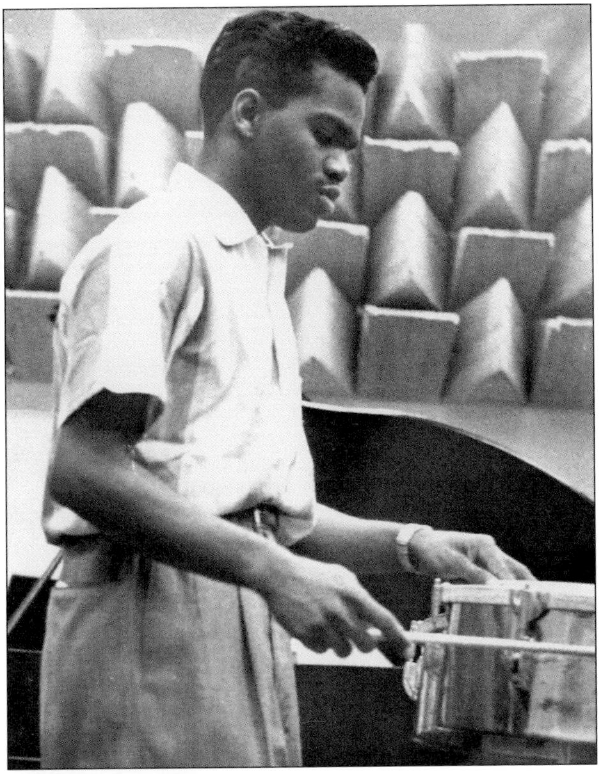

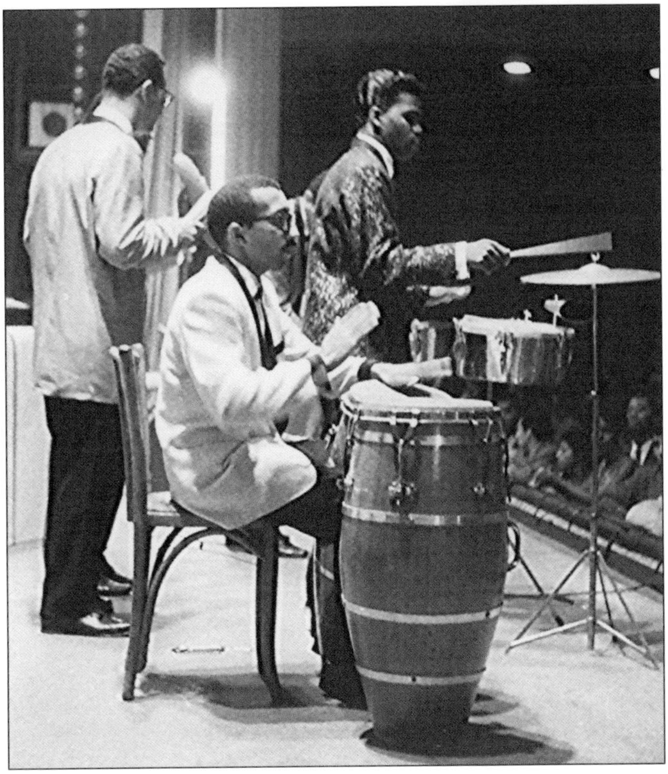

An impeccable dresser and superior dancer, Kako always looked good whenever he appeared. His stage clothes were unique, setting trends that were copied by other groups. He appears here in 1956 wearing an iridescent jacket at the Hunts Point Palace in the Bronx. John Palomo is playing congas.

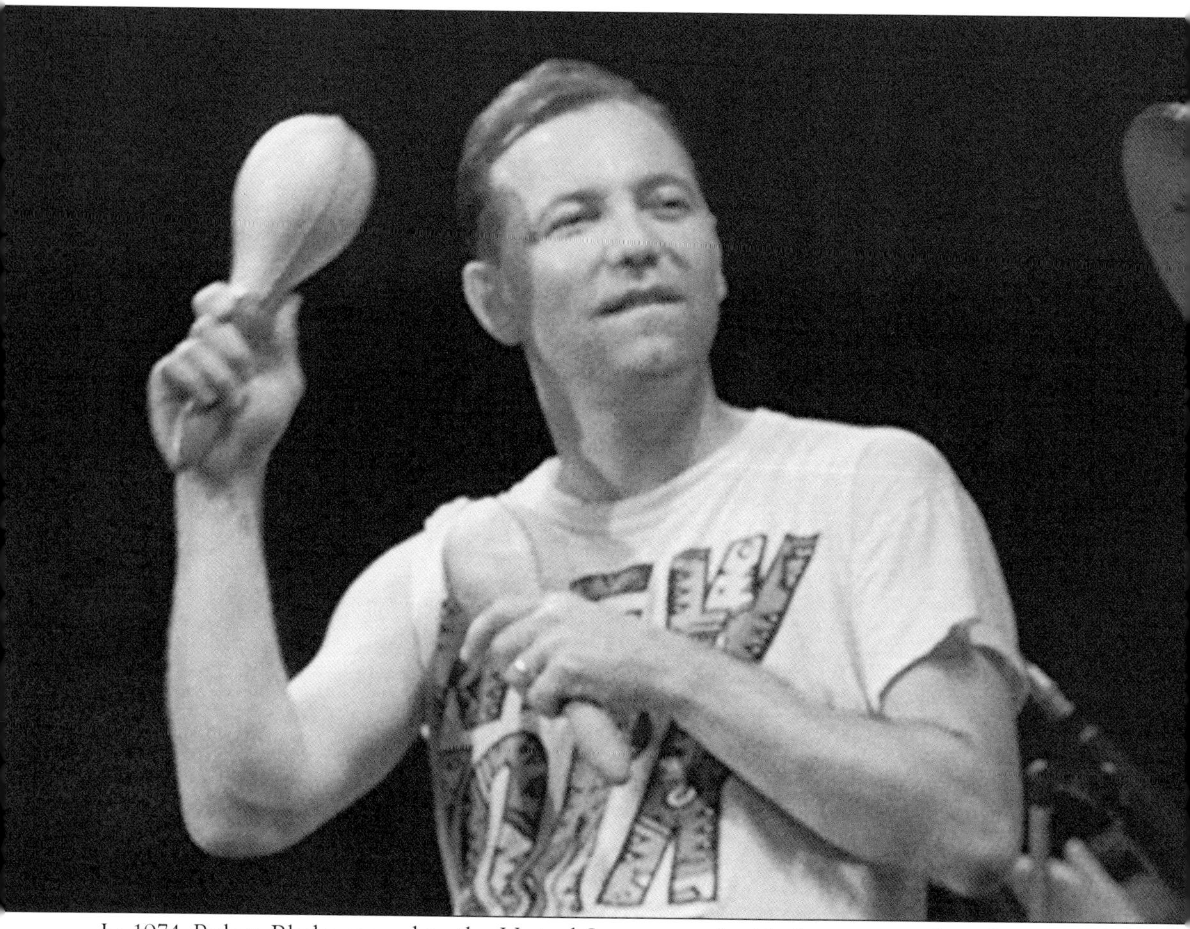

In 1974, Ruben Blades moved to the United States armed with degrees in political science and law from Panama's Universidad Nacional. He obtained a job in the mail room of Fania Records. It was there that Blades began his musical career. He soon found work performing with the bands of Larry Harlow and Ray Barretto. In 1982, he performed at the Trade Tech College in Los Angeles.

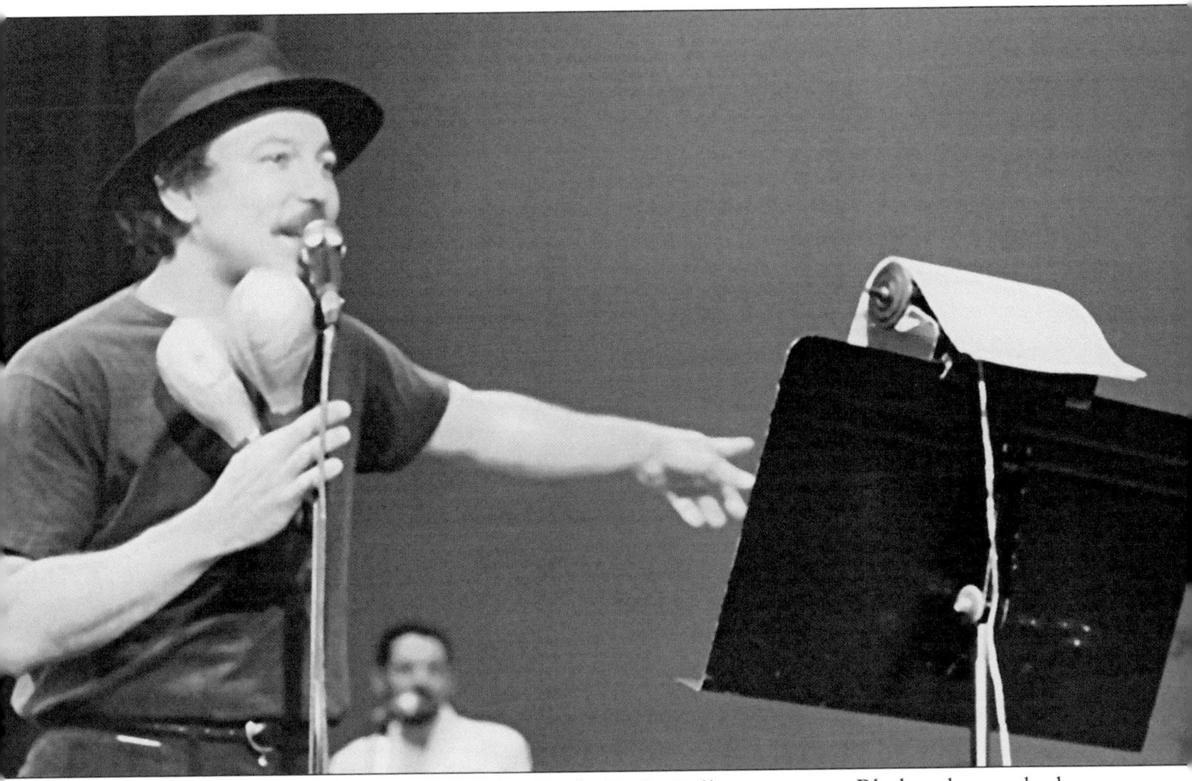

This photograph was taken in 1982 at the Trade Tech College concert. Blades also worked as an actor starting in 1982, when he made his first movie, *The Last Fight*. In addition to acting, composing, and singing, Blades has run for president in his native Panama and is currently the minister of tourism.

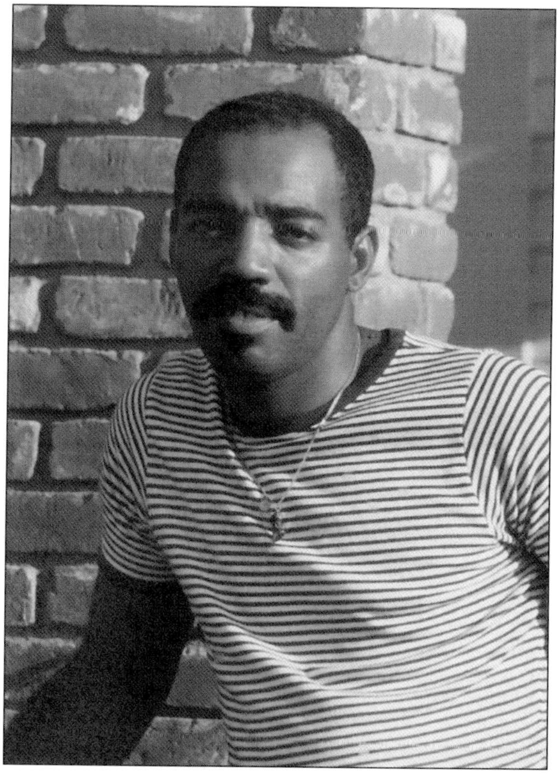

Willie Bobo, seen in this 1965 image, is standing on the front steps of the author's home in Los Angeles. He came to play with his own group at a local nightclub called Maverick's Flat, which is now defunct. Born and raised in Spanish Harlem as William Correa, Bobo grew up knowing all the popular musicians because of his talent and charismatic personality. He easily mastered all the percussion instruments and started playing professionally at an early age.

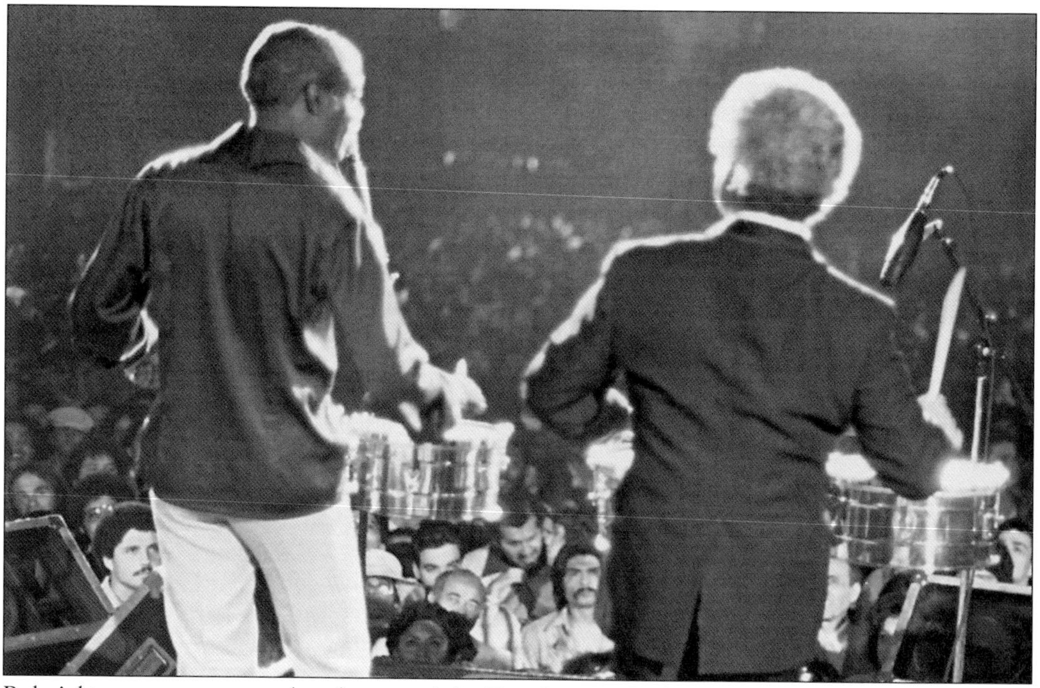

Bobo's big moment came when he joined the Tito Puente Orchestra and played alongside one of his idols, Mongo Santamaria. This back view of him dueling with Puente was taken at a concert in Los Angeles in 1979.

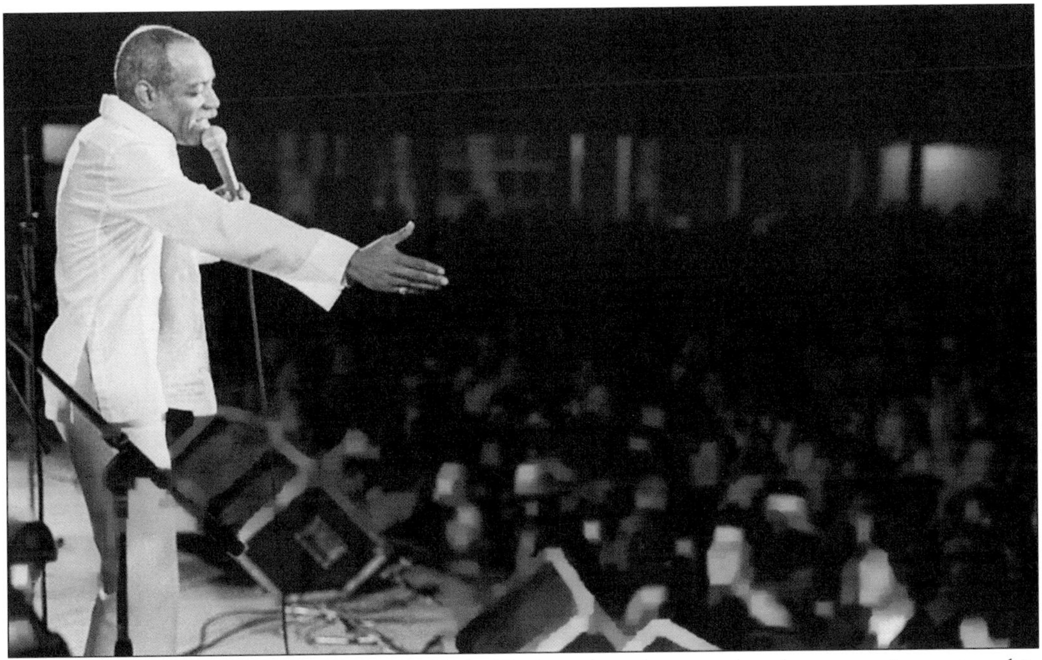

Bobo's love for singing led him to ballads. Endowed with a modest but engaging voice, his recording of "Dindi" on his 1970 album *Lost and Found* brought him one of his first hits. In this photograph he is singing the above-mentioned song at a concert in 1979 at the Los Angeles Sports Arena.

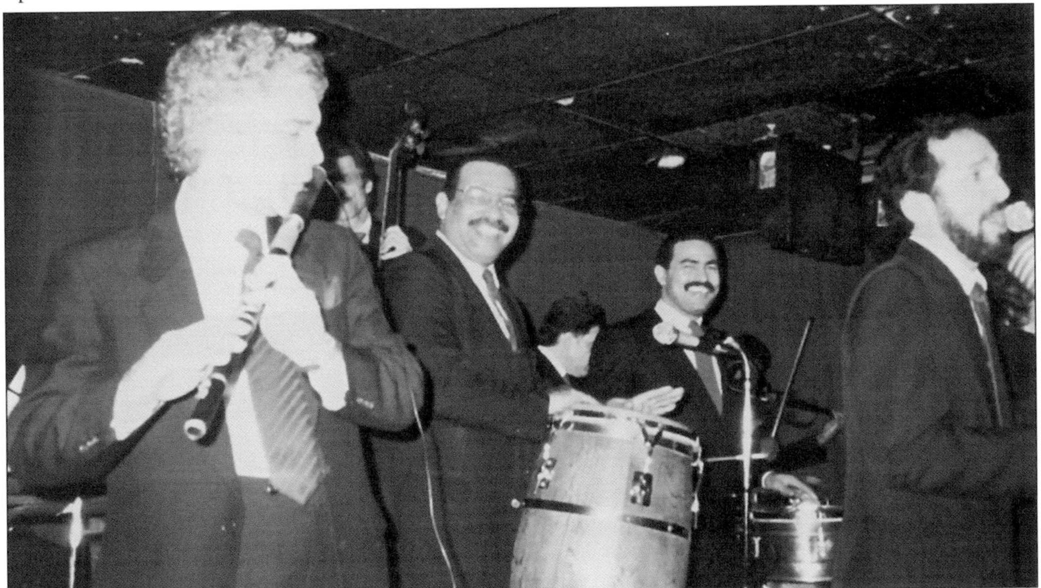

George Maysonet played conga with groups led by Alfredito Valdés, Johnny Pacheco, Eddie Palmieri, Willie Rosario, Típica Novel, and Orquesta Broadway before organizing La Charanga America in 1977. Eventually it became a family affair when his wife, Margaret (vocals), and their sons George Jr. and Eliot joined the group playing percussion. Here George Sr. is playing conga, George Jr. is playing timbale, Bobby Nelson is on flute, and Hector "Tempo" Alomar is doing the vocals at New York City Club Maganette in 1985.

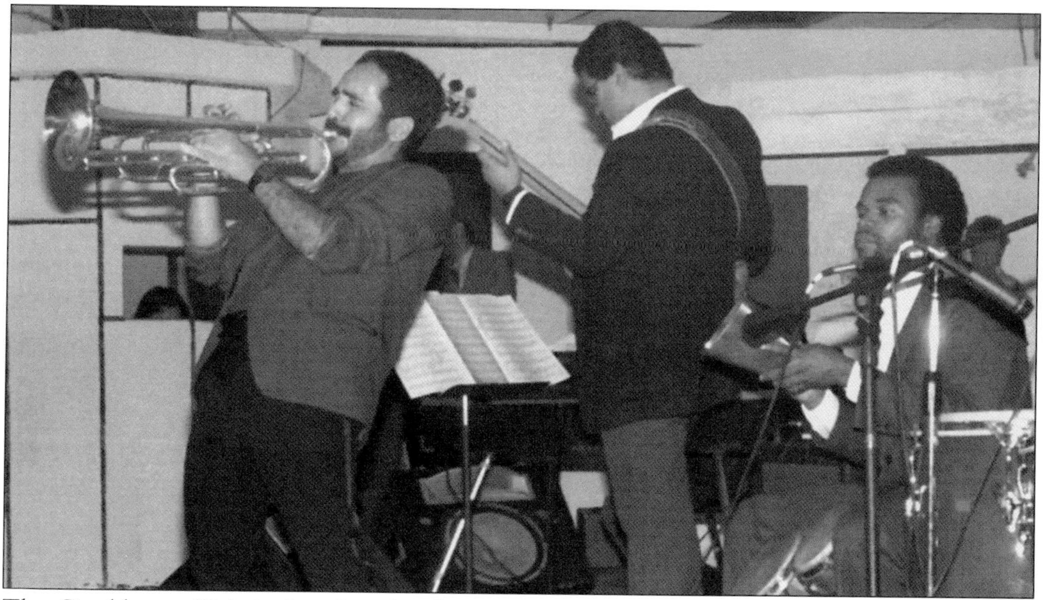

The Casablanca Club in Los Angeles during the 1970s booked a good number of New York bands because salsa music had become very popular through the efforts and popularity of the Fania Record label and radio station KXLU-FM and its program "Alma Del Barrio." With the help of disk jockeys like Carmen Rosado, Eddie Lopez, Emilio Vandanedes, Alan Geik, and the late Nina Lenart, salsa music received greater airplay. Willie Colon and his band played at the Casablanca several times and are seen here in 1979 taking a base trombone solo.

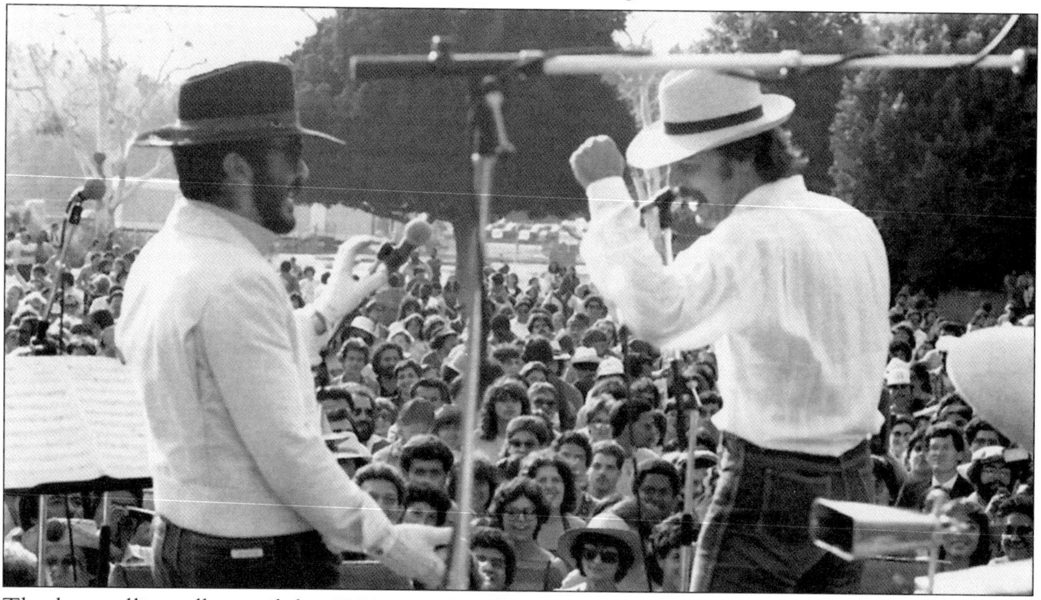

The best-selling album of the 1970s was *Siembra*, recorded by Willie Colon and Ruben Blades and released in 1978 on the Fania label. It instantly caught the attention of the New York Puerto Rican population with its exciting dance music and lyrics full of social commentary written by Blades. When they performed music from this recording the audience knew every word and inflection that Blades sang. In 1979, they appeared on the campus of the University of California, Los Angeles (UCLA) at a free concert to celebrate El Dia De La Raza.

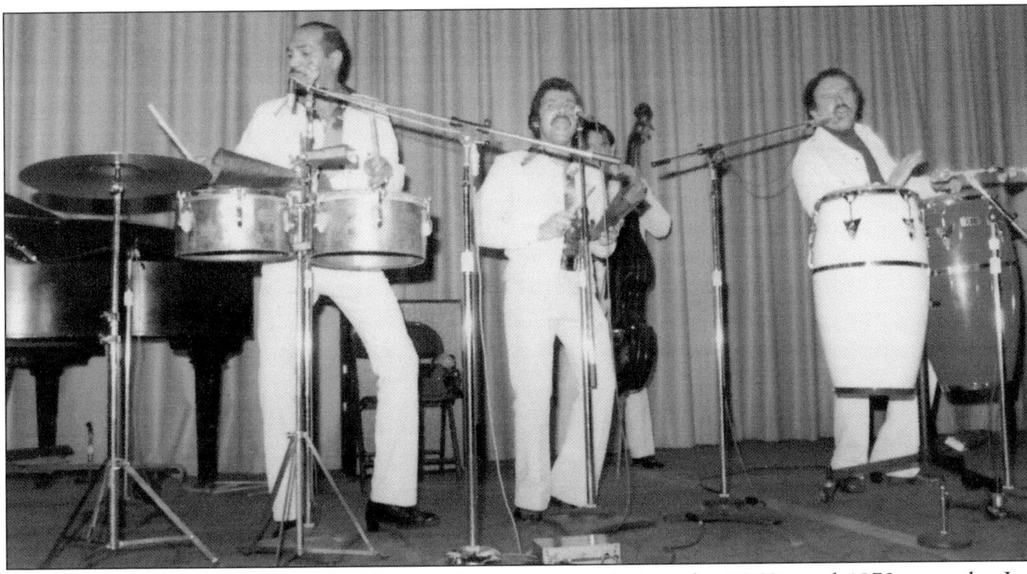

One of the hottest small groups that made an impact during the 1960s and 1970s was the Joe Cuba Sextet. Gilbert Calderon, also known as Joe Cuba, recorded his first album called *Bang! Bang! Push, Push, Push* in 1966. This gave the sextet its first big hit and ushered in the Boogaloo era. Cheo Feliciano, Willie Torres, and Jimmy Sabater recorded tunes with Spanish and English lyrics furthering their popularity with the non-Latino community. Pictured here from a 1974 Los Angeles appearance at the California Club are Joe Cuba on conga, Jimmy Sabater on timbal, Mike Guagenti on vocals, and Jules "Slim" Reyes Cordero on bass.

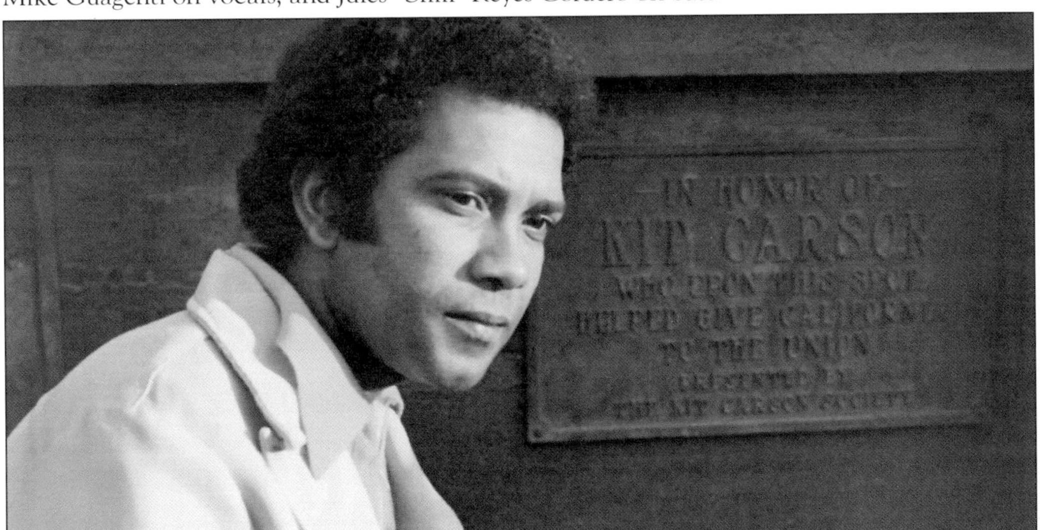

Born in Ponce, Puerto Rico, Feliciano came to live in New York City in the early 1950s at the age of 17 and began his professional career as a percussionist with a group called Ciro Rimac's Review. He went on to work as a *conguero* with Luis Cruz's Conjunto Marianaxi and with the orchestra of Kako y su Trabuco. He was also the band boy for the Tito Rodriguez orchestra, and it was Rodriguez who recommended Feliciano for the singing spot in the new Joe Cuba sextet. Cuba's recording of "A la Seis," "El Ratón," "Como Ríen," and "El Pito" became great hits with Feliciano on vocals. This photograph was taken in front of the Kit Carson statue in Los Angeles when Feliciano visited Los Angeles in 1972.

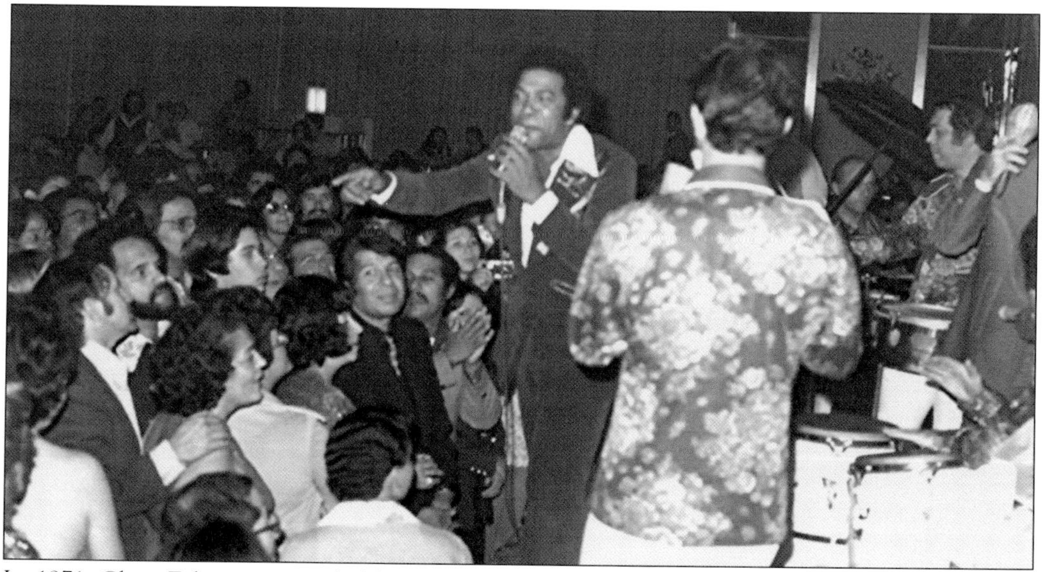

In 1971, Cheo Feliciano recorded his solo debut album called *Cheo*. It was a runaway success due to the coproduction and songs written by his good friend the late Catalino "Tite" Curet Alonso. "Anacanona," the hit song on the album, sold more than 140,000 as a single. With an all-star band made up of great musicians such as Johnny Pacheco, conga; Larry Harlow, piano; Bobby Valentin, bass; Louie Ramirez, vibes; Orestes Vilato, timbales; Johnny Rodriguez, bongos; Ismael Quintana, maracas and clave; Vinnie Bell, electric guitar; and Charlie Rodriguez, tres, how could he go wrong? He is pictured here in 1978 at the Biltmore Hotel in Los Angeles.

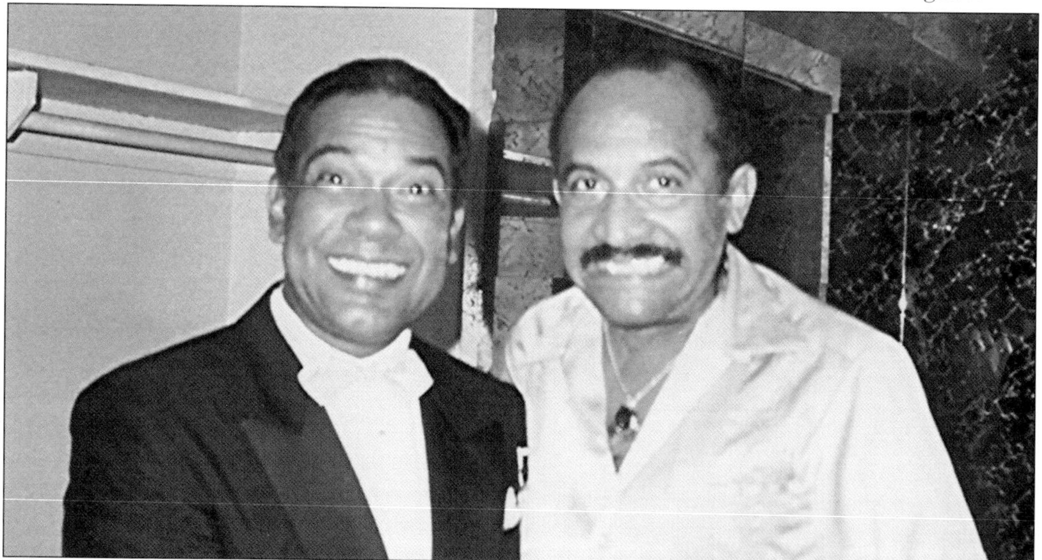

Feliciano's ability to sing romantic ballads and swing a *guaracha* has made him a huge success all over Latin America. His interest in having socially provocative songs in his repertoire (almost all written by Tite Alonso) has endeared him to his audiences, whom he refers to as "familia." Unlike many *soneros* that engage in the *guaperia* (bold) style of singing, Feliciano prefers to use a more smooth and friendly approach, a quality that has made him a favorite to audiences worldwide. Feliciano (left) and the author are making funny faces in this photograph taken backstage at the Hollywood Palladium in Los Angeles in 1983.

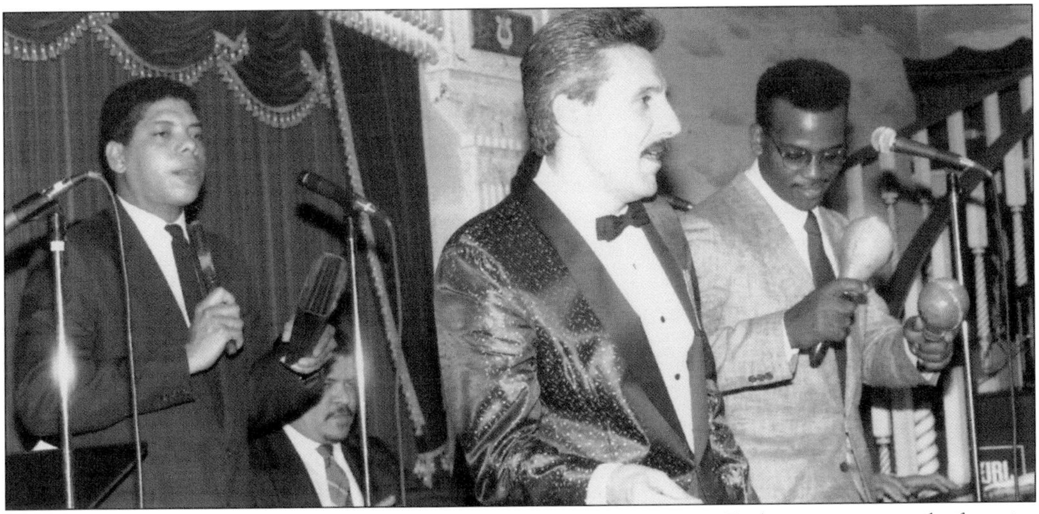

A talented singer, songwriter, bandleader, and painter, Henry Fiol remains a cult favorite appreciated mainly by the Latin music cognoscenti here and abroad. A native New Yorker of Italian and Puerto Rican parents, Fiol has a fine arts degree from Hunter College in New York City but chose to become a full-time musician in 1969. For several years he played conga in bands in the New York area until 1974 when he cofounded the band Saoco. Fiercely independent, he has suffered from distribution of his recordings. His early album covers used his original paintings and musical compositions. He is pictured here in 1983 in a club in Los Angeles. From left to right are Ramon Ramos (cowbell), Jose "Papo" Rodriguez (conga), Henry Fiol, and Nenge Hernandez (maracas).

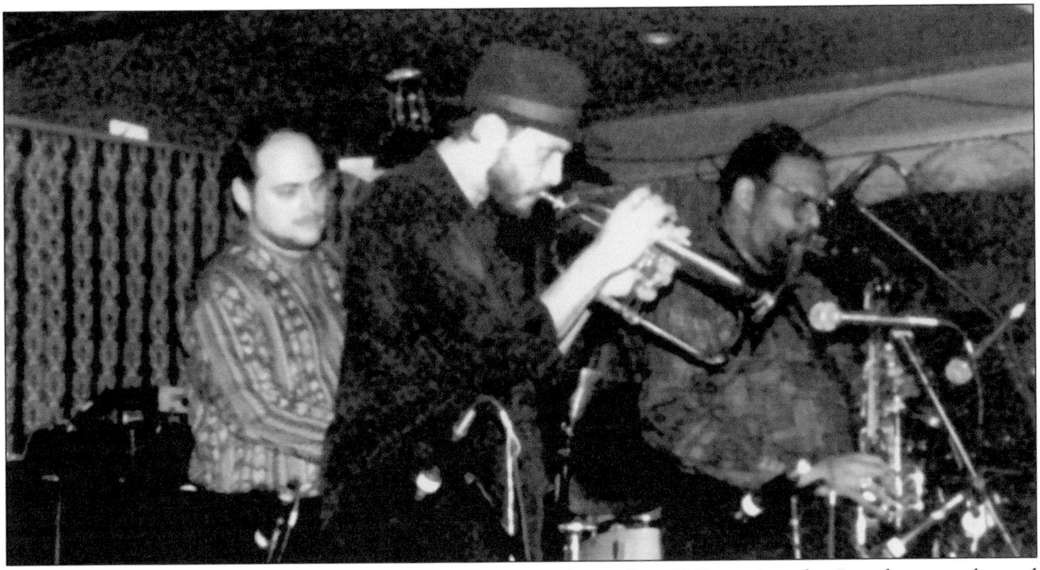

Jerry Gonzalez's first album, *Ya Yo Me Curé, Jerry Gonzalez & Fort Apache Band*, was released in 1980, and immediately this conguero/trumpeter received instant notice from the Latin and jazz music communities. The Fort Apache Band brought a new approach to Latin jazz, and Gonzalez's distinctive conga style using the rumba element gave a fresh interpretation to the music of Theolonious Monk, Wayne Shorter, Benny Golson, Dizzy Gillespie, and Bud Powell. Pictured here in 1983 at Steven's Steak House in Los Angeles is Andy Gonzalez (bass), Jerry Gonzalez (flugelhorn) and Joe Ford (alto sax).

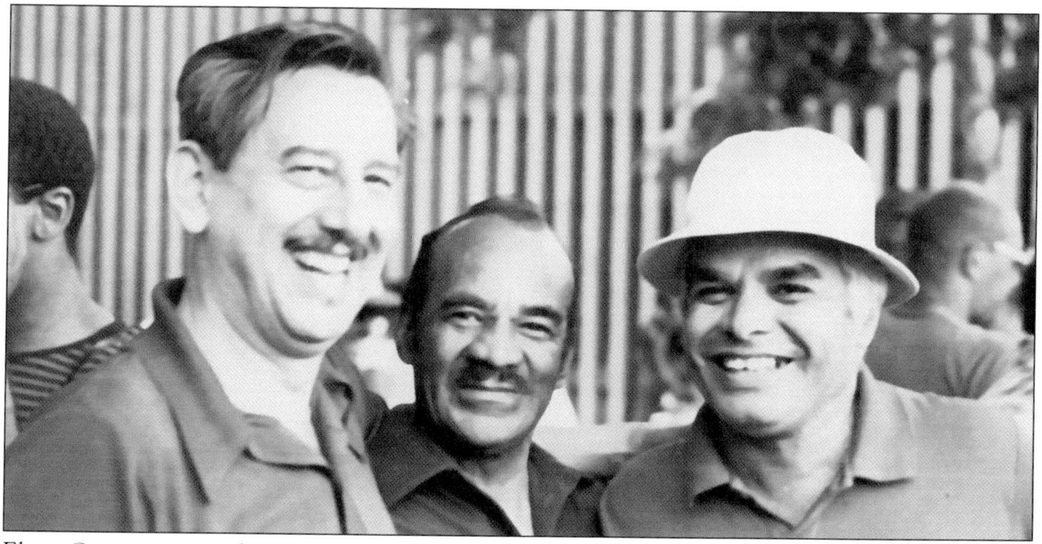

Elmo Garcia, pictured in the middle of this photograph, never recorded an album or CD in all the years that he led a band in New York City. In the 20 years as a leader he employed many of the young musicians coming up during the late 1940s and 1950s. Ray Armando, Tony Matos, vocalist Olquita Melendez, and Johnny Palomo are four that come to mind. Garcia's talent came in organizing and acquiring work for the group. His band was always featured as the opening band when promoters gave large dances with five or six orchestras on the bill. In this photograph, from left to right, are the late Jules "Slim" Reyes Cordero (bassist for the Joe Cuba Sextet), Elmo Garcia, and Tony Quintana.

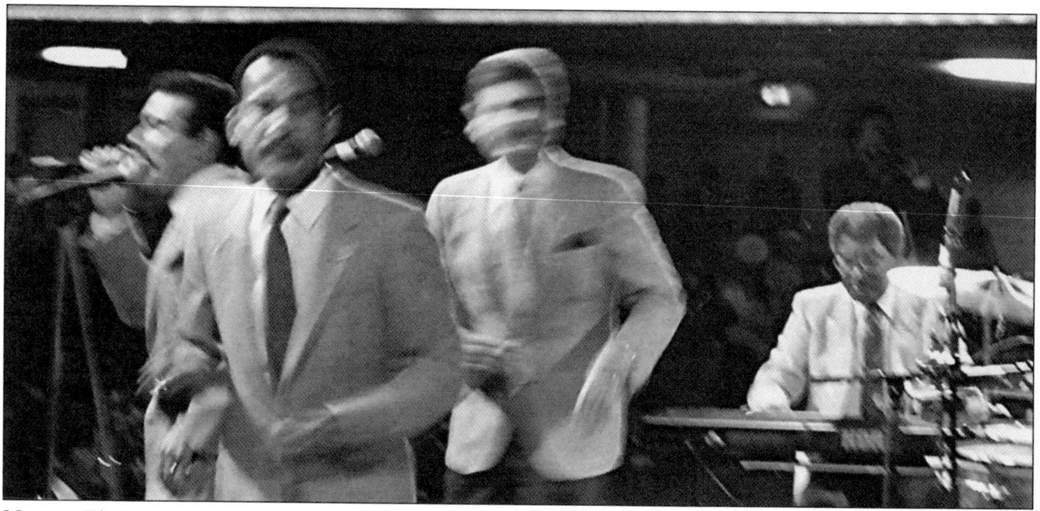

Here is El Gran combo, performing since 1962 when they first started in Puerto Rico. This group grew out of the remnants of the combo of the late Rafael Cortijo. Pianist Rafael Ithier took over the helm, and they have been together ever since. New York City, with its large Puerto Rican population, has always been a main stop on their tours. Their music is never complicated and purposely kept simple for the dancing public. They have been doing it this way for over four decades, and just recently Ithier started conducting, giving up the piano chair to a younger musician named Willie Sotelo, formerly with the Roberto Roena organization. The Hollywood Palladium was also a stop on their tours, and here is part of the group in 1983, with Itier at the piano and, from left to right, singers Charlie Aponte, Jerry Rivas, and Papo Rosario at the microphone.

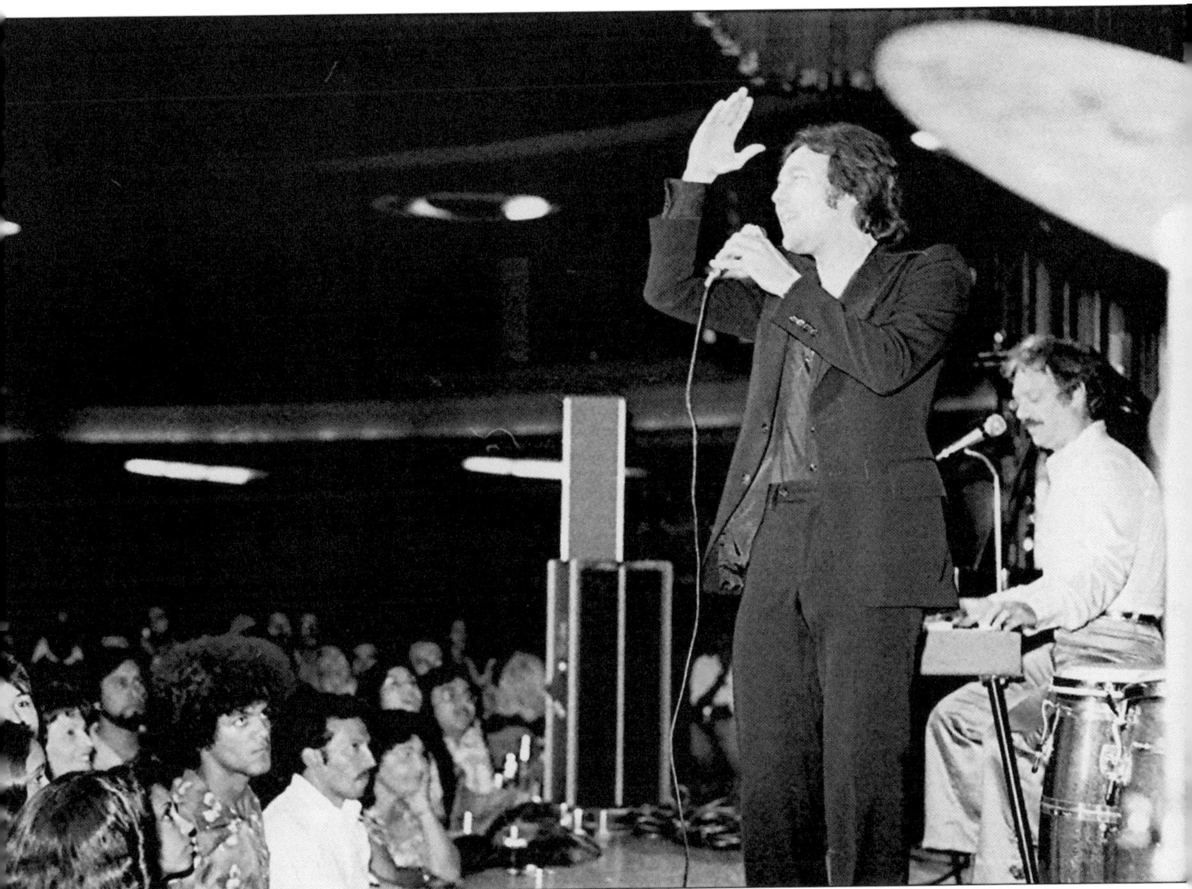

Ruben Blades was the featured vocalist with Larry Harlow's orchestra in this photograph taken at the Hollywood Palladium in 1983. In 1975, the Fania record label released Harlow's *El Judio Maravilloso* (the Marvelous Jew). To the New York Latin listening audience he was truly marvelous at playing Cuban-tinged salsa music. Born in Brooklyn, Harlow graduated from the New York High School of Music and Art, and his exposure as a teenager to the music and culture of the New York Latino community fascinated him. He went to Cuba and studied all the branches of Afro Cuban music, from the religious to the popular dance music and became a full-fledged initiate in the religion of Santeria. Harlow has produced dozens of albums and has written original compositions for documentaries and theater presentations. The musicians he has used on his projects are the most talented available. Now living in Florida, he continues to work at his craft by traveling all over the United States and Latin America.

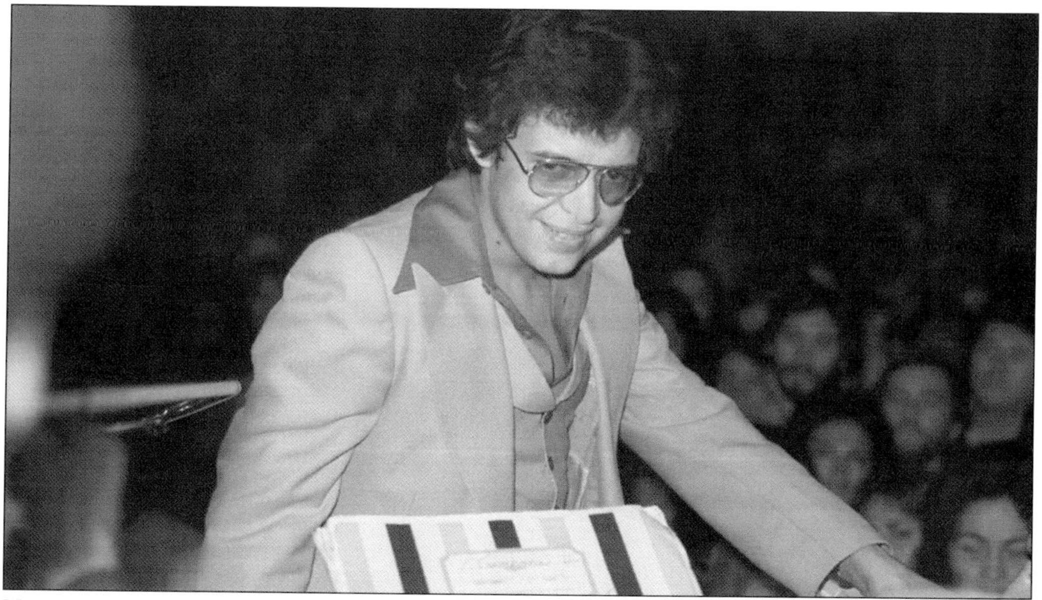

Hector Lavoe is shown here at the Hollywood Palladium in 1979 where he appeared with his own band. His improvisations as a *sonero* were filled with negative references to female battery and guaperia (street tough). Ironically women seem to idolize him and men thought he was quite the macho man. Lavoe received limited musical training at Juan Morel Campos Public School of Music in his native Ponce, Puerto Rico. He was blessed with good looks, natural singing ability, and a good ear for music.

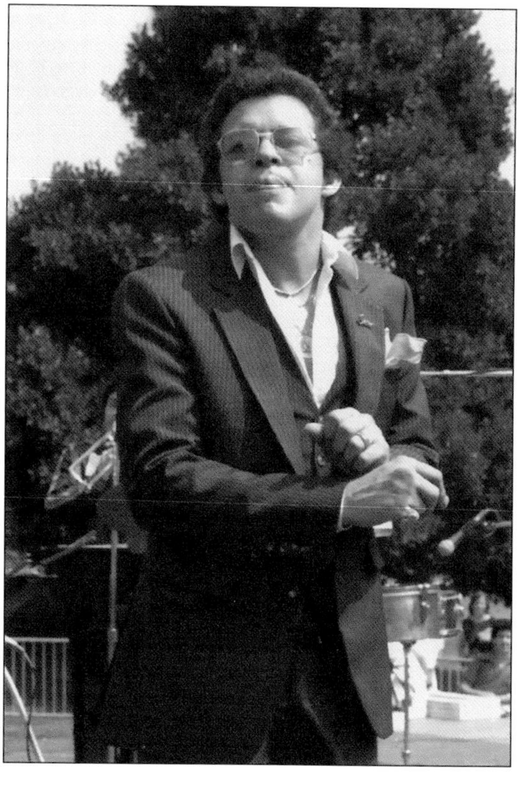

Lavoe arrived in New York City in 1963 at the age of 17, and after working with a few of the local groups he met Willie Colon through Johnny Pacheco, the co-owner of Fania Records. *Malo*, their first recording, was an immediate success and from 1967 to 1983, they made 10 recordings together. He went on to form his own group and made more than 10 recordings as a soloist. He also recorded with Tito Puente and the Fania All-Stars. At this writing, two films are in production based on Lavoe's life, one produced by Marc Anthony and Jennifer Lopez in which they also play the lead roles, and the other by Linda Viera Caballero, also known as "La India." Lavoe died on June 29, 1993, in New York City, not yet 47.

This photograph is of Israel "Cachao" Lopez leading his orchestra at Hunter College in Manhattan during a 1985 concert. Cachao was well known among Cuban music aficionados long before he came to the United States from Cuba in the early 1960s. His *descarga* recordings, originally called *Concerts in Miniature*, recorded in Cuba in the mid-1950s, turned the Afro-Caribbean music world on its ear. What they heard was the exceptional advanced playing of Tata Guines on conga, Guillermo Barreto on timbales, and Cachao on bass, with the rest of his soloists blowing stupendous jazz licks on their horns.

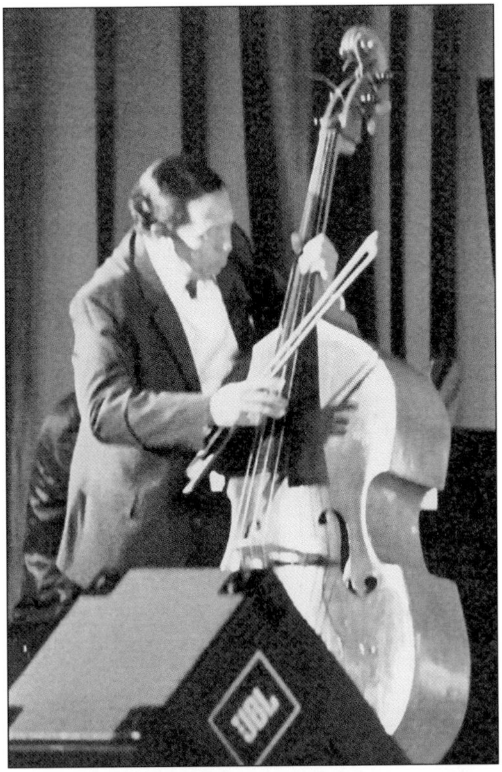

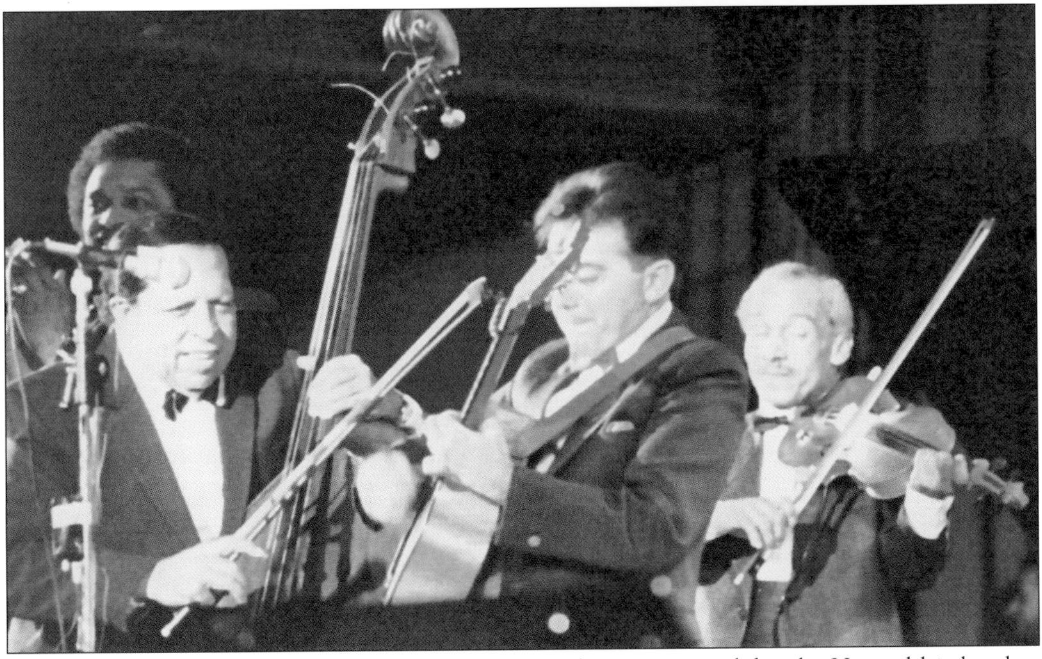

A trained classical musician, Cachao came from a famous musical family. He and his brother Oreste wrote music and played for Arcaño y Sus Maravillas, Cuba's famous charanga orchestra. Here he is shown on bass, Charlie Rodriguez on tres, and Felix "Pupi" Legaretta on violin at Hunter College. Cachao is still occasionally performing at the age of 88.

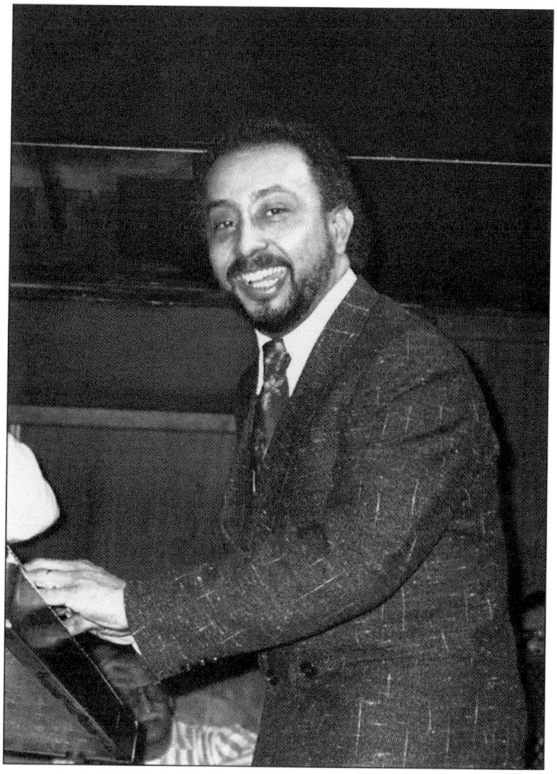

Enrigue "Papo" Lucca has led La Sonora Ponceña for 45 years. La Ponceña was originally started by his father, Enrigue "Quique" Lucca, in the city of Ponce, Puerto Rico. This group has maintained its popularity both on the island and in the United States and has recorded more than 25 albums. Papo is seen on the left at the Hollywood Palladium in 1986 with his father, Quique, singing *coro* (backup) with the band below.

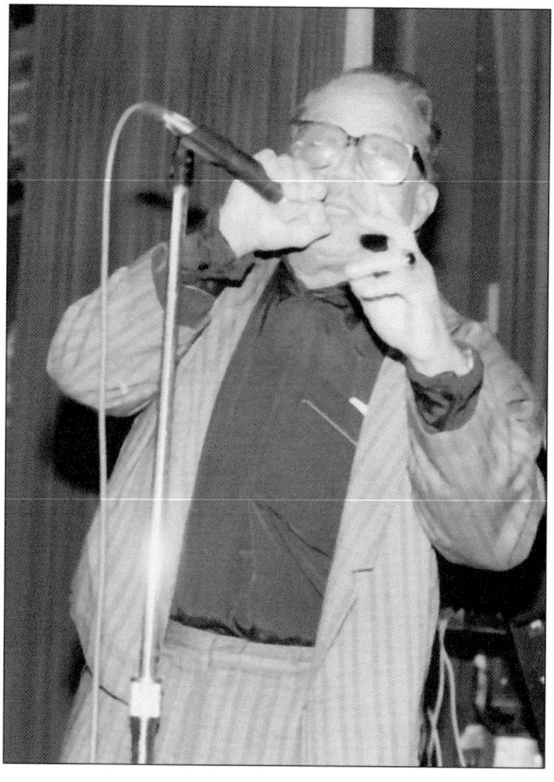

Puerto Rico's master percussionist Angel "Cachete" Maldonado was the founder in 1980 of Batacumbele, an innovative ensemble that fused Afro Cuban salsa and jazz with African and Puerto Rican folkloric polyrhythms. He spent many years on the island and in New York City playing with Larry Harlow, Luis "Perico" Ortiz, and many top groups of the salsa world. This photograph was taken in his home in Puerto Rico in 1992.

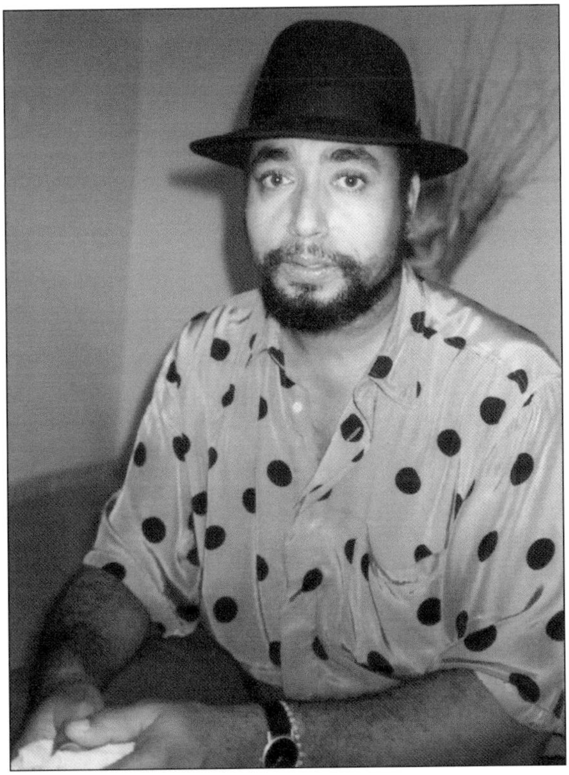

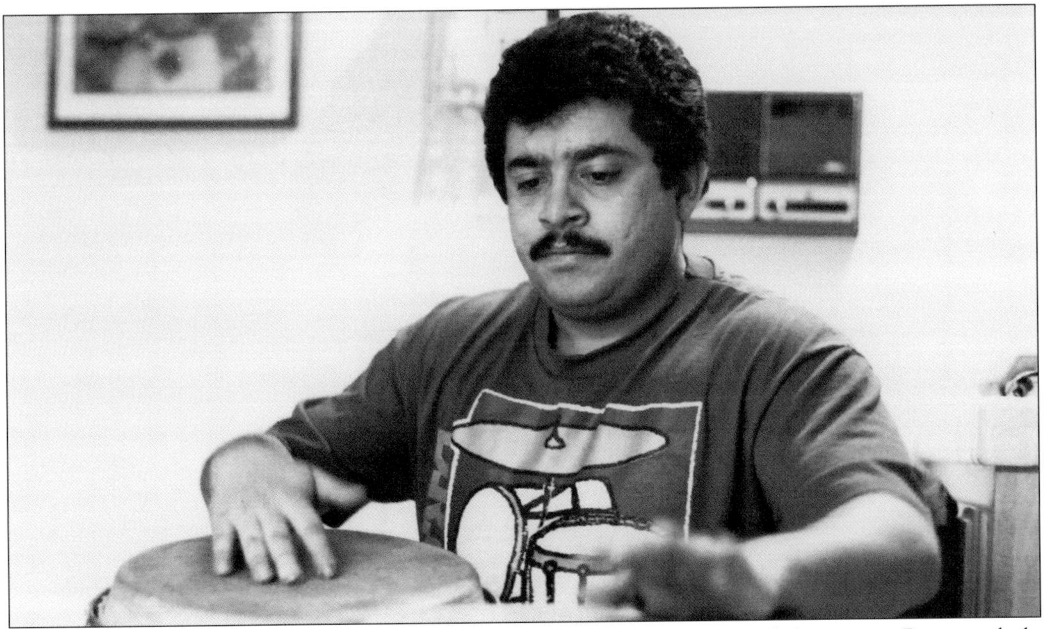

Giovanni Hidalgo became known outside of Puerto Rico as part of the group Batacumbele founded by Cachete. Unfortunately the group disbanded after several years and only made a few recordings. Hidalgo has gone on to become one of the world's leading percussionists. Using the technique that drummers use with sticks, Hidalgo uses his hands and plays with very fast precision. This photograph was taken at the author's home in 1993.

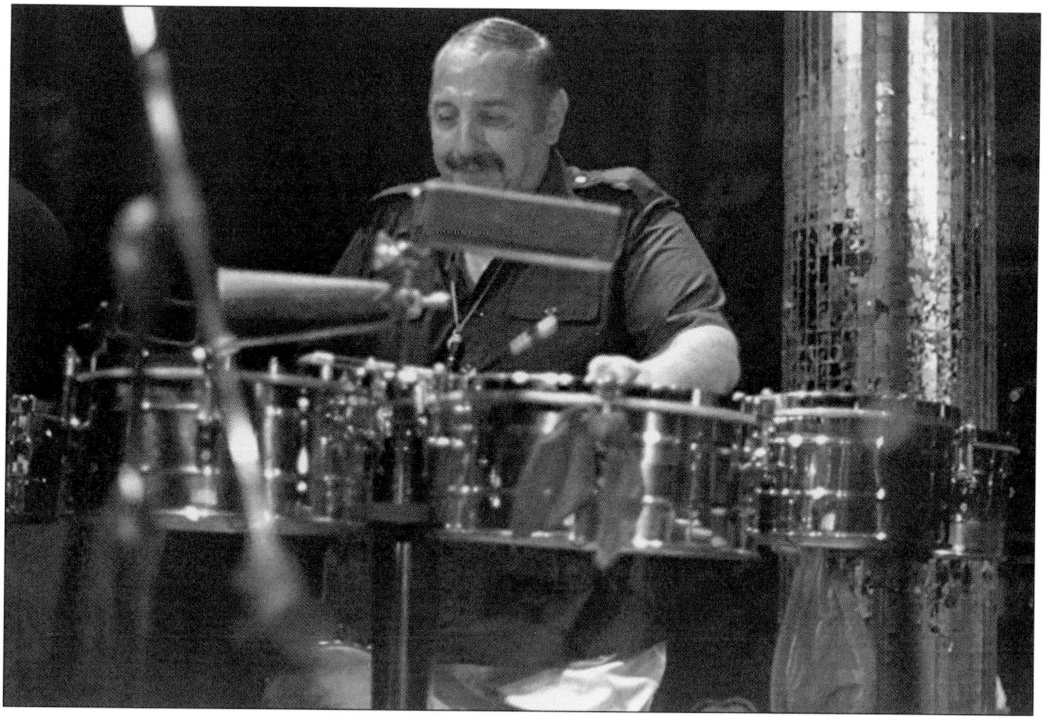

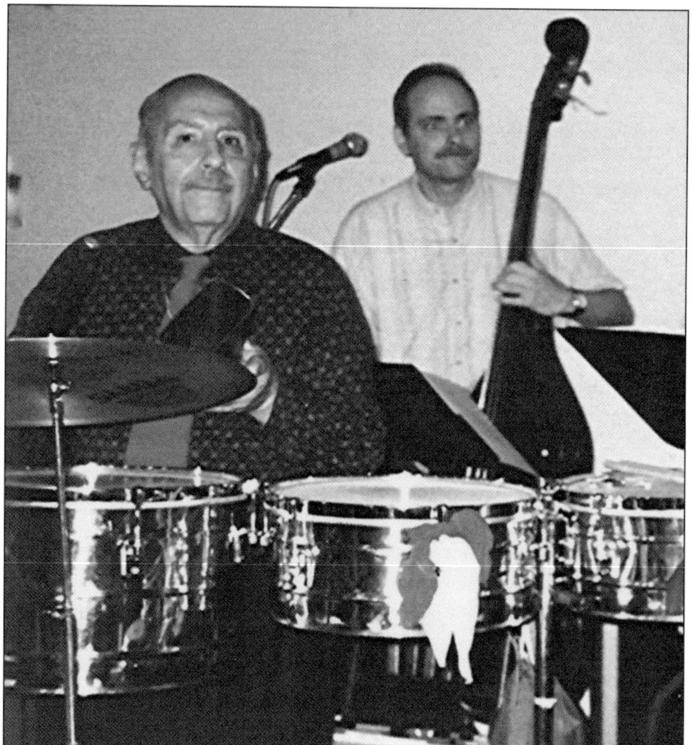

Manny Oquendo has been a musician for 50 years and a coleader with Andy Gonzalez of the group called Libre for 25 years. A seasoned percussionist, Oquendo has played with every major band and has the distinction of being the *timbalero* in the band that backed Chano Pozo's first public appearance in New York City in 1949. Oquendo and Gonzalez are shown in these photographs at Catalina's Bar and Grill in Hollywood in 1984.

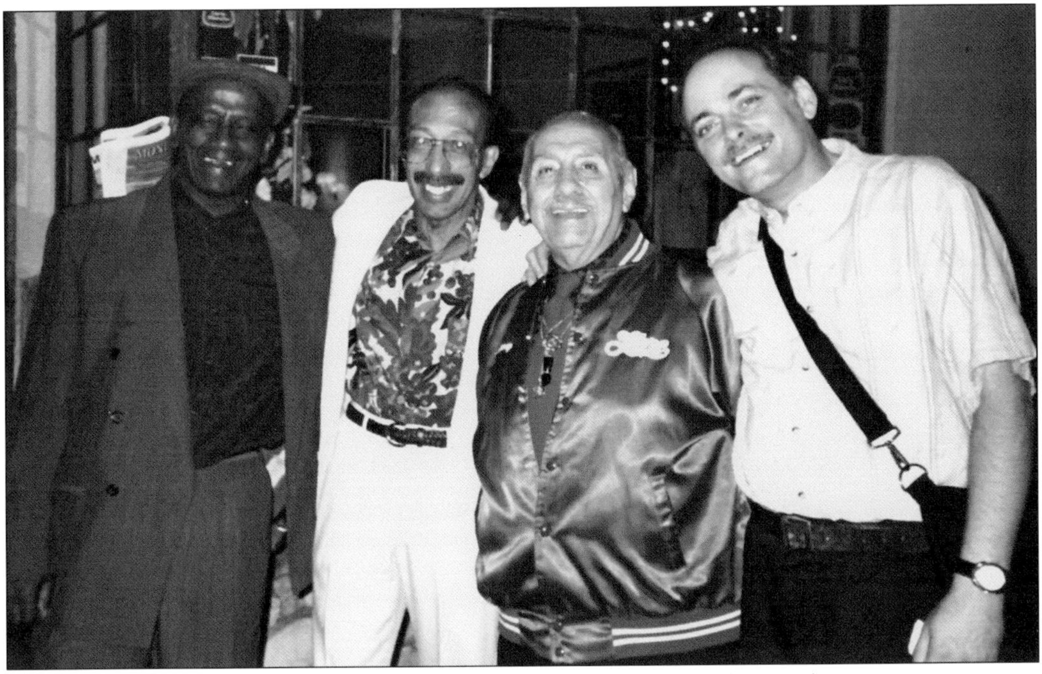

Outside Catalina's Bar and Grill in Hollywood in 1984, from left to right, are percussionists Francisco Aguabella and Johnny Palomo, Manny Oquendo, and bassist and coleader of Libre, Andy Gonzalez.

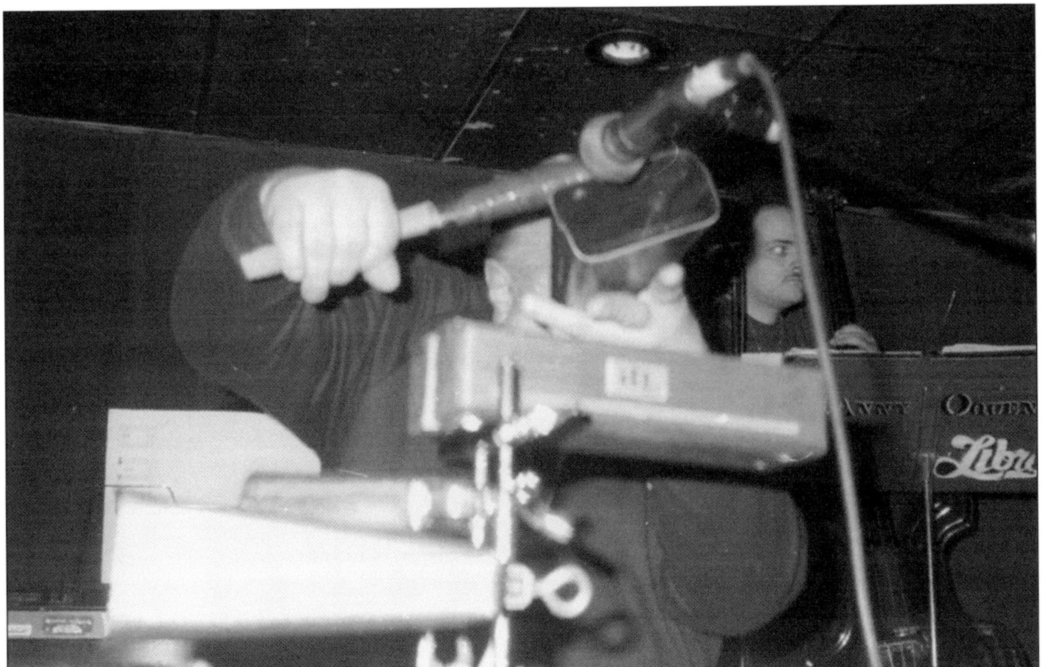

Taken in 1983 at the Maganette in New York City, Oquendo was captured executing an accent sound on his cowbell. Gonzalez is in the background.

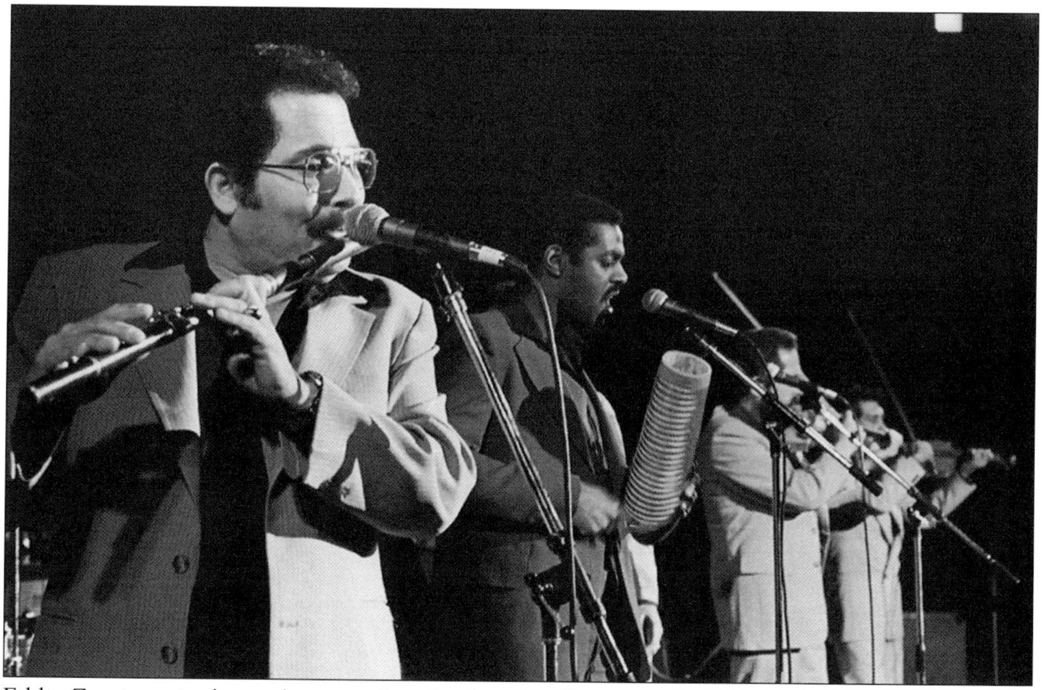

Eddie Zervigon is shown here on flute leading his Orquesta Broadway, a group that has been together for over 40 years in the New York City area. This charanga group is shown here at the Maganette in 1987. Playing quiro is Rafael "Felo" Barrio.

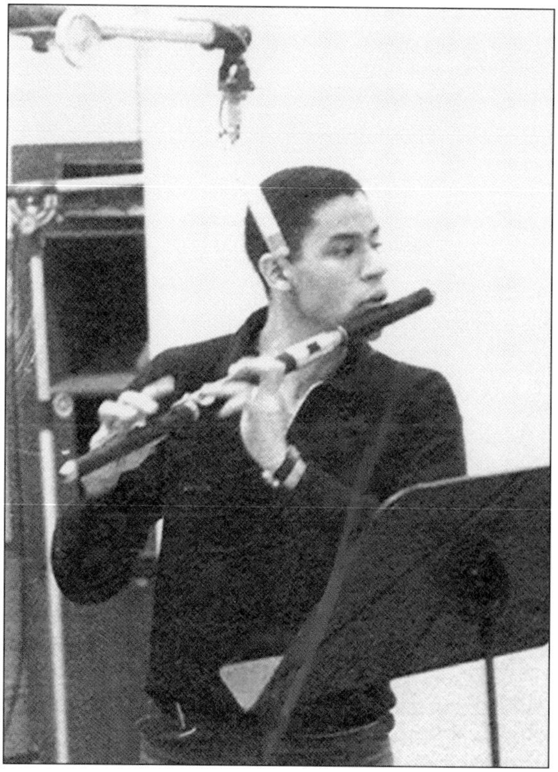

Here is a very young Johnny Pacheco during a 1957 recording session for "Charanga: Orquesta La Duboney" featuring Pacheco, Vitin Aviles, and Charlie Palmieri.

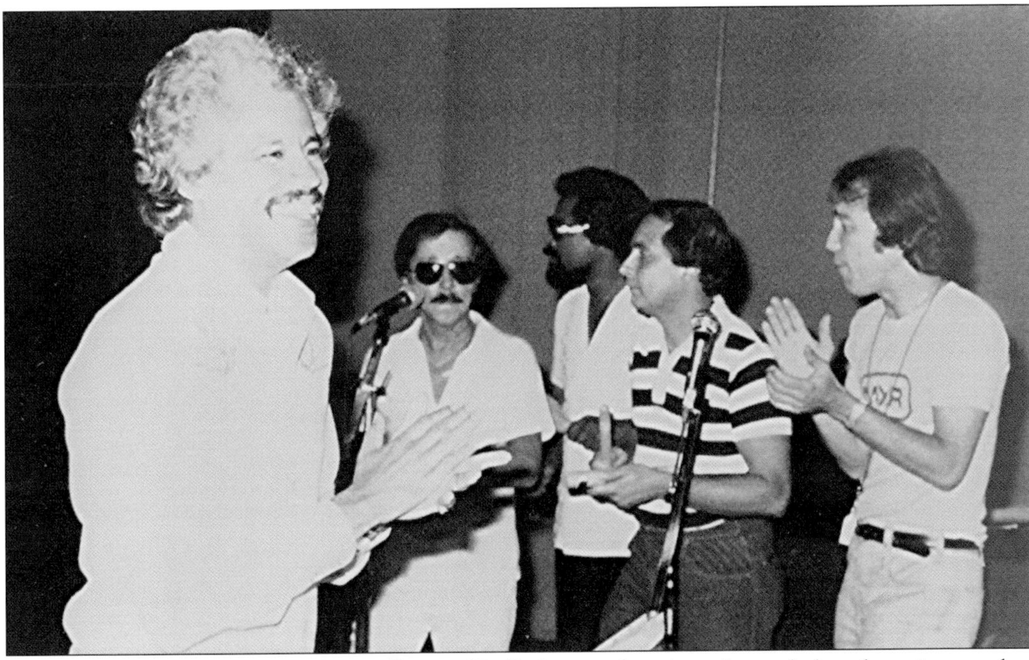

The Fania All-Stars came to the Hollywood Palladium in Los Angeles and played to a jam-packed house. This 1983 photograph was taken during rehearsal for the show; from left to right are Johnny Pacheco, the late Santito Colon, the late Pete "El Conde" Rodriguez, Ismael Quintana, and Ruben Blades.

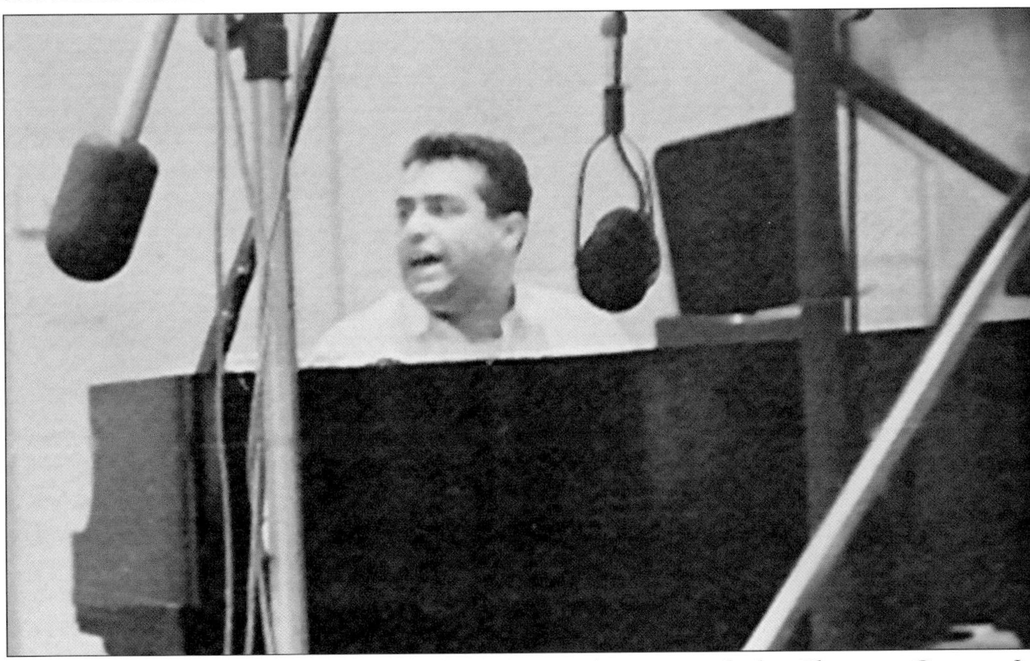

Charlie Palmieri is at the piano during the 1957 recording session for his *Charanga: Orquesta La Duboney Con Johnny Pacheco & Vitin Aviles*. The older brother of Eddie Palmieri, Charlie was a seasoned musician at this time, having played with numerous groups in New York City before he decided to form his own charanga group.

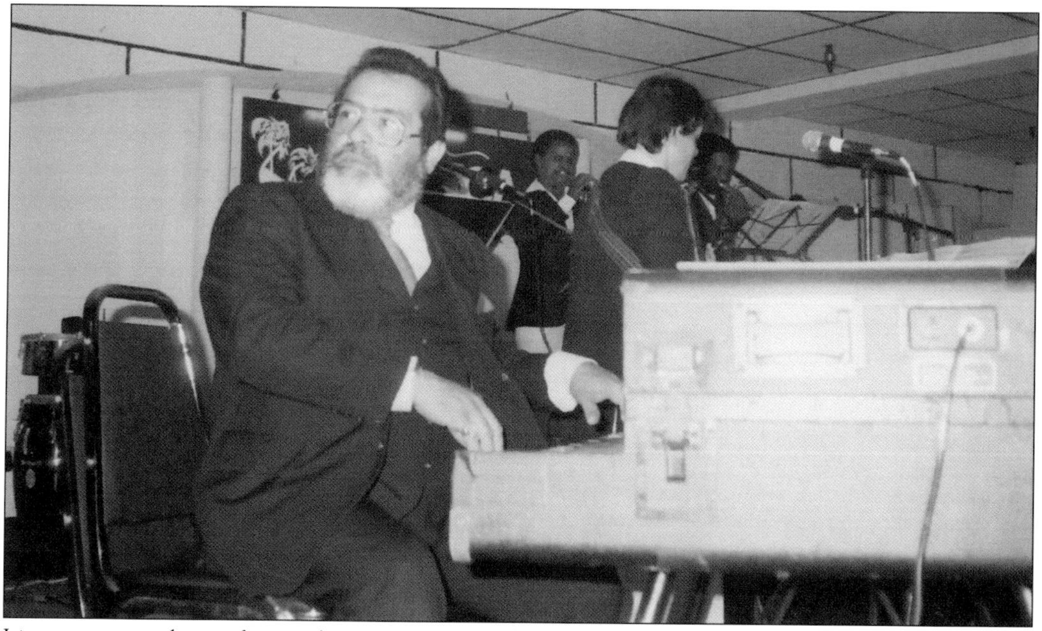

Live music is always featured at the Annual Old-Timers Reunion on 111th Street and Fifth Avenue in New York City. Charlie Palmieri came with his group one Sunday in 1985 and played to a standing-room-only crowd. He recorded over 15 albums during his short career that ended when he passed away on September 12, 1988.

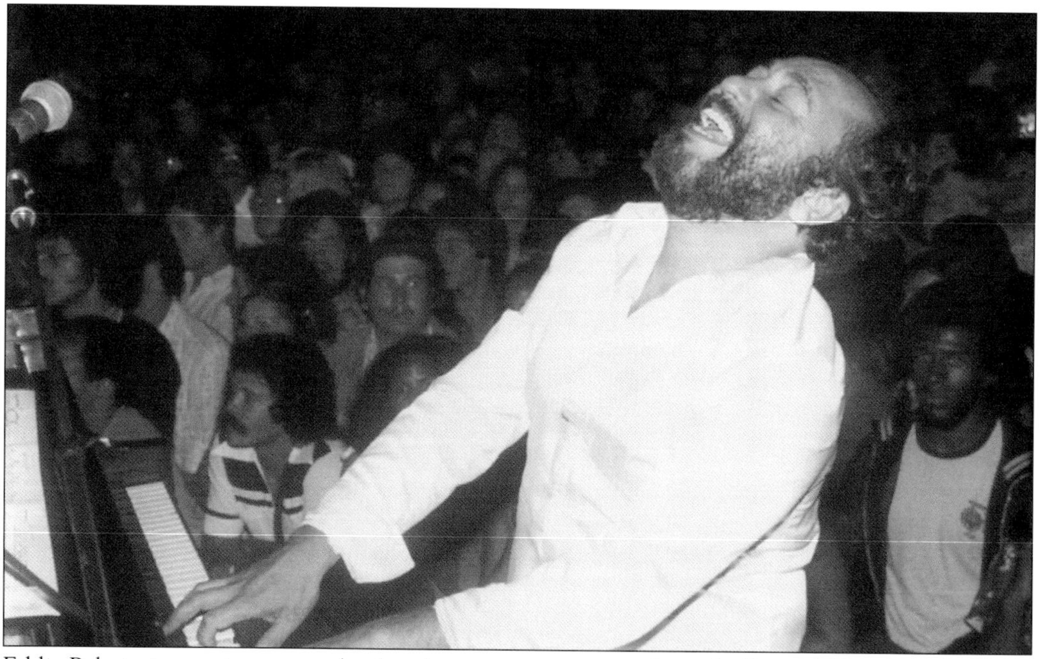

Eddie Palmieri was a joy to watch when he was appearing in dance halls or club dates because his playing was aggressive and adventurous. With Manny Oquendo on bongos and Tommy Lopez on conga, his trombone conjunto La Perfecta took New York City by storm. Formed in 1961 when he left the Tito Rodriguez Orchestra, La Perfecta quickly became New York's most sought after bands. Here is Palmieri at the Hollywood Palladium in Los Angeles in 1978.

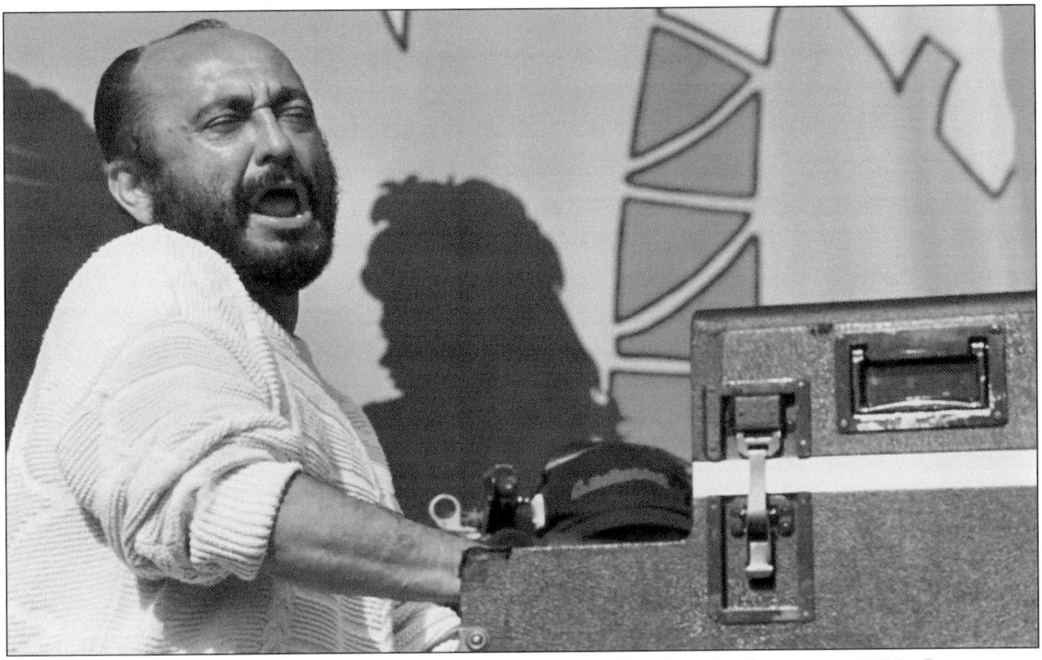

Eddie Palmieri is shown at an outdoor concert in Long Beach, California, in 1990. Starting in 1975 with his recording of *The Sun of Latin Music*, Palmieri has won an unprecedented eight Grammies and continues touring all over the world with his all-star group of musicians. He has more than 20 recordings under his name.

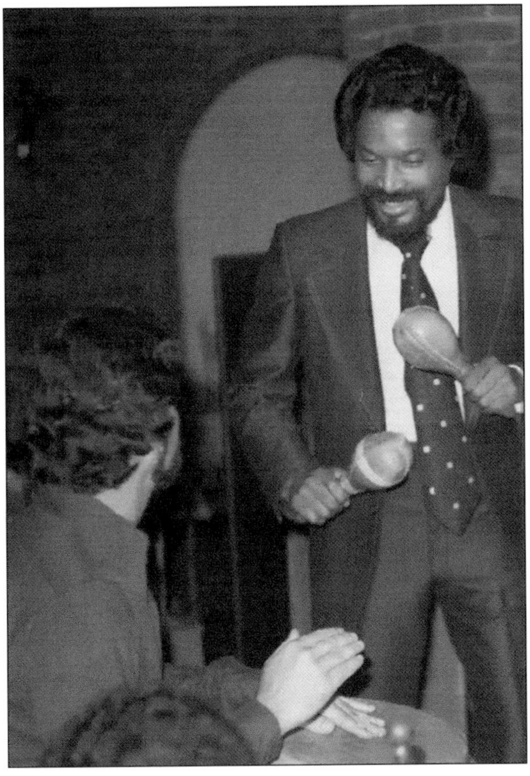

Pete "El Conde" Rodriguez always appeared well dressed when he performed. This was immediately noticeable when one saw El Conde (the count) in person. Born in Ponce, Puerto Rico, he was bestowed this nickname because of his royal stage presence. A percussionist and singer in his native Ponce, he left for New York in the early 1950s, and with the help of Johnny Pacheco, he quickly made a name for himself as an excellent improviser, conguero, maraca player, and dancer. He once remarked that any conga player that played in his band "had to play better than me." The Maganette in New York City was the place for this photograph, taken in 1986.

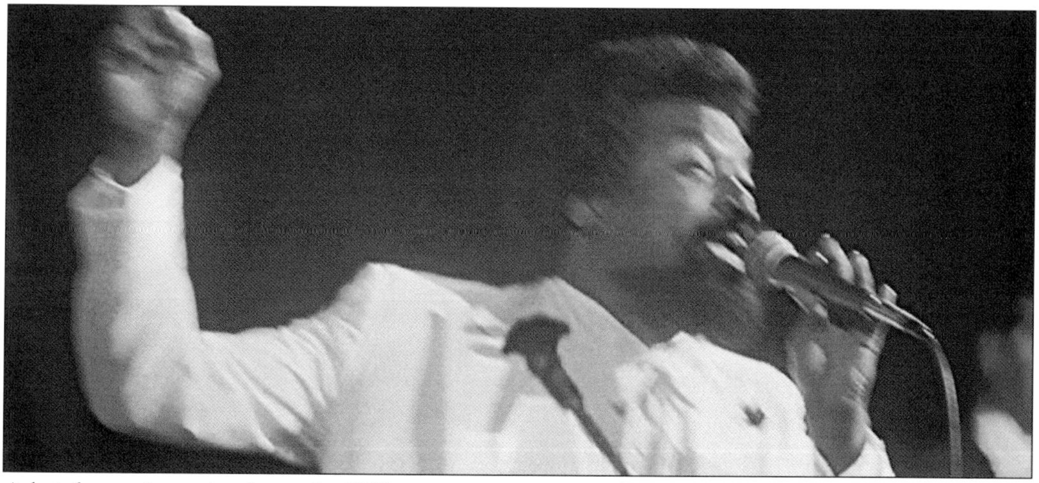

A brief experience in the early 1950s as a paratrooper at Fort Bragg, North Carolina, impacted Pete "El Conde" Rodriguez greatly. As a Black Puerto Rican, he lived the humiliation of racism in the American South. His union with Johnny Pacheco proved to be very beneficial for his career. However, it was when he struck out on his own and recorded "Catalina La O," written by Johnny Ortiz, and "Pueblo Latino," written by Catalino "Tite" Curet Alonso, that El Conde found his groove. All his hit albums of the 1970s were arranged by the incomparable trumpet player/arranger Jose Febles, now deceased. Most of his albums contained at least one tune by Tite Curet Alonso, a composer who addressed the history of the Afro-Puerto Rican. El Conde remained an important member of the Fania All-Stars. This photograph is from a concert at the Los Angeles Sports Arena in late 1979. El Conde died on December 2, 2000.

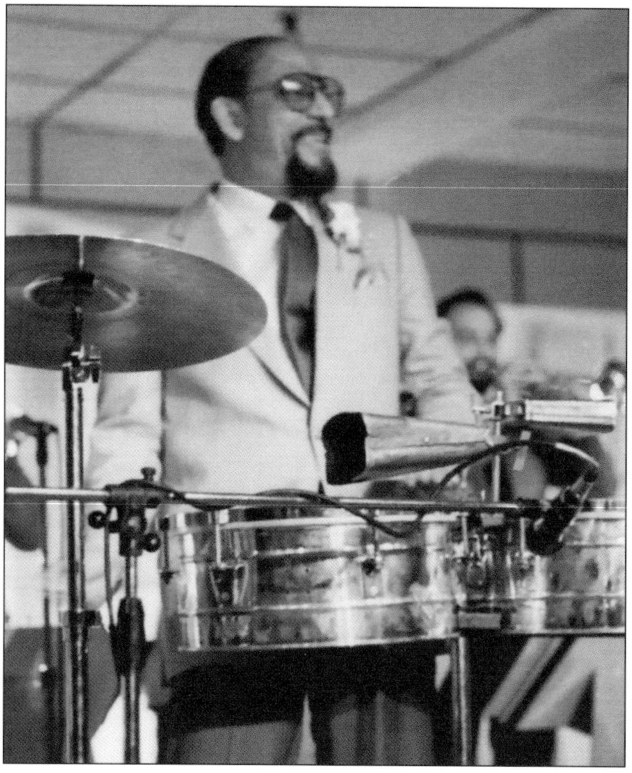

A native of Coamo, Puerto Rico, Willie Rosario received his basic musical education on the island but moved to New York City in his teens. Tito Puente, Tito Rodriguez, and Machito were beginning to make their impact by enlarging the form of Afro Cuban music. After getting experience playing with groups in the New York City area, Rosario started his own orchestra in 1958 with charts given to him by Rodriguez and Puente. After some hardships in New York City, he moved back to Puerto Rico in the 1970s and found success using fresh new talent on the island. His band is known as a university because of the well-known musicians that have been members. He is photographed here in Los Angeles in 1985 when he played at the Casablanca Ballroom.

Referred to as "El Caballero de la Salsa" (the gentleman of salsa), Gilberto Santa Rosa has been a sonero (salsa singer) for over 30 years. He started his career in 1976 in his native Puerto Rico with the band of Mario Ortiz and then went on to work with Tommy Olivencia, Elias Lopez, and Rosario. Known for his exceptional ability to improvise, his records have enjoyed great popularity, especially with his female admirers. Taken in 1993, this photograph shows him leading his orchestra at Myron's Ballroom in Los Angeles.

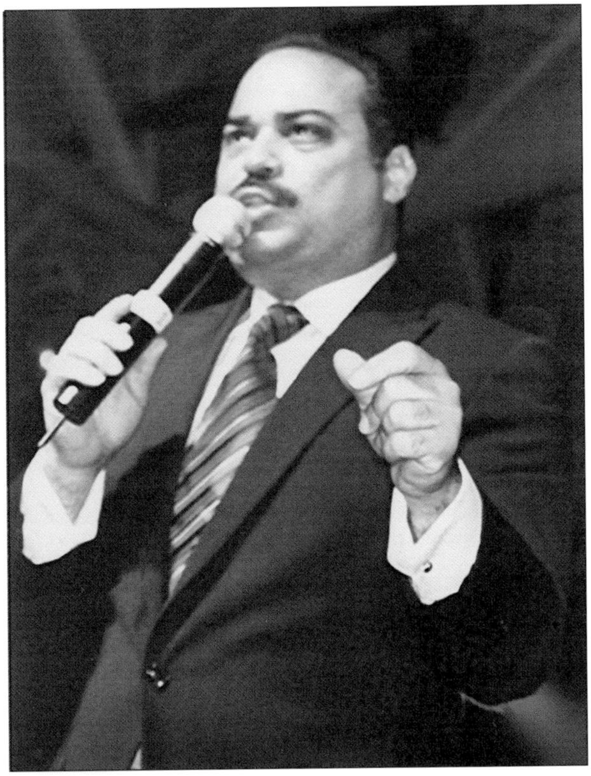

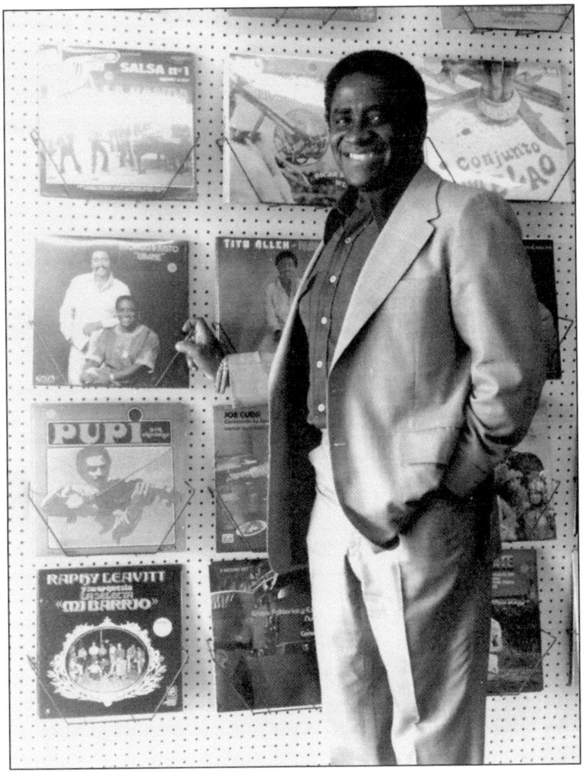

"Afro Blue," composed by Mongo Santamaria in 1958, has become a standard in the Latin jazz and jazz world and brought him success. Arriving in New York City from his native Cuba in the early 1950s, Santamaria played with the orchestras of Perez Prado, Tito Puente, and Cal Tjader until he formed his own group in 1959. His first album as a leader was *Our Man in Havana*, released in 1960. Santamaria has over 30 recordings to his credit, employing a roster of musicians that have gone on to become important stars. At the author's 1976 grand opening of the Alma Latina Record Shop in Gardena, California, Mongo made an appearance and signed autographs for his many fans.

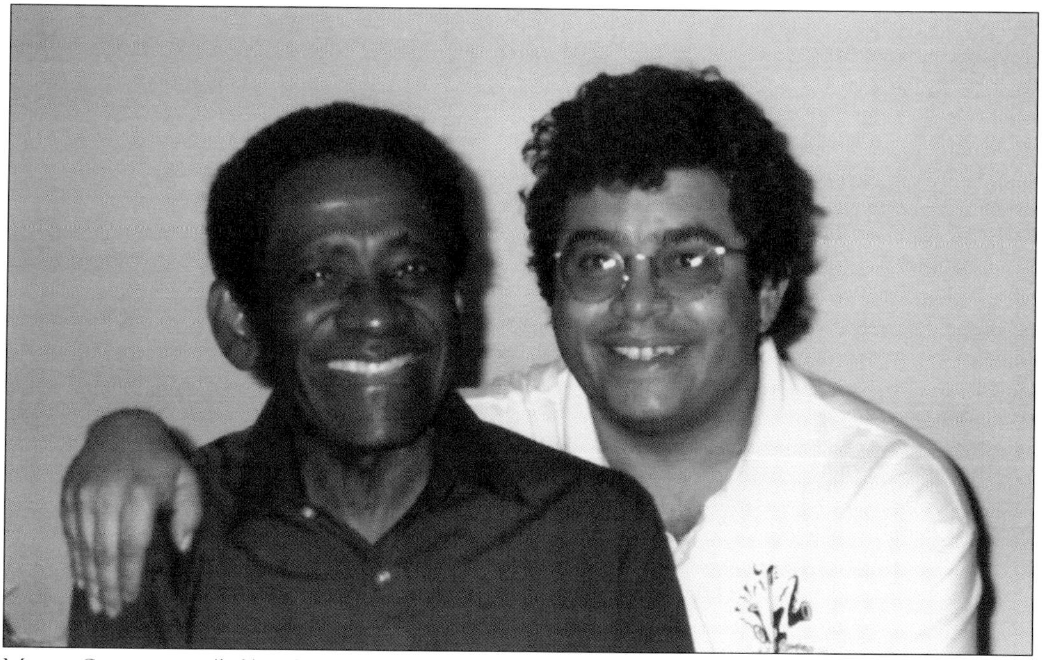

Mongo Santamaria (left) influenced many percussionists. Here he is shown with Giovanni Hidalgo, the current conga wizard, who is passing it on to future generations. This photograph was taken in Santamaria's hotel room in Los Angeles in 1997 prior to an appearance with the Tito Puente Orchestra. Santamaria passed away in February 2003 in Miami. He was 85 years old.

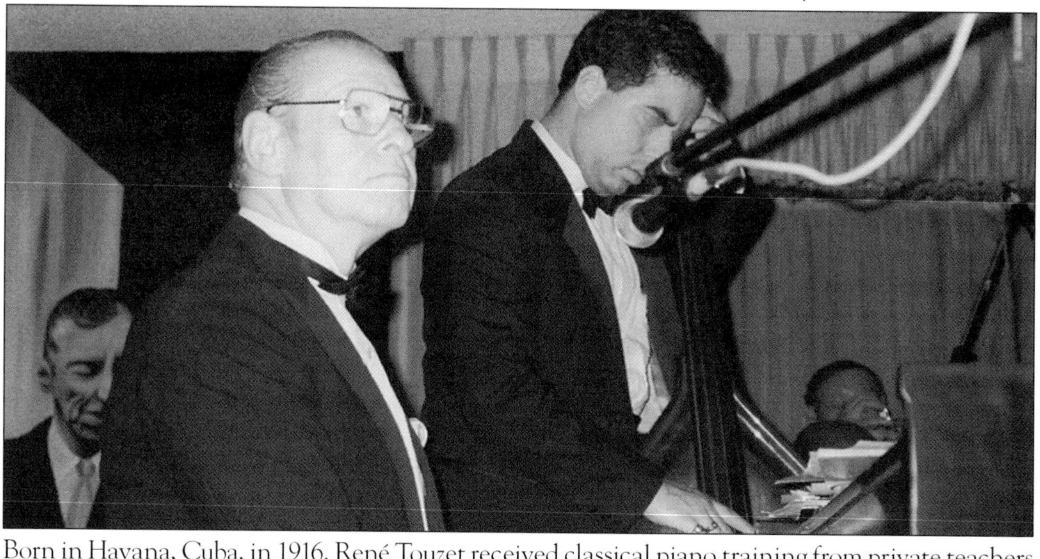

Born in Havana, Cuba, in 1916, René Touzet received classical piano training from private teachers before entering the entertainment world. At the age of 15, he wrote his first composition, a waltz dedicated to his teacher. Touzet formed his first band when he was in his late teens and developed into one of Latin America's foremost composers of boleros. He decided to try his luck in the United States and in 1945 headed to New York City. His reputation as a songwriter helped him land a job in a band led by the Spaniard Enrique Madriguera and work in Hollywood with the Desi Arnaz Orchestra. He is shown here working in a club in Los Angeles in 1993 with his orchestra. Pictured also is Eddie Resto on bass. Touzet died of heart complications on June 15, 2003.

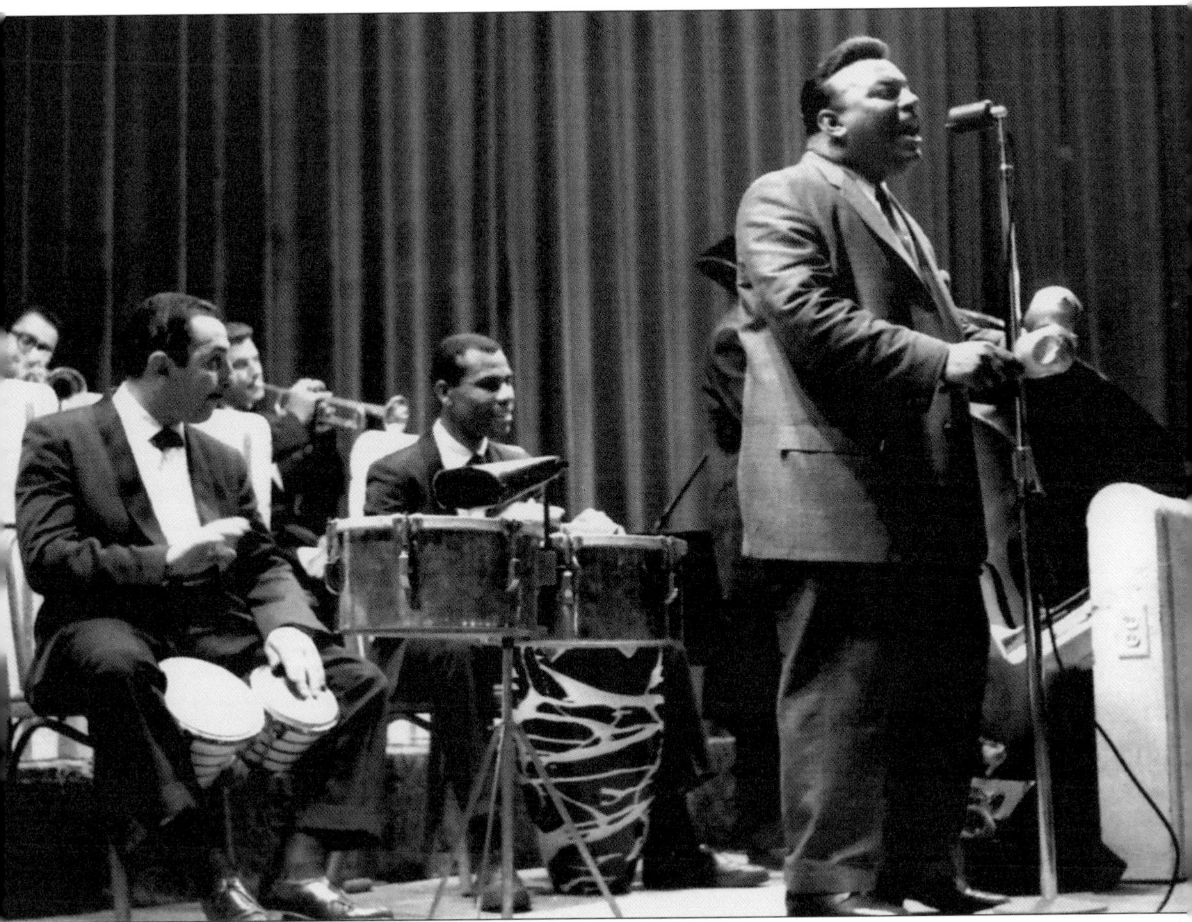

Considered one of the all-time greatest Cuban singers, Vicentico Valdés was born in the year 1921 in Havana, Cuba. Almost all the members of his family were musicians who worked with famous groups in the Havana area. After spending a few years in Mexico, Valdés moved to Los Angeles in 1948 and later to New York. Between 1948 and 1954, as the vocalist with the Tito Puente Orchestra, he recorded "Arrollando," "Ran-kankán," and "Babarabatibiri." These recordings made him famous with both the New York City and Latin American dancing public. The SECCO recordings (1953 and 1958) of "Decídete," "Una aventura," "Yo no soy guapo," "Solo por rencor," and "Los aretes de la luna" in Havana with the Sonora Matancera band started his fame as a bolerista. Valdés organized his band in 1959 and employed some of the brightest young musicians in New York City. This 1959 photograph shows him working at a dance hall with Manny Oquendo on bongos and conguero Tommy Lopez.

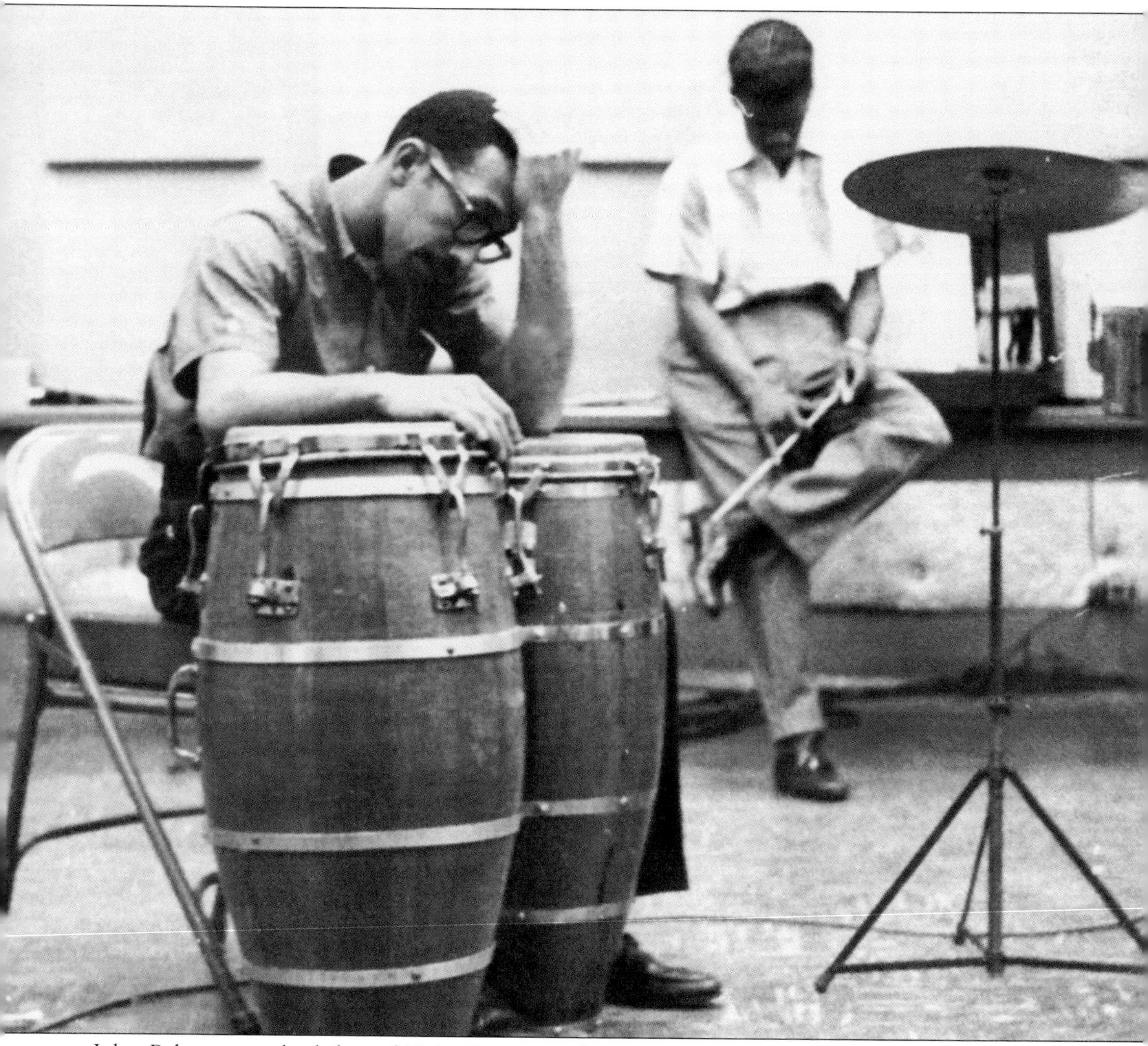

John Palomo, on the left, and Kako Bastar are listening to a studio playback in this photograph taken in 1957. Bastar became artistic director and general manager for the Alegre Record Label and recorded classic albums featuring some of the top musicians of that era. He died in July 1994.

Four

THE SIDEMEN

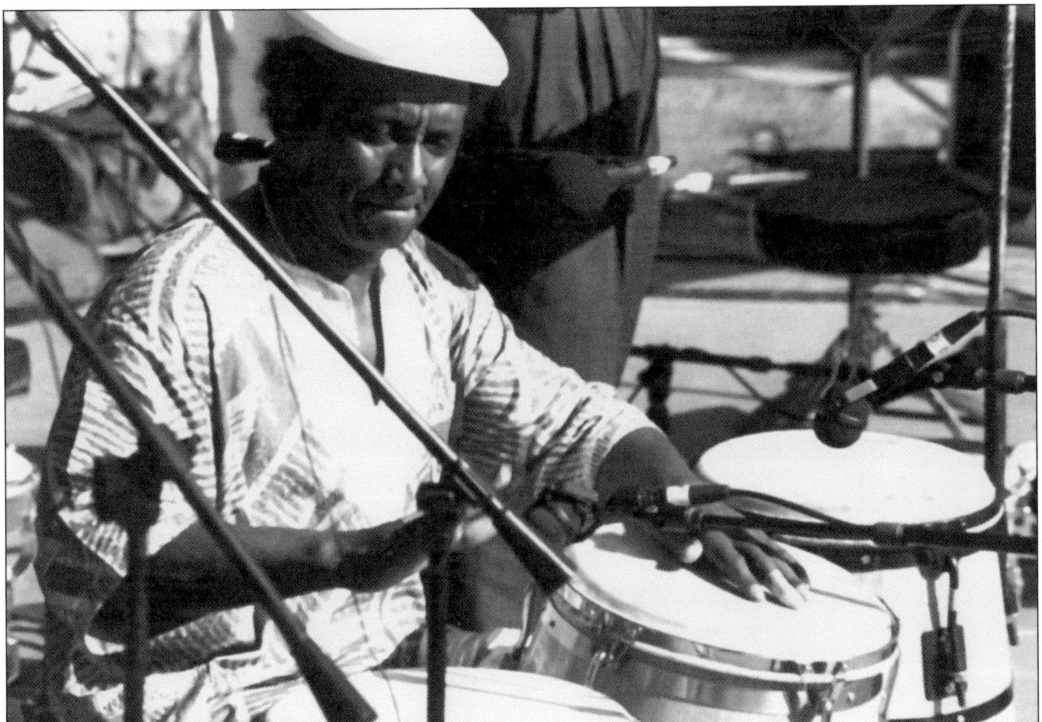

At an outdoor concert in Long Beach, California, in 1990, Francisco Aguabella plays with the Eddie Palmieri Orchestra. One of Cuba's important legends, he remains active in the Los Angeles area.

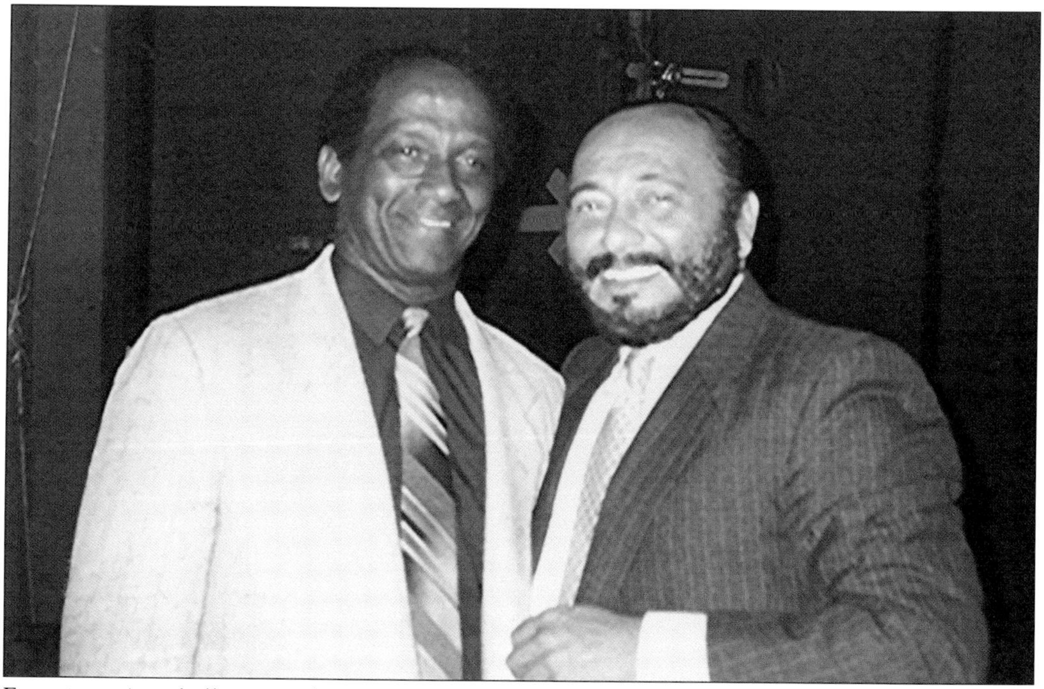

Francisco Aguabella was photographed with Eddie Palmieri backstage at the Hollywood Palladium in 1988.

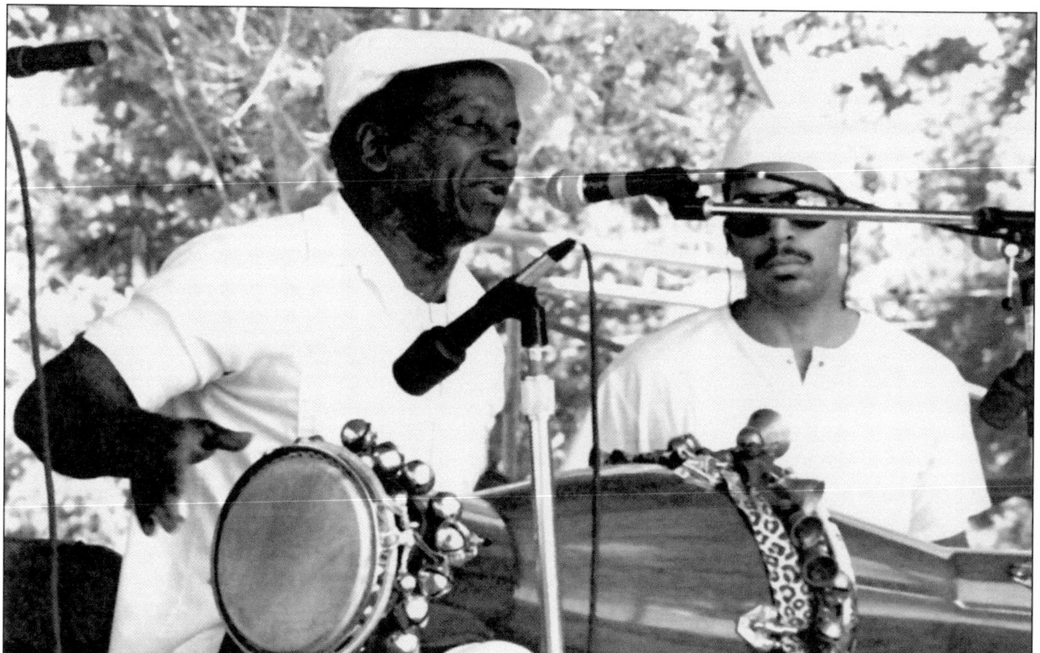

Noted for his religious as well as his secular percussion work, Aguabella is shown playing the sacred batá drum used in the Yoruba/Lucumi religion at a Watts Festival in Los Angeles in 1983.

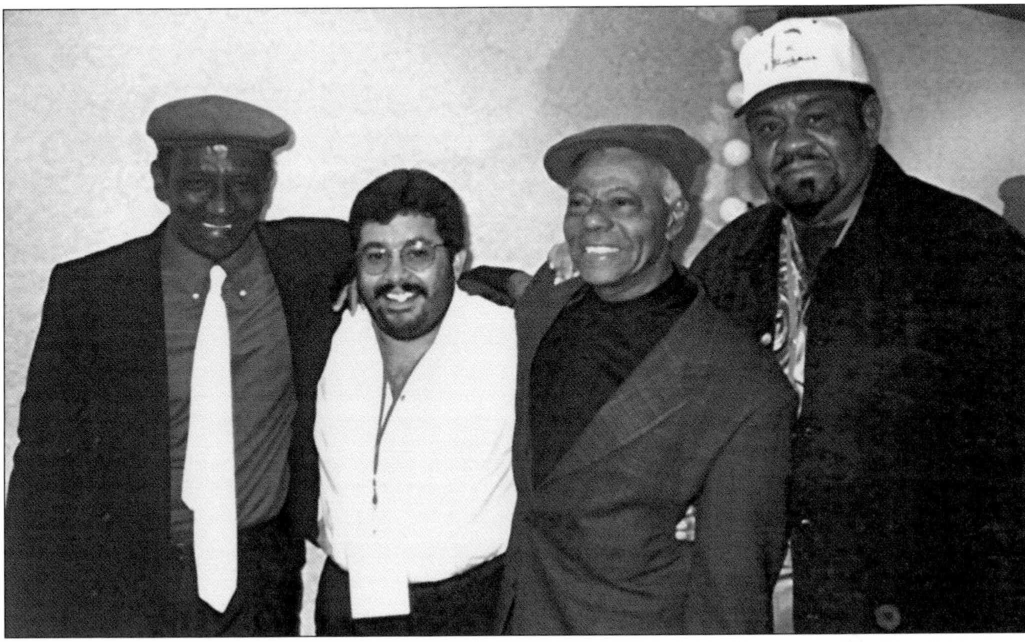

The past and the present come together in this 1996 photograph backstage at the Greek Theater in Los Angeles. Shown here, from left to right, are Aguabella, Giovanni Hidalgo, Armando Peraza, and bassist Al McKibbon.

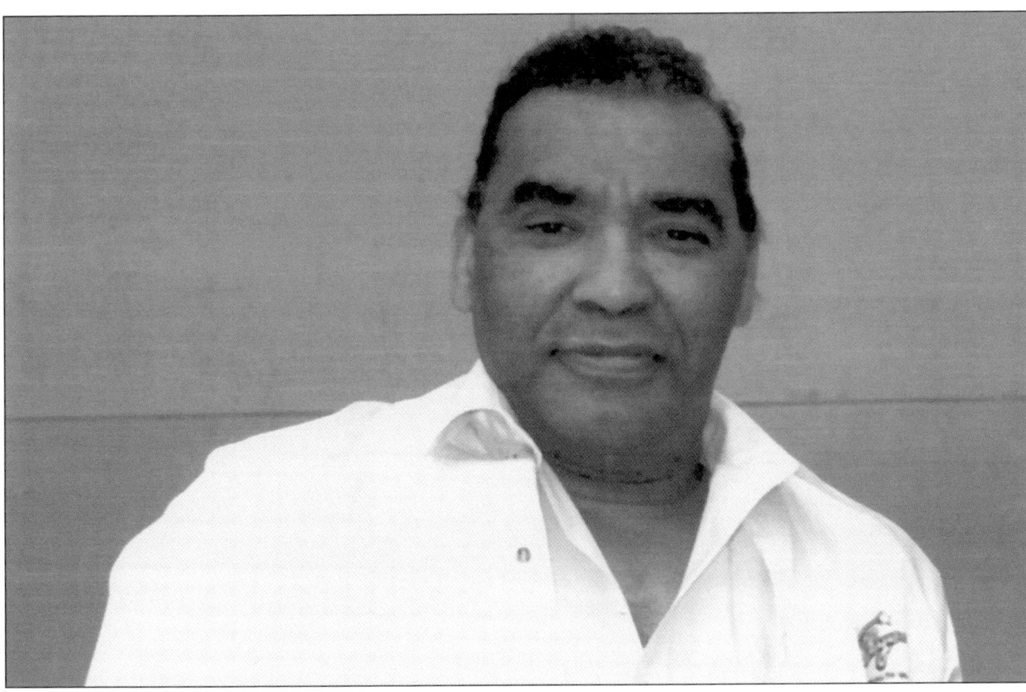

Pedro Aguilar, also known as "Cuban Pete," is pictured in 1993 on the set of *The Mambo Kings*, where he served as a dance consultant. During the late 1940s and 1950s, Cuban Pete was one of the principal dancers that gave exhibitions at the legendary Palladium Ballroom.

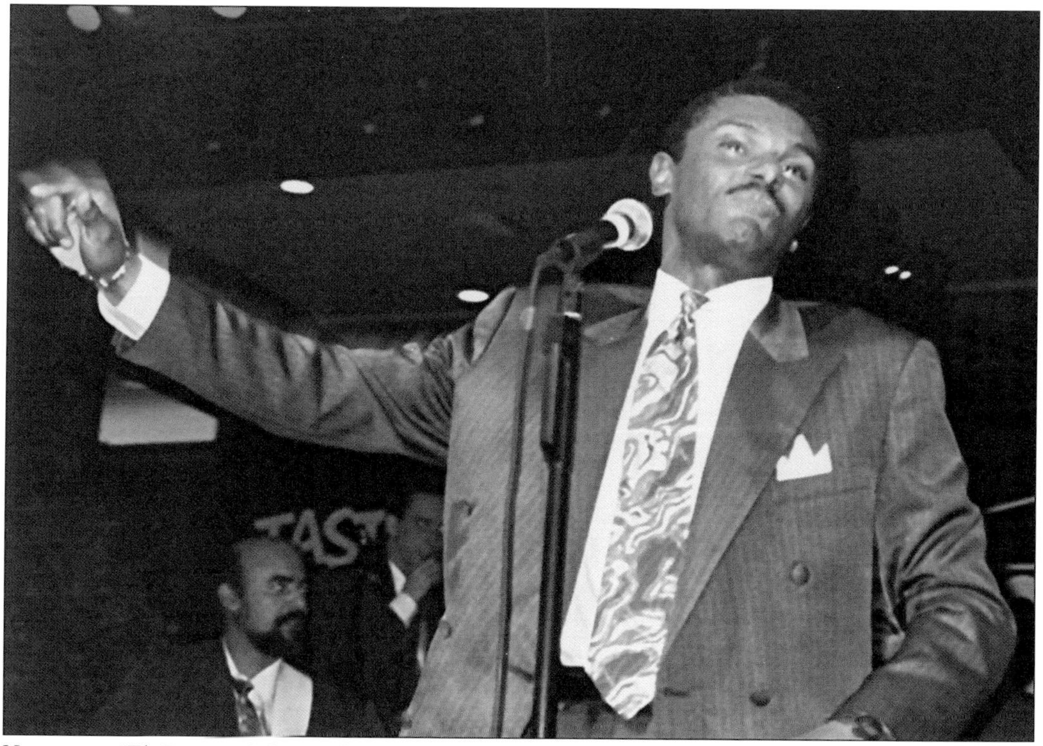

Known as "El Canario," Jose Alberto moved to Puerto Rico at the age of seven from his native Dominican Republic. He received his musical education in Puerto Rico before moving to New York City in the early 1970s. Alberto soon found employment with Tipica 73, one of the hottest groups during that era. In this 1995 photograph, he leads his own orchestra in a club in Los Angeles.

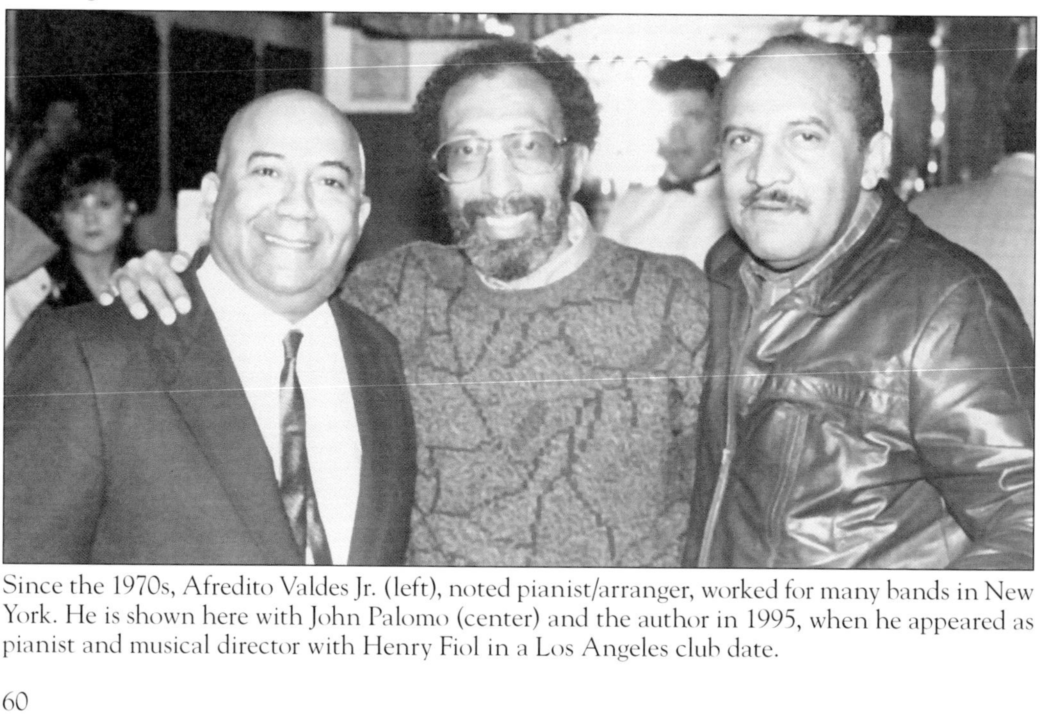

Since the 1970s, Afredito Valdes Jr. (left), noted pianist/arranger, worked for many bands in New York. He is shown here with John Palomo (center) and the author in 1995, when he appeared as pianist and musical director with Henry Fiol in a Los Angeles club date.

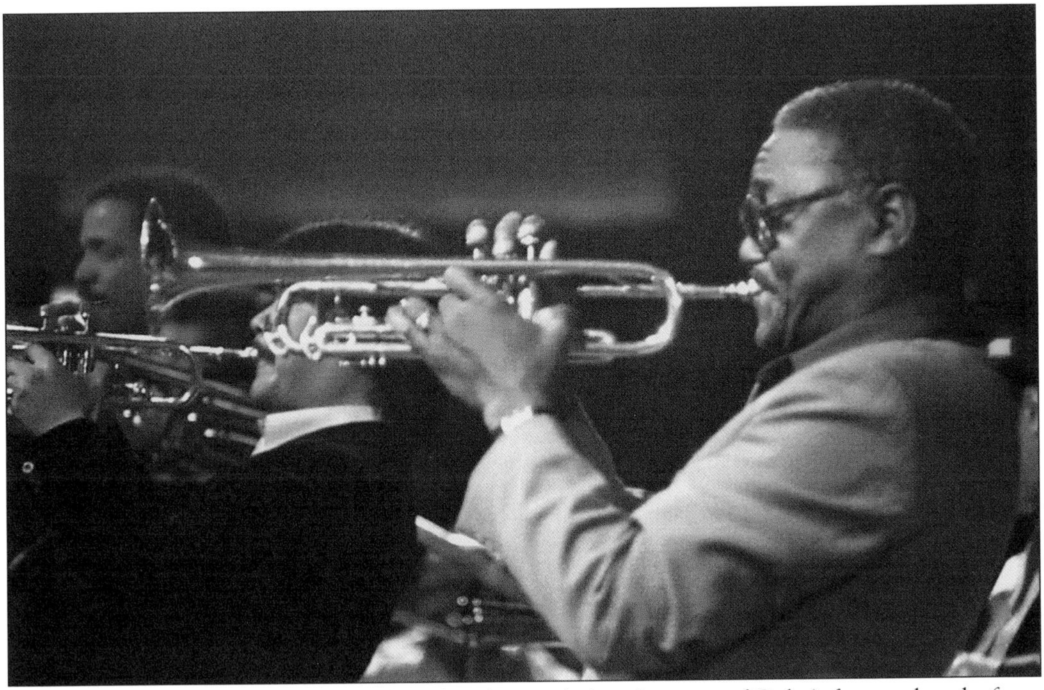

Alfredo "Chocolate" Armenteros played and recorded with many of Cuba's famous bands, from Septeto Habanero to Beny Moré, before coming to the United States in the mid-1950s. He is seen here at the Hollywood Palladium in 1993.

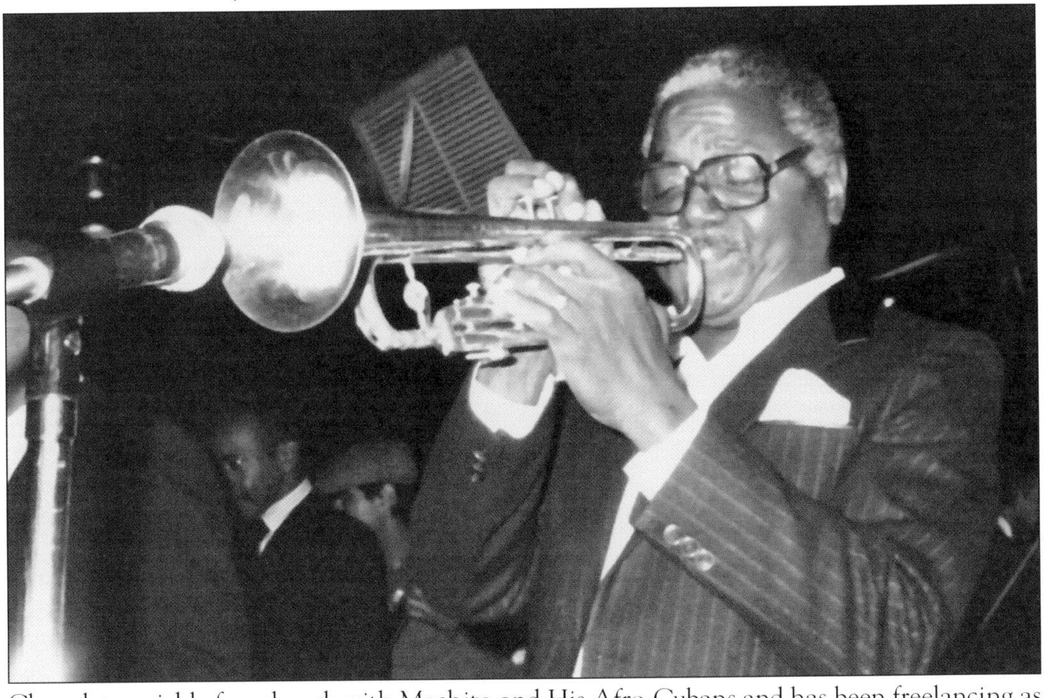

Chocolate quickly found work with Machito and His Afro-Cubans and has been freelancing as a number one trumpeter ever since. Known for his clear tone and deliberate phrasing, he is seen here at Club Side Street in the Bronx in 1998.

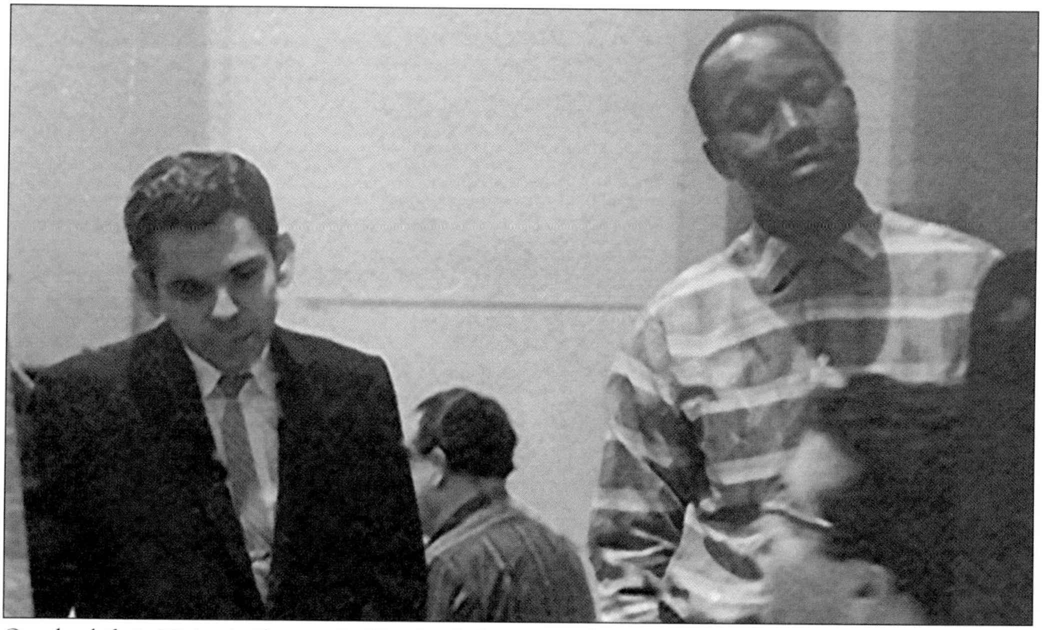

On the left is Vitin Aviles, with Charlie Palmieri at the piano and Leonel Bravet standing on the right. This photograph was taken at the 1957 recording session of Palmieri's album *Orquesta La Duboney con Johnny Pacheco and Vitin Aviles*. Born in Mayaguez, Puerto Rico, Aviles came to New York during the 1950s and worked with Xavier Cugat, Enrique Madriguera, Noro Morales, and many bands of that era.

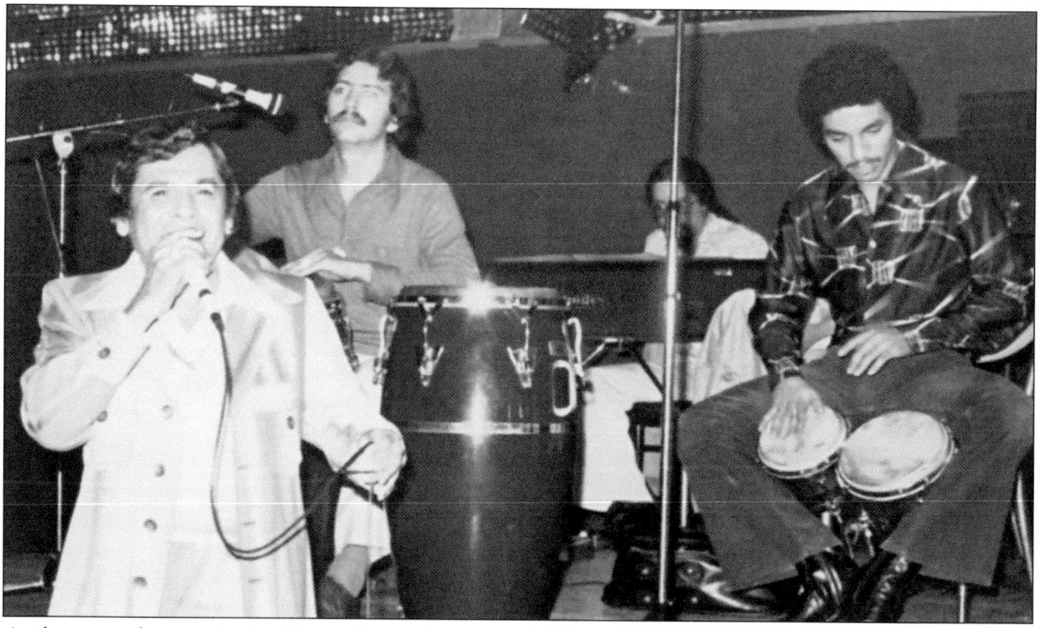

Aviles toured extensively all over Latin America. He was able to sing up-tempo guarachas as well as love songs. His extensive list of recordings with boleros earned him the title of "El Cantante Del Amor" (the love balladeer). In this 1996 picture, he is shown at a Los Angeles nightclub where he hired local musicians. Pictured on conga is Luis Conte, and playing bongos is the late Hector Andrade. Aviles died on January 1, 2004, in New York City.

In 1994, Eddie Palmieri played at the Pasta House in Los Angeles. Ismael Quintana, Palmieri's featured singer, is joined here by Luis Camilo "Azuquita" Argumedes.

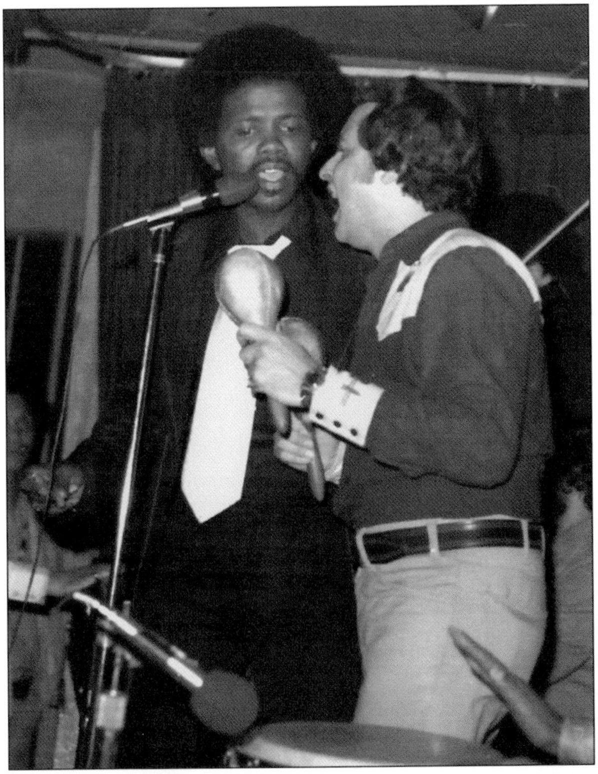

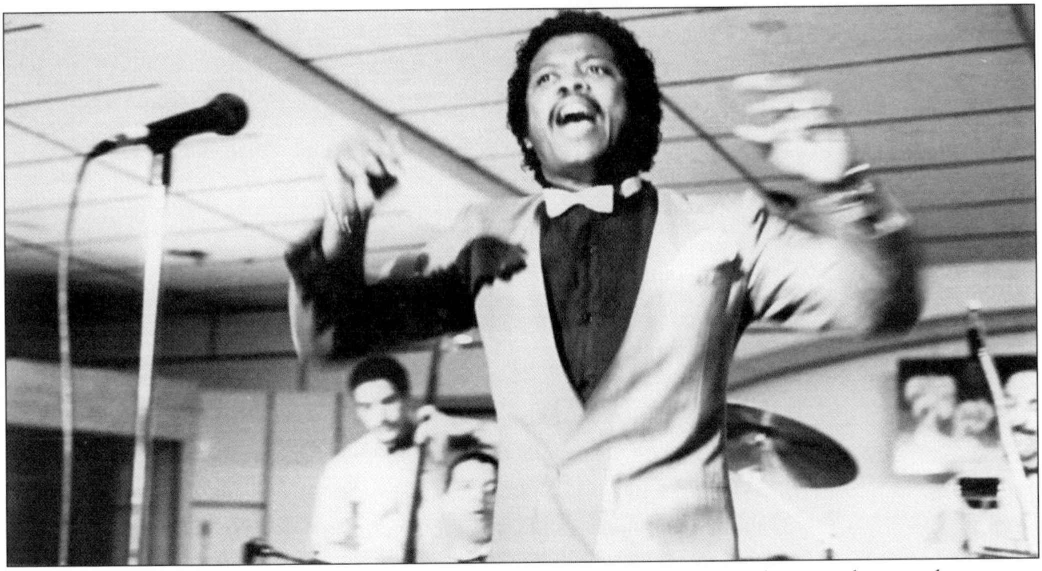

Azuquita has had a vast amount of experience as a sonero (salsa singer). Since leaving his native Panama, he has traveled to many cities throughout Latin America and Europe leading his own groups. He gained important recognition in New York when he joined Tipica 73 as featured vocalist in the 1970s and continued to do the same in Puerto Rico and Los Angeles. At an important dance club in Los Angeles called Casablanca, he gave outstanding performances in 1993 with his own band. Tony Rosa can be seen on the left on congas, and Kevin Ricard is on timbales, on the right.

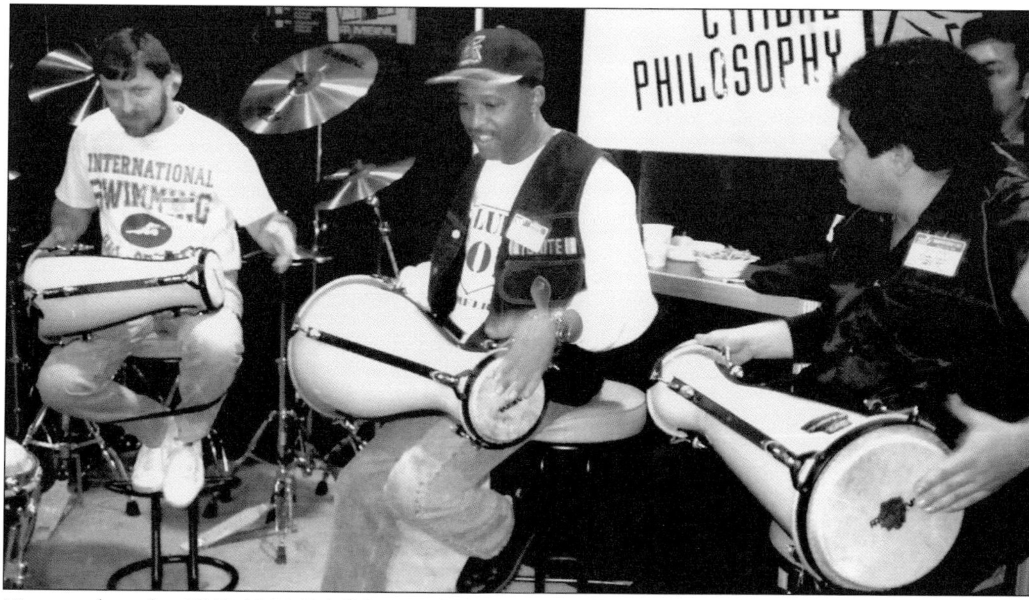

Captured at the 2003 NAMM (National Association of Music Merchants) show in Anaheim, California, are three important percussionists who have been active playing salsa dance music since the 1970s. Here they are playing the commercial version of the sacred batá drums used in the Yoruba/Lucumi religious ceremonies. Pictured here, from left to right, are Michael Spiro (San Francisco), Giovanni Hidalgo (Florida), and Bill Summers (New Orleans).

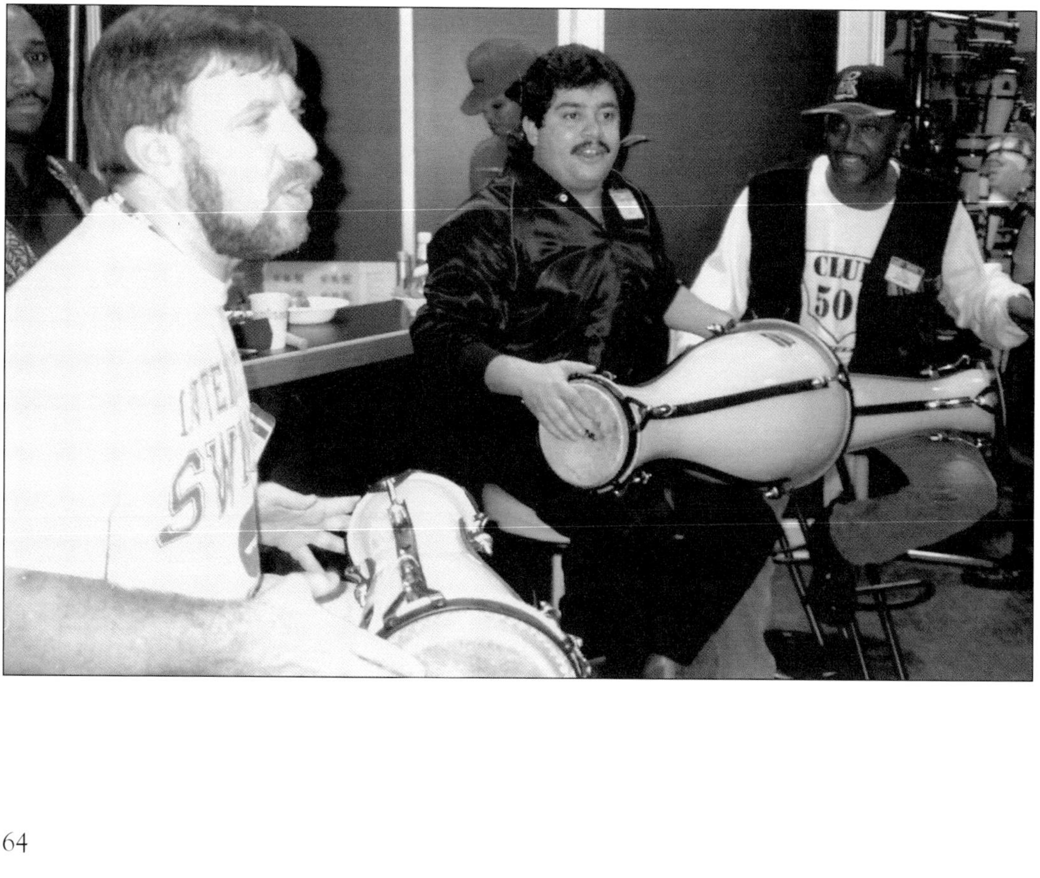

One of New York's finest all-around percussionists, Steve Berrios is shown here in 1993 with the Fort Apache Band at Steven's Steak House in Los Angeles. Andy Gonzalez is on bass. His father, Steve Sr., was a drummer with the major Latin bands of the 1940s and 1950s, including Noro Morales, Miguelito Valdez, and Pupi Campo. He was influenced by Willie Bobo and Julio Collazo, the legendary master of the batá sacred drum. Steve became a percussion apprentice under Collazo and at the same time, Collazo became his spiritual mentor in Ifa, the Yoruba-based rites that are the wellspring of all serious Afro Cuban music. At 19 he became a member of Mongo Santamaria's group and in 1981, a founding member of the Latin jazz group the Fort Apache Band.

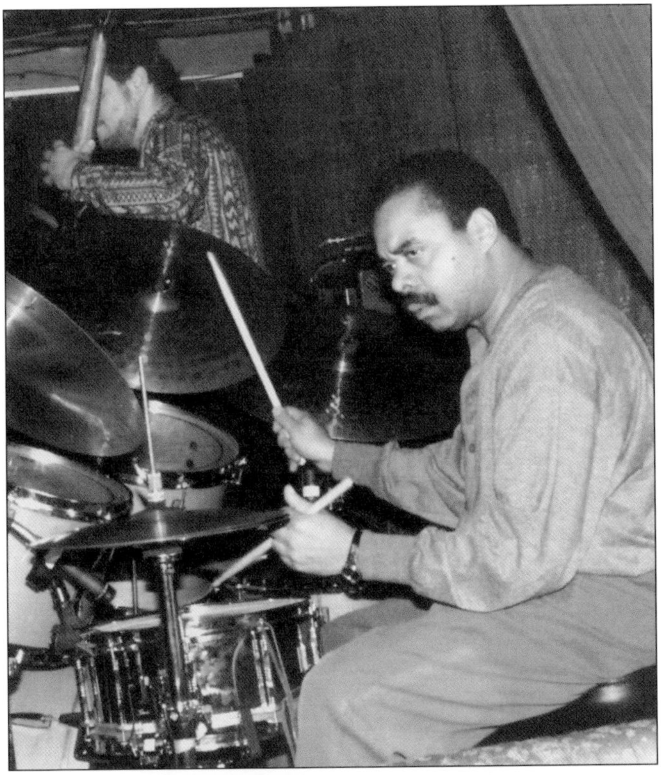

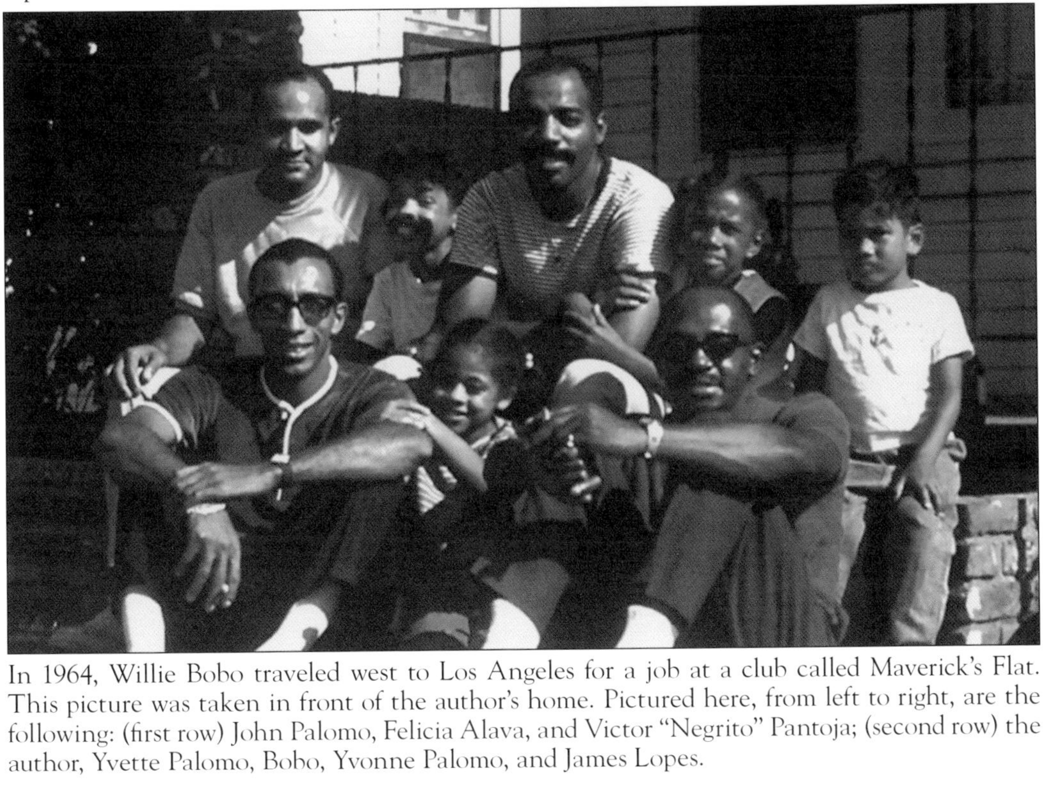

In 1964, Willie Bobo traveled west to Los Angeles for a job at a club called Maverick's Flat. This picture was taken in front of the author's home. Pictured here, from left to right, are the following: (first row) John Palomo, Felicia Alava, and Victor "Negrito" Pantoja; (second row) the author, Yvette Palomo, Bobo, Yvonne Palomo, and James Lopes.

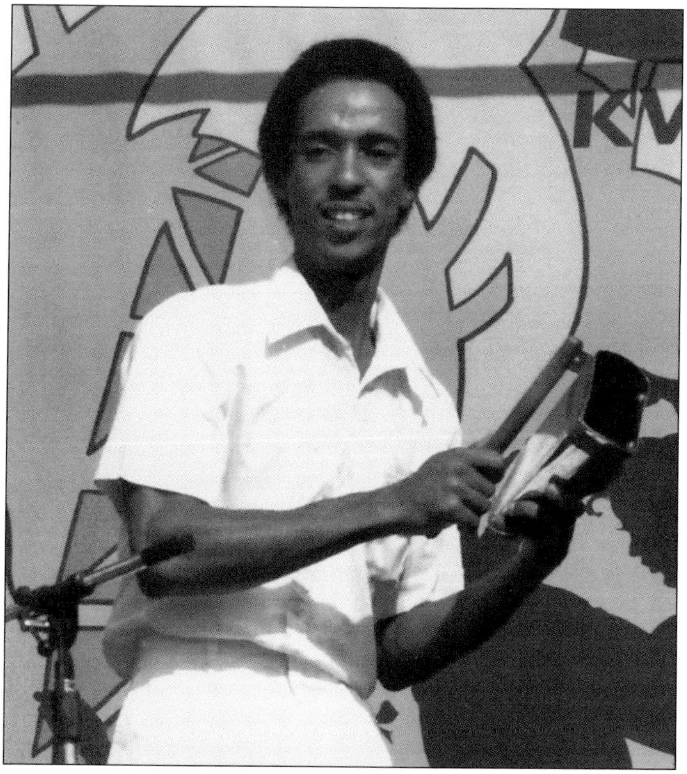

One of Puerto Rico's finest percussionists, Anthony Carrillo has had ample experience since the late 1970s when he played bongos with some of the islands leading groups. His extensive talents became well known with the group Batacumbele, founded by Angel "Cachete" Maldonado. This group also featured new conga wizard Giovanni Hidalgo. Together they became a dynamic duo in the rhythm section of numerous bands. He is shown here with the Eddie Palmieri Orchestra at an outdoor concert in Long Beach, California, in 1994.

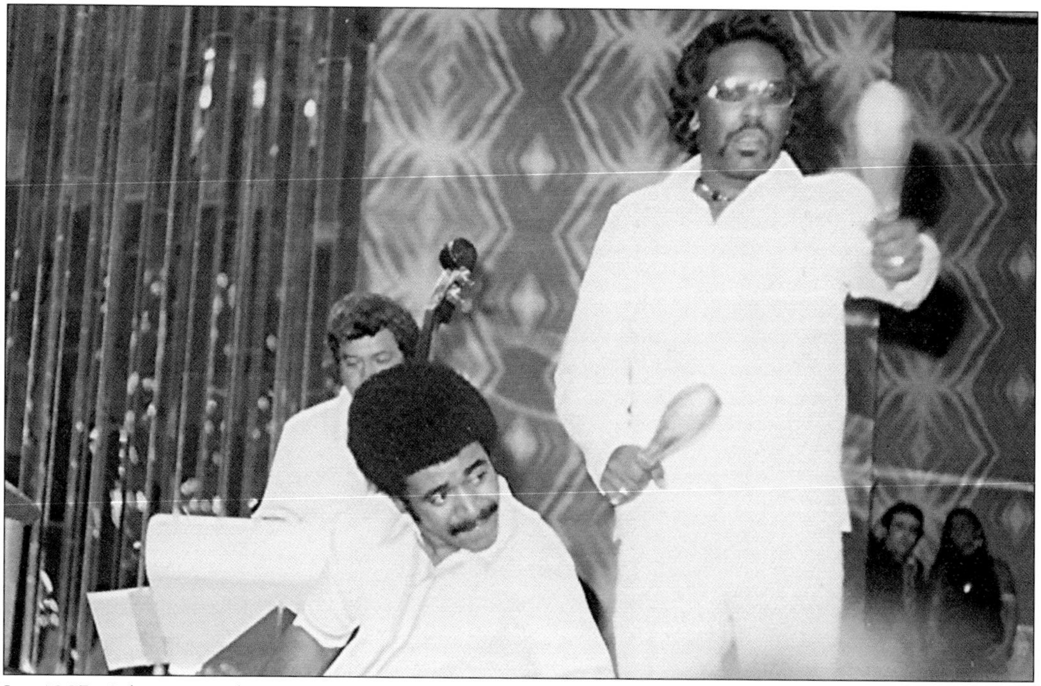

In 1987, Johnny Pacheco's group accompanied Celia Cruz's appearance at the Hollywood Palladium. With the group were Hector Casanova, singer and maraca player, and Jose Mangual Jr. playing bongo.

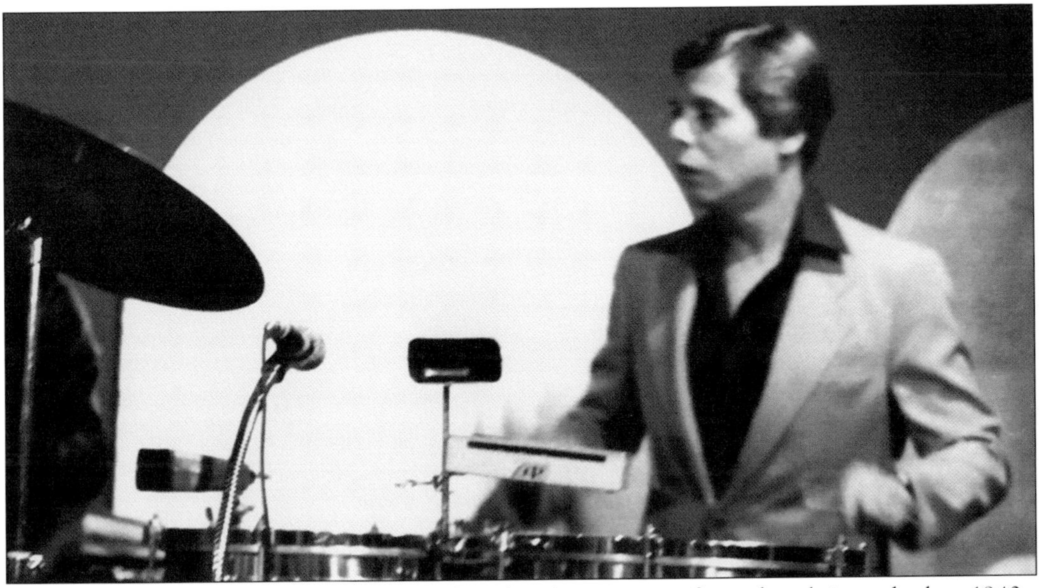

Mike Collazo, a native New Yorker, has played with every significant band since the late 1940s. Known as a fine drummer as well as a timbalero, one of his first jobs was with the band of Marcelino Guerra. A stint with Vicentico Valdes followed before he became a member of Eddie Palmieri's group La Perfecta. Tito Rodriguez and Tito Puente have also used his talent. This picture was taken in 1994 when he was a member of Orquesta Broadway at Club Maganette in New York City.

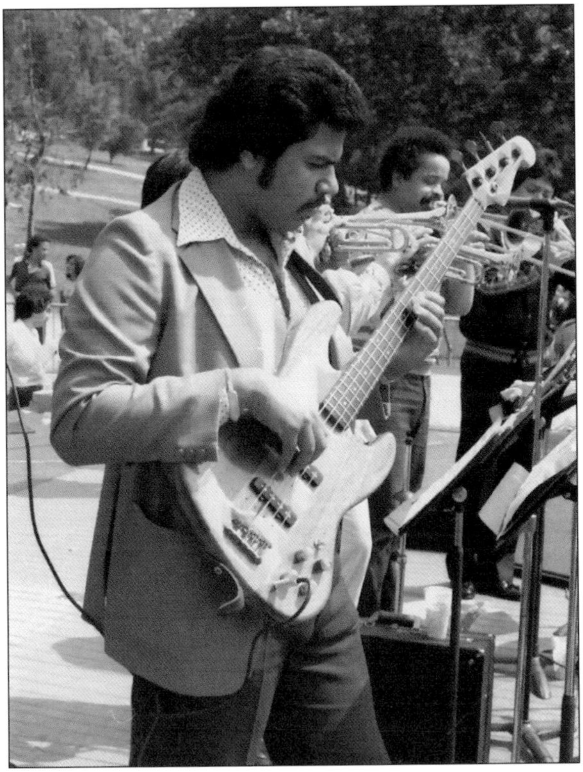

Taken in 1989 at an outdoor concert with the Willie Colon band at the University of California Los Angeles, this picture shows Salvador (Sal) Cuevas on fender bass. One of the first to use this type of bass in salsa dance music, he contributed some of the funk feeling used in rhythm and blues. He worked and recorded during the 1970s with Ruben Blades, Ray Barretto, Willie Colon, and many other salsa greats.

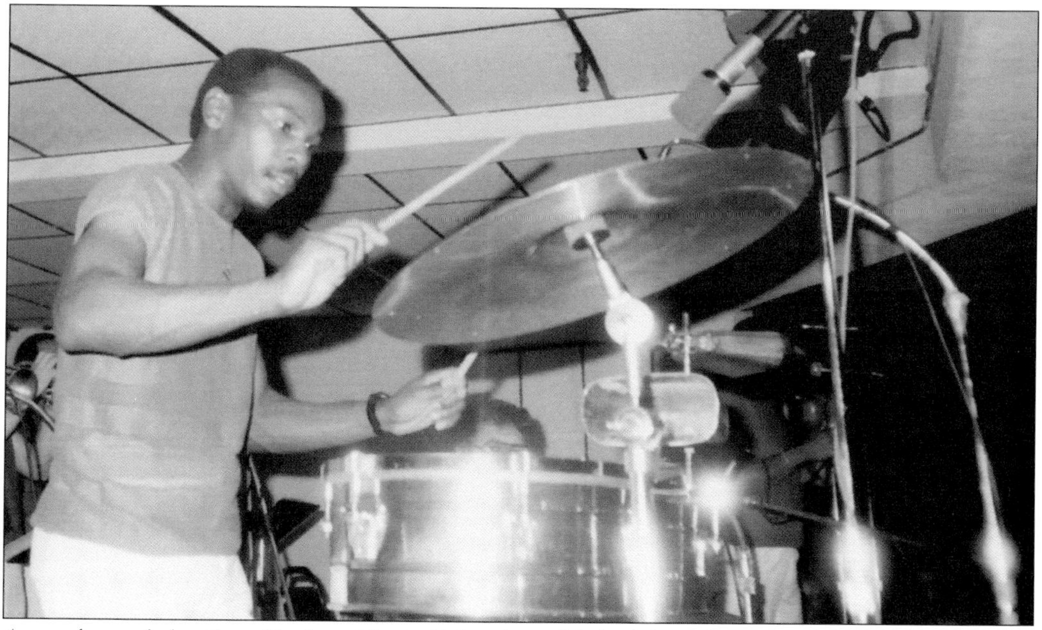

A product of the East Harlem Music School established by Johnny Colon, Jimmy Delgado exhibited his talent at a very young age. By the early 1970s, Delgado had established himself as a major timbale player with bands such as Orchestra Cimarron, Eddie Palmieri, Ray Barretto, Willie Colon, Ruben Blades, Ismael Quintana, and Tipica Novel, to name a few. He is shown here at the Hollywood Palladium in 1987 with Ray Barretto.

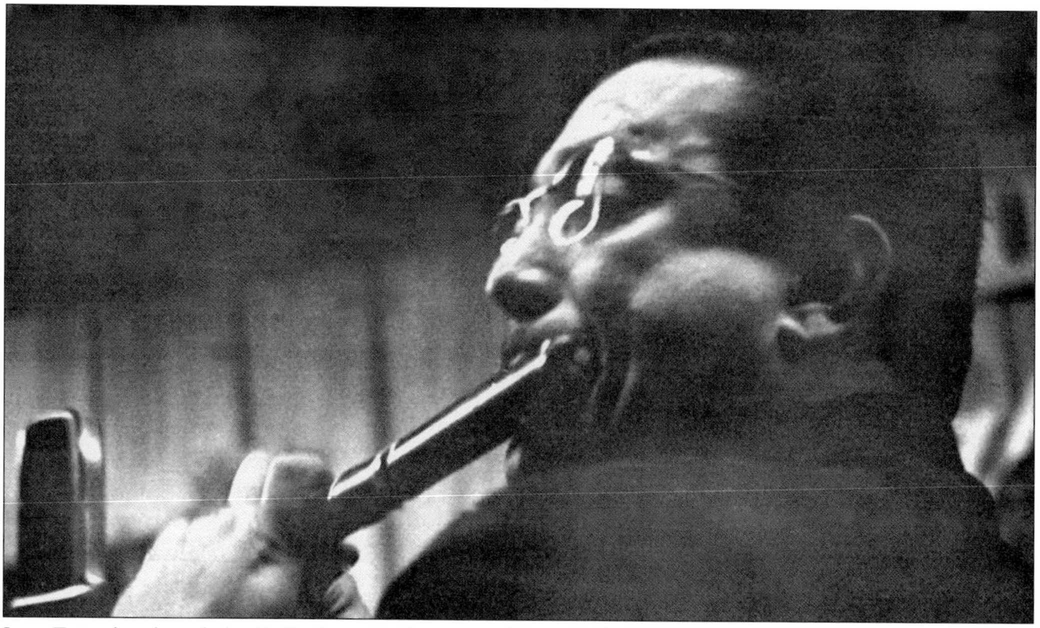

Jose Fajardo played the Palladium Ballroom in New York City with his charanga band in 1958. His band was one of the first charanga bands to come from Cuba. The hall was mobbed that night because in his band was a young Tata Guines. Cachao's popular recording *Concerts in Miniature* was known to all the percussion aficionados, and word spread quickly that the "percussion sensation" featured on that album would be there.

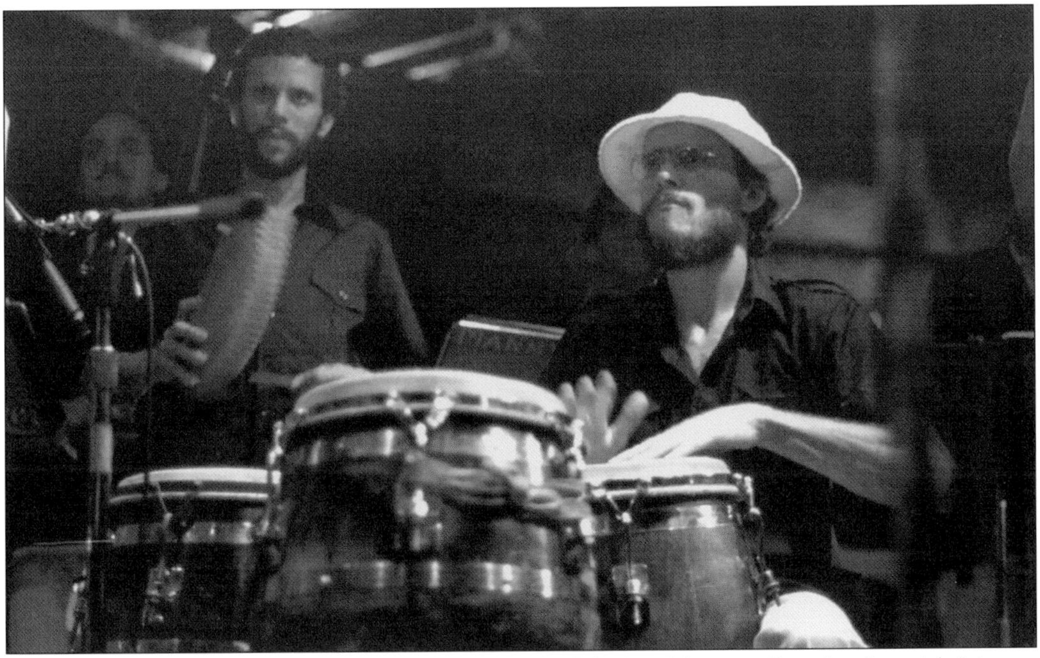

Jerry Gonzalez (right) is pictured here in 1985 at Club Candilejas in Los Angles with Manny Oquendo's group Libre. Gonzalez started playing trumpet at age 12 as a student in junior high school. His interest in percussion began as a teenager participating in jam sessions on tenement rooftops, in the streets, and particularly in Central Park in New York City.

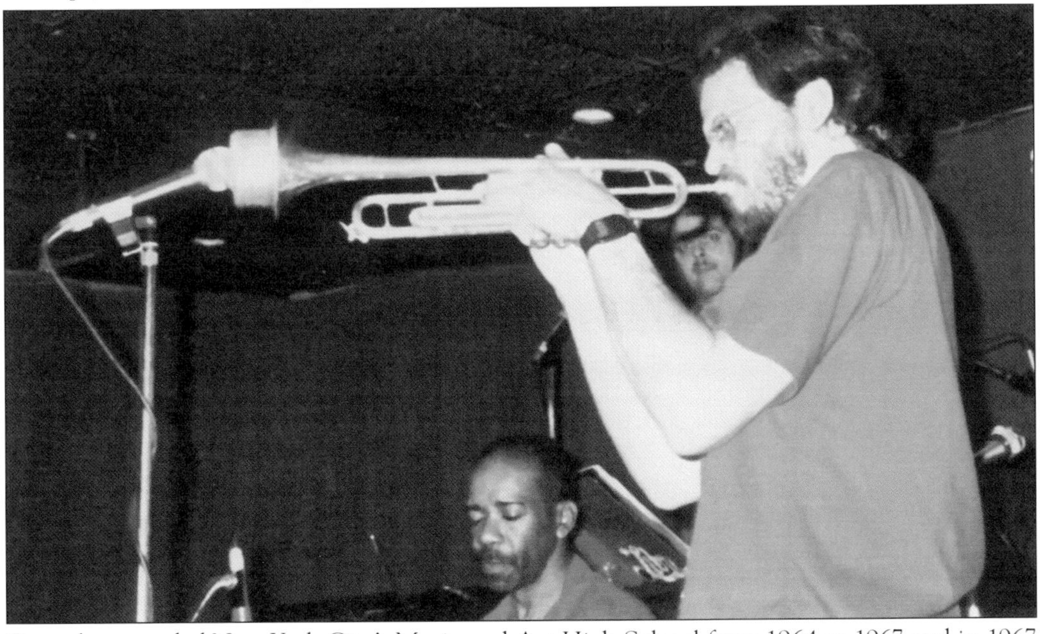

Gonzalez attended New York City's Music and Art High School from 1964 to 1967 and in 1967 received a scholarship to New York College of Music, where he was influenced by jazz trumpeter Kenny Dorham. Taken at Steven's Steak House in Los Angeles in 1985, this image shows him playing trumpet with his Latin jazz group the Fort Apache Band. A musician for over 30 years, he has played and recorded with many important salsa and jazz groups.

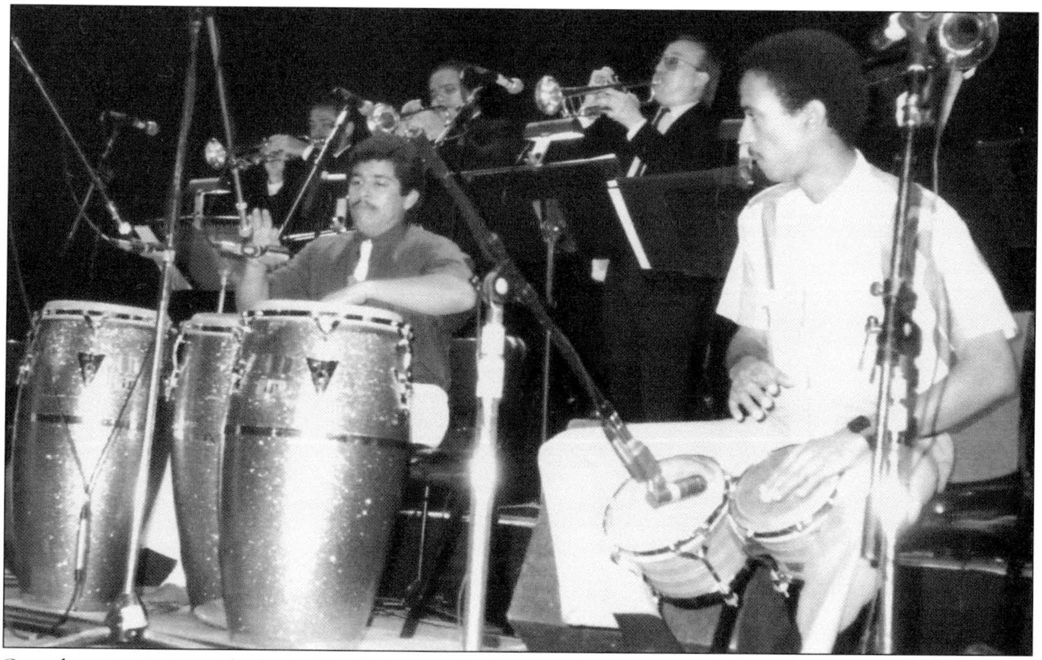

Seen here in 1994 with the Eddie Palmieri Orchestra, Giovanni Hidalgo, on conga, and Anthony Carrillo, playing bongo, are former members of the Latin jazz group Batacumbele. Musicians since their early teens in their native Puerto Rico, they have become world renowned as a salsa dance band duo.

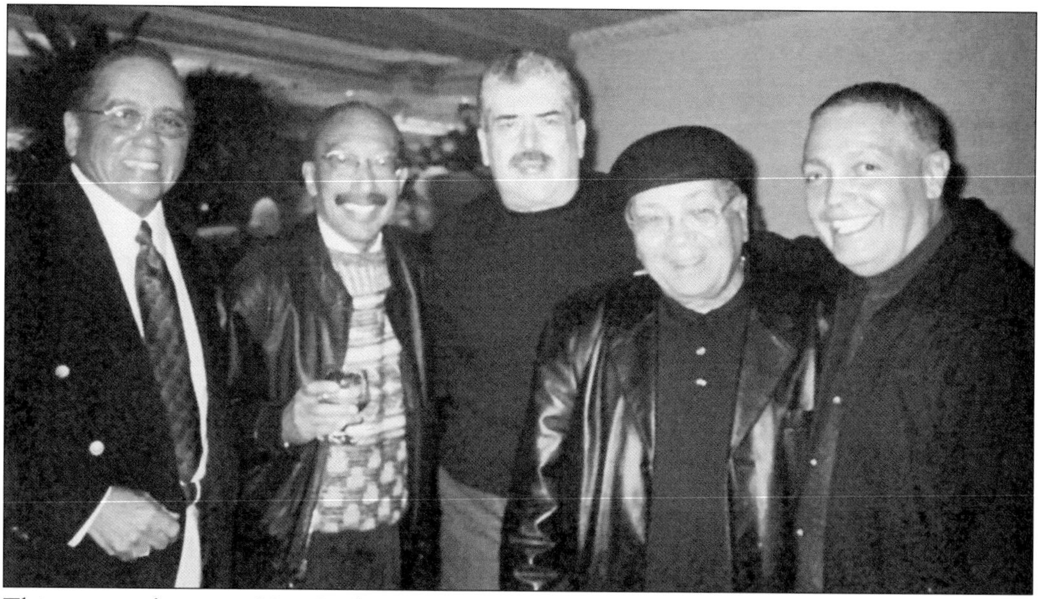

This group of veteran New York percussionists became known as the Latin Rat Pack. The photograph was taken on a Monday night at the Mandalay Bay Hotel and Casino when several Las Vegas resident musicians met to welcome two other musicians who were in town. Luis Miranda and Pat Rodríguez were guests of honor at the Coral Reef Lounge where Rick Arroyo and his Latin jazz ensemble were featured. Pictured from left to right are Luis Miranda, John Palomo, John "Dandy" Rodriguez, Pat Rodriguez, and Joe Torres.

Living in the United States since the mid-1950s, Felix "Pupi" Legarreta has been a member of practically all the charanga groups formed in the New York area. He was also a member of the Cesta All-Stars, the Alegre All-Stars, and the Fania All-Stars. A flute player as well as a violinist, this picture is from a Cachao Lopez concert at Hunter College in 1978.

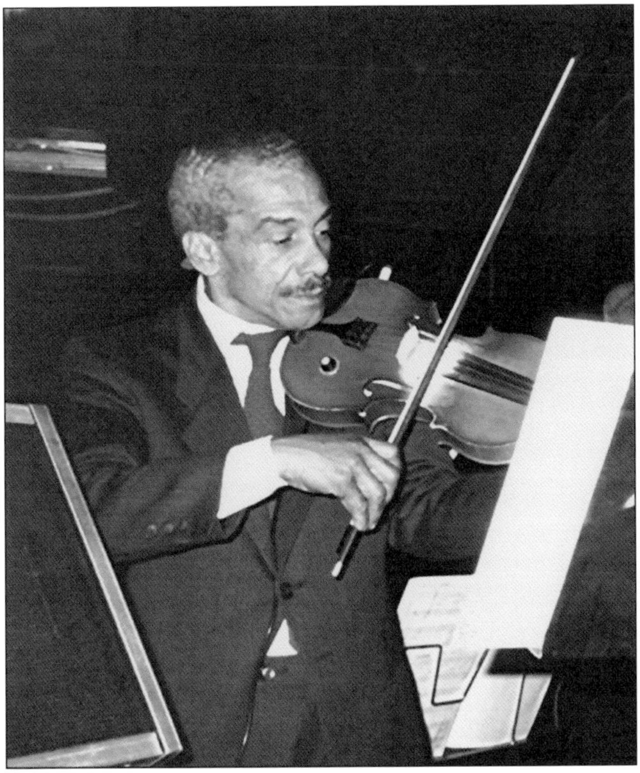

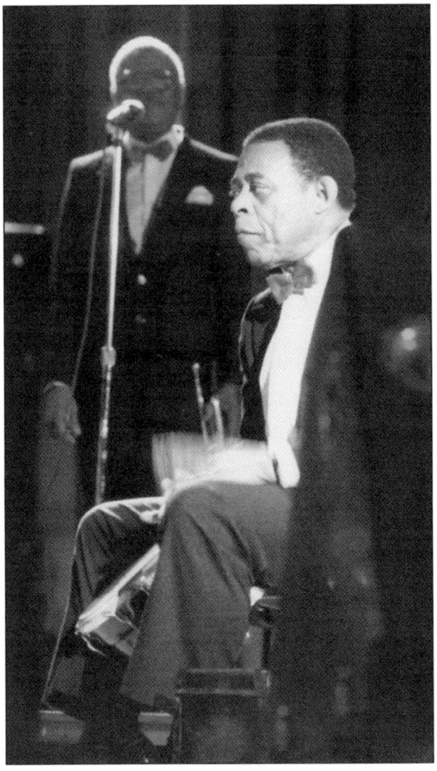

This same Cachao Lopez concert at Hunter College in 1978 featured veteran *bongocero* Jose Mangual Sr. of the famous Machito and His Afro-Cubans. Looking on with trumpet in hand is Alfredo "Chocolate" Armenteros.

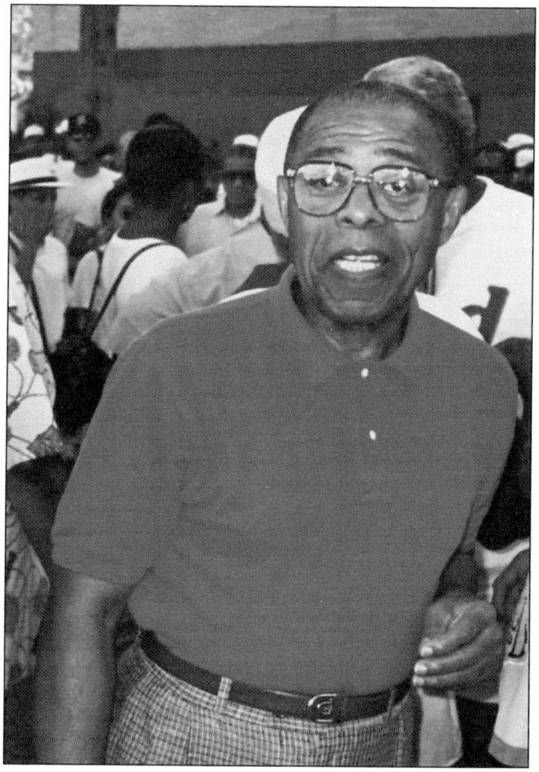

Here Jose "Buyu" Mangual Sr. is at the Annual Old-Timers Reunion held on 111th Street and Fifth Avenue in 1996. After he left the Machito organization, Mangual began doing studio work and then became the percussionist with the Erroll Gardner Trio. Gardner traveled extensively, which gave Mangual the opportunity to see other parts of the United States and Europe. Mangual died in 1998.

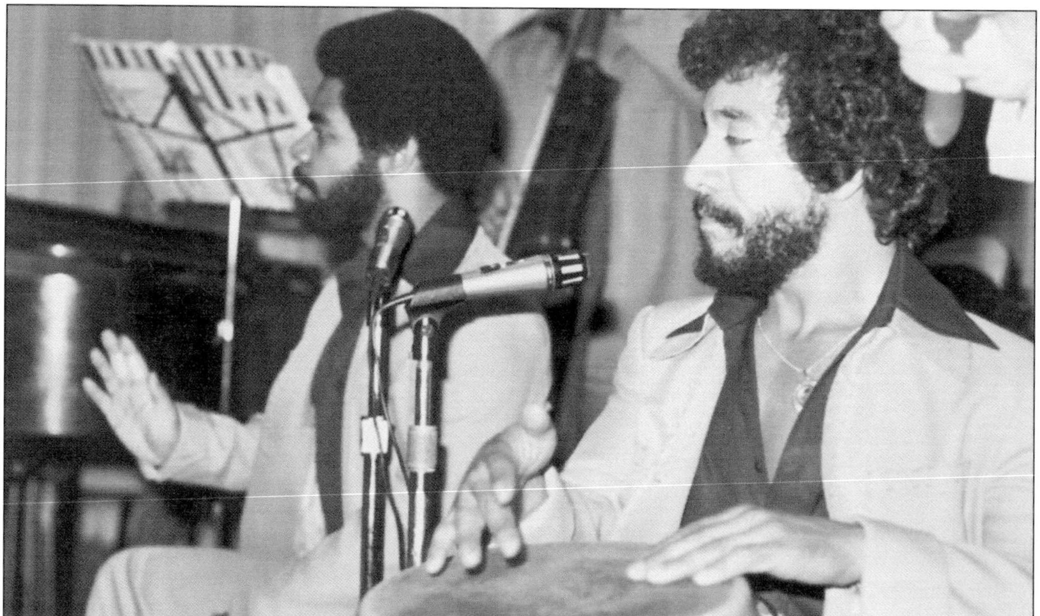

Jose Mangual Jr., playing the bongo, is pictured with Milton Cardona, playing the congas, in 1982 with the Hector Lavoe Orchestra. Born and raised in Spanish Harlem, Mangual was tutored by his father and has become one the industry's finest bongo players. He and his spiritual brother, Milton, became a dynamic duo with the Willie Colon band and did studio recordings for many artists.

Appearing in 1996 at the Greek Theater in Los Angeles, Jose Mangual Jr. is pictured with Papo Pepin on congas in front of his own group, Son Boricua.

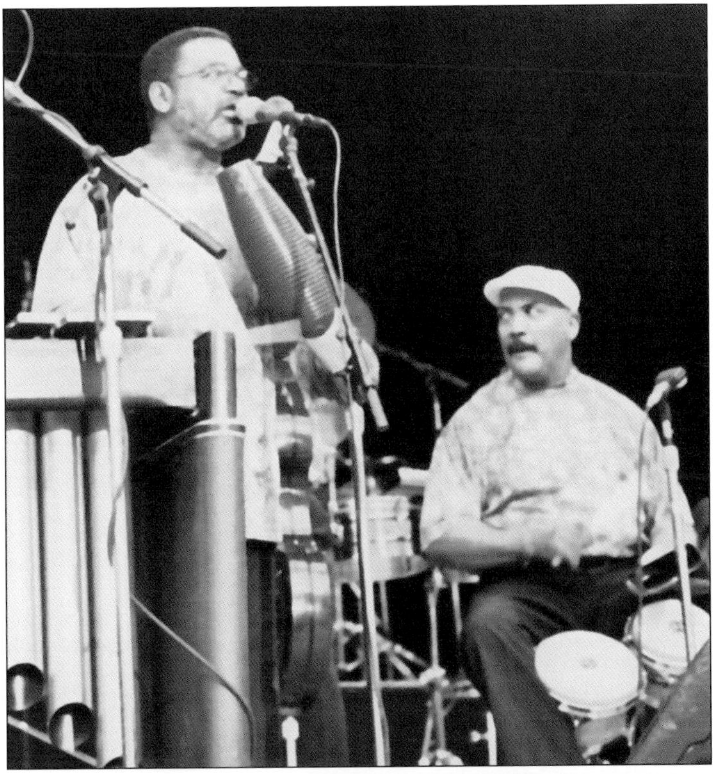

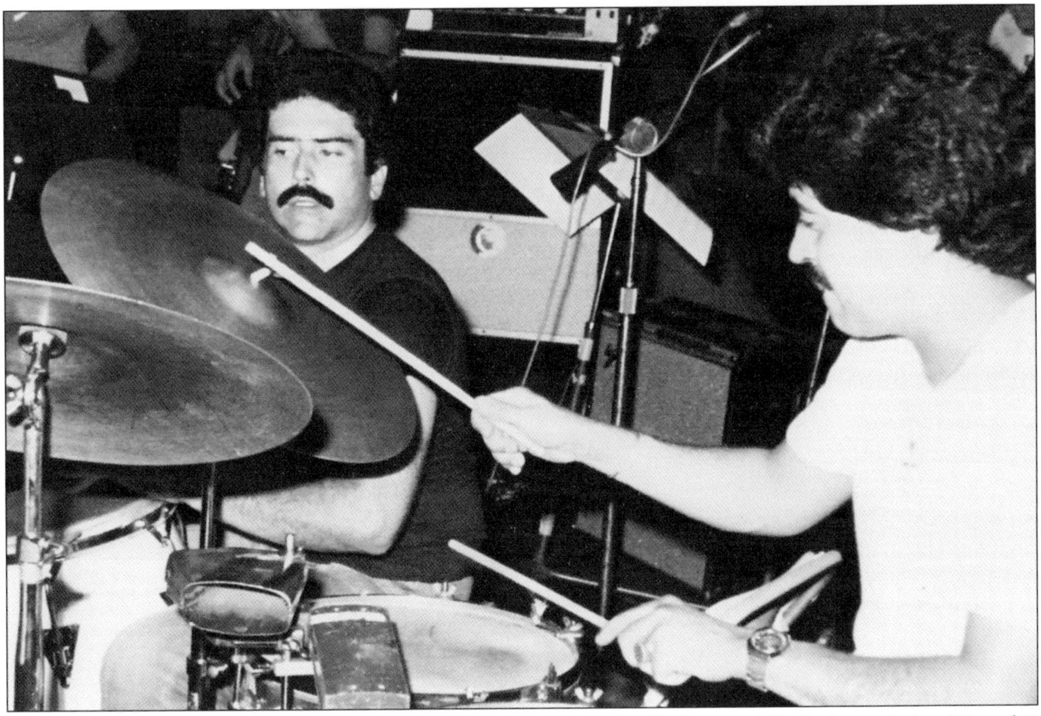

In 1983, during a Fania All-Stars rehearsal for a show at the Hollywood Palladium, John "Dandy" Rodriguez is on congas and Nicky Marrero is shown on timbales.

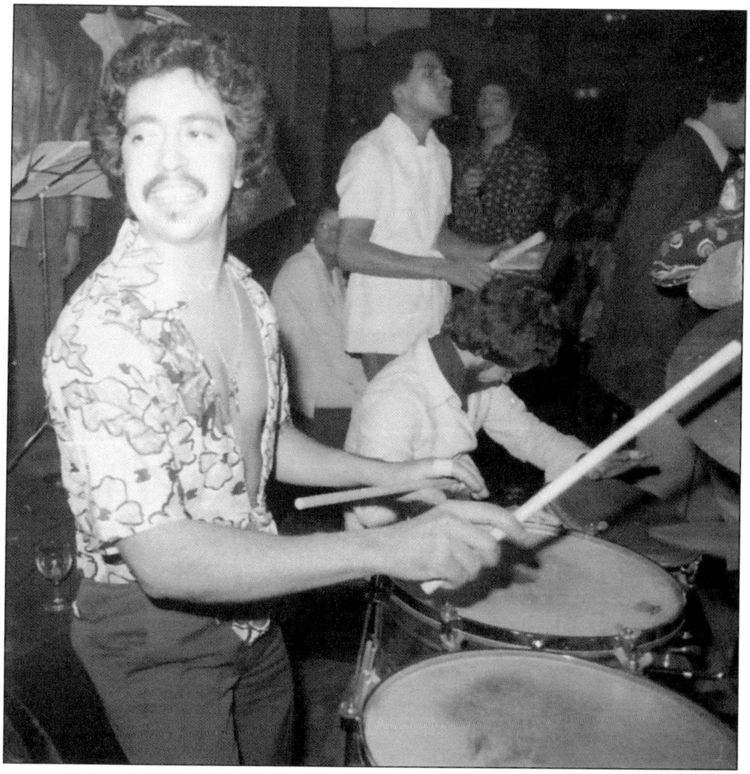

Nicky Marrero is shown on timbales, and Chuckie Lopez is playing cowbell with the Eddie Palmieri band in Los Angeles in 1987. Chuckie is the son of legendary conguero Tommy Lopez of the early Palmieri group La Perfecta.

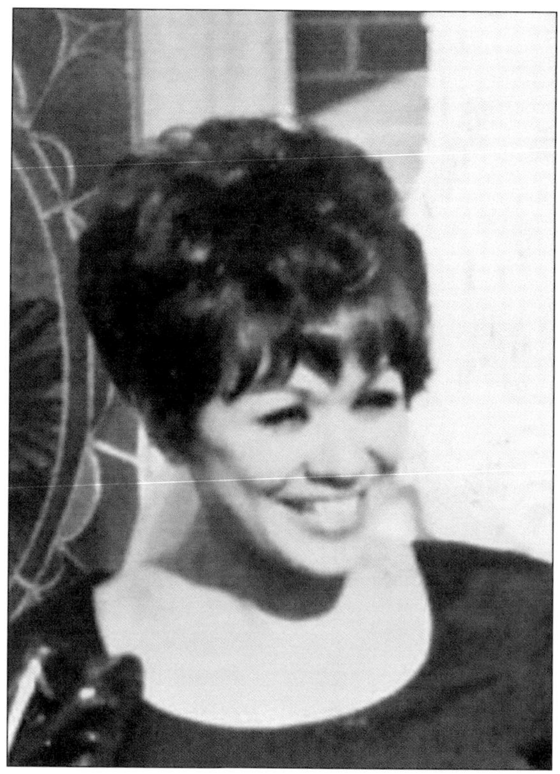

Olguita Melendez was an original, born and educated in Spanish Harlem, who went on to enjoy a short-lived fame as a singer during the golden era of Latin music in New York City. Blessed with a great sense of humor and joy for life, she sparkled with radiance to all who met her. She started her professional career in the late 1940s as a teenager with the band of Eddie Forrester, and went on to sing with the Elmo Garcia organization. She, along with Mechita, were the only female singers attempting to make a living in the male-dominated world of band singers. In the late 1950s, she moved to Los Angeles where she found employment with the Modesto Duran and Al Escobar bands. She was the featured singer on Duran's recording "Pachanga, Anyone?" She eventually moved to Las Vegas because of the abundance of work there and put down roots for many years. Her sexy and raucous laughter is something that will be remembered by those that knew her. Melendez died in 2006.

After moving to New York City from Puerto Rico at the age of 17, Ismael Miranda joined the band of Joey Pastrana. They had a hit in 1967 with "Rumbon Melon." Eventually Miranda joined the Larry Harlow Band as the lead singer and recorded more than six albums that established him as a superior sonero. As a member of the Fania All-Stars, he toured all over Europe and Latin America. He is seen singing here in 1978 at a club in Los Angeles where he was backed up by the Johnny Nelson Band under the direction of Miranda's musical arranger, Jorge Millet.

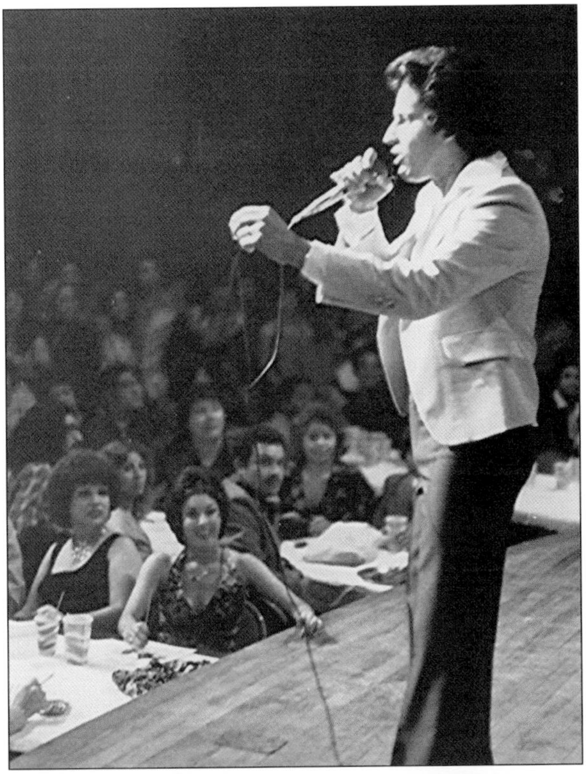

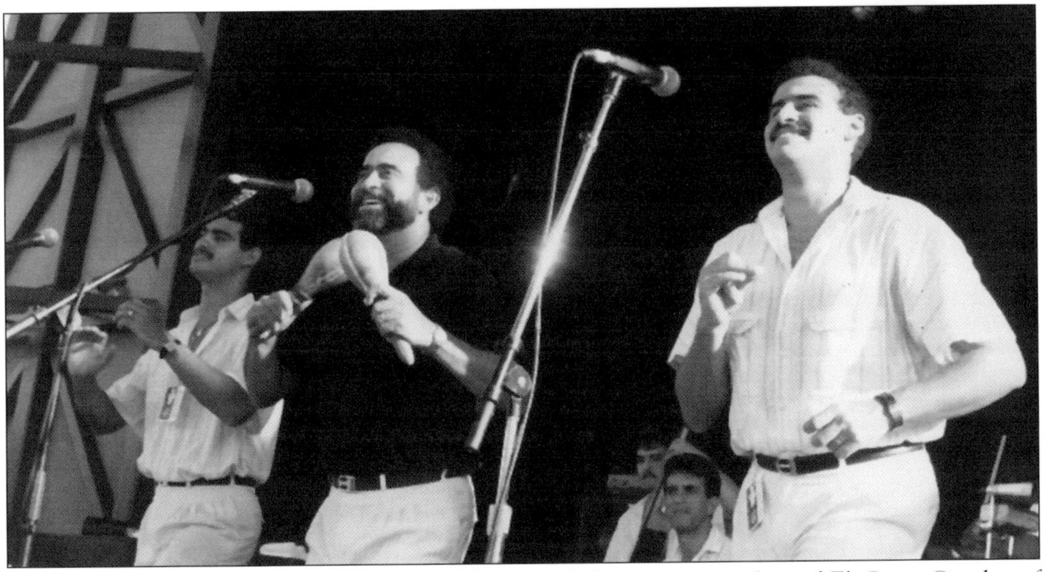

Andy Montanez Sr. (shown in the middle), gained fame as a member of El Gran Combo of Puerto Rico, a group that has been together for over 40 years. His greatest hits came with songs like "Hojas Blancas" (white leaves), "Un Verano en N.Y." (a summer in N.Y.), "El Barbero Loco" (the crazy barber), and "Julia." Montanez has had his band for the last 20 years, occasionally using his two sons as backup singers. Harold (left) and Andy Jr. (right) are shown with him here at a performance at Universal Studios in Los Angeles in 1987. The music on his latest recordings shows a blend between salsa and reggaeton using rappers like Daddy Yankee and Julio Voltio.

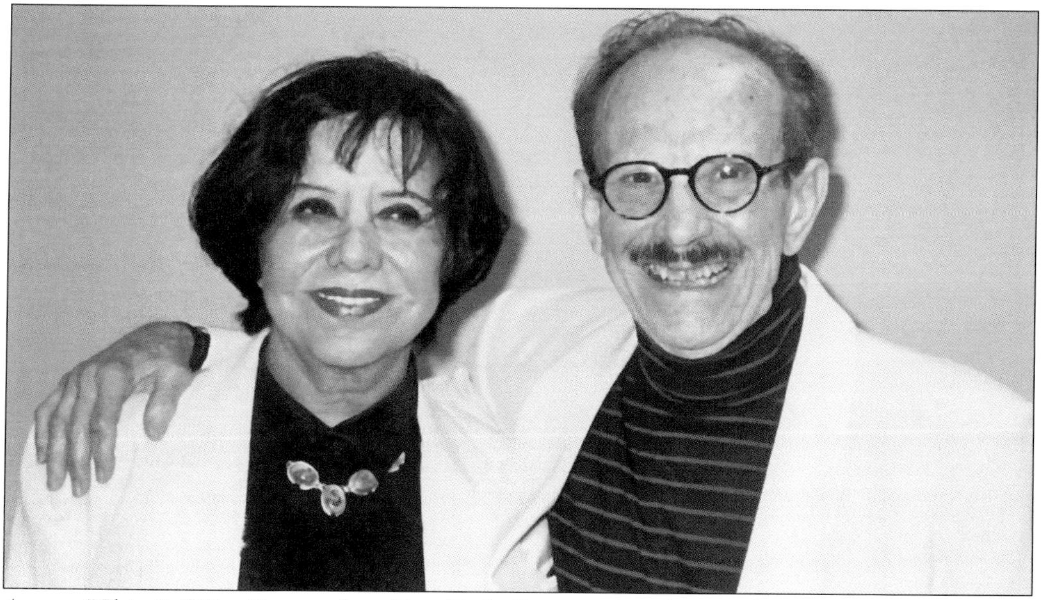

Arturo "Chico" O'Farrill moved to New York City in 1948 from Cuba, where he worked as a ghostwriter for arranger Gil Fuller before obtaining a job writing for Benny Goodman. Soon he began working with some of the most influential musicians of the Afro Cuban movement: Dizzy Gillespie, Machito, and Noro Morales. Chico's original compositions and arrangements have credited him with being one of the great architects of Latin jazz. He is pictured here with his wife, Lupe, backstage after a concert in Los Angeles in 1996. Chico died in June 2001.

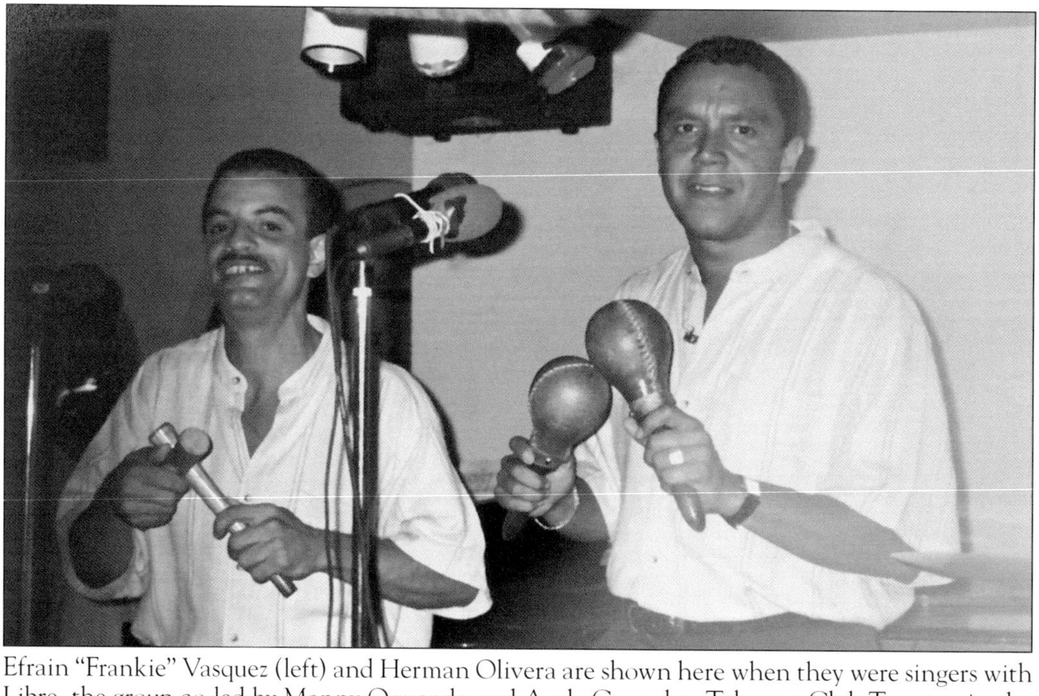

Efrain "Frankie" Vasquez (left) and Herman Olivera are shown here when they were singers with Libre, the group co-led by Manny Oquendo and Andy Gonzalez. Taken at Club Tapestry in the Bronx in 1983, Vasquez and Olivera have become sought-after musicians and have recorded with numerous leading groups.

Olivera leans back to let out one of his clever "inspiraciones" (improvisations) while singing with Libre at the Maganette in New York City in 1986.

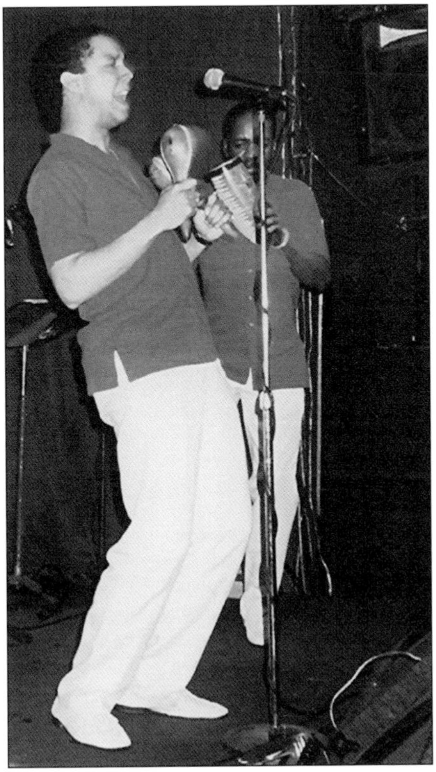

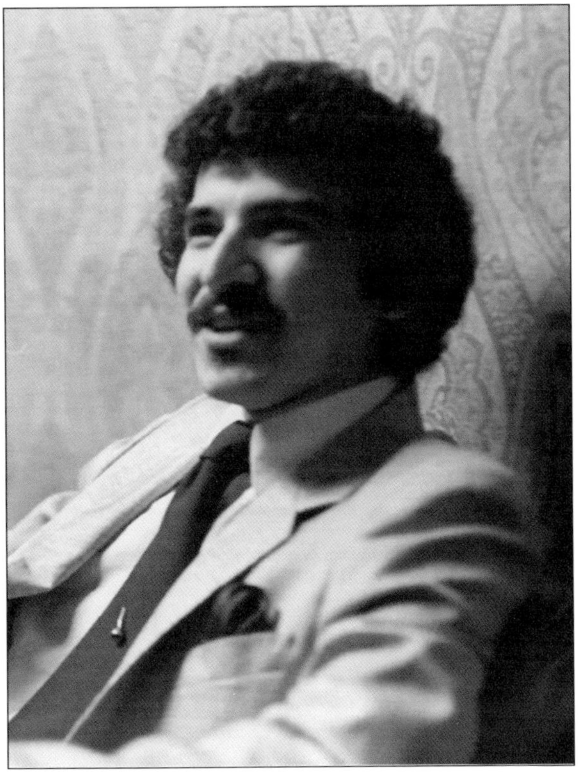

Taken backstage at the Hollywood Palladium in 1985, trumpet sensation Luis "Percio" Ortiz sits relaxing and talking to visiting fans. One of Puerto Rico's outstanding instrumentalists and a University of Puerto Rico music graduate, Perico played professionally in the Symphony Orchestra as a guest soloist at the age of 18 with Pablo Casals as its director. He has worked for all the television stations in Puerto Rico and has served as first trumpeter for many of the hotel orchestras that backed up major stars like Ann Margaret, Dionne Warwick, Diahann Carroll, Trini Lopez, Engelbert Humperdinck, Sammy Davis Jr., Tony Bennett, Paul Anka, and the Supremes, to name a few. In 1970, Perico moved to New York to record and lead his own salsa band.

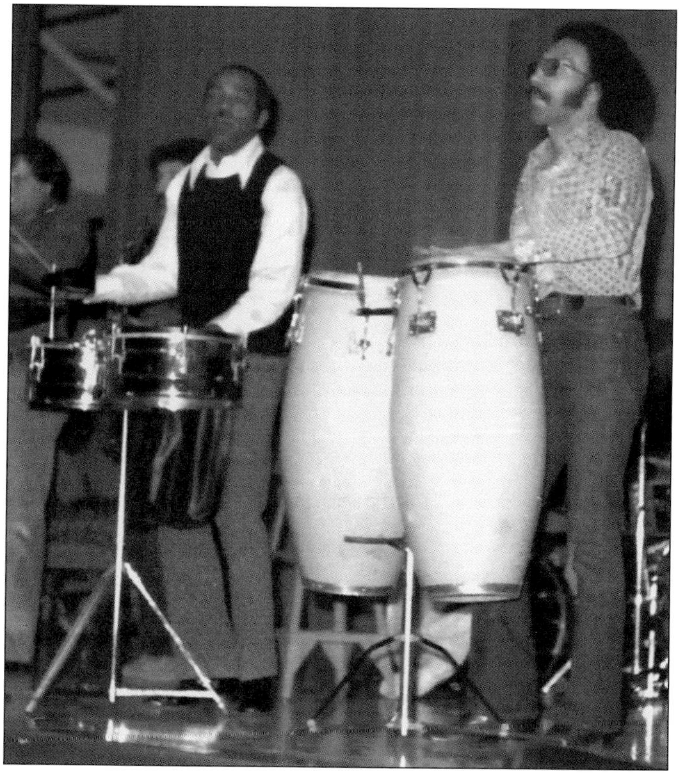

John Palomo joined Willie Bobo's group for a few months during 1978 and played all over Los Angeles. They are seen here at Concerts by the Sea on the pier in Torrance, California.

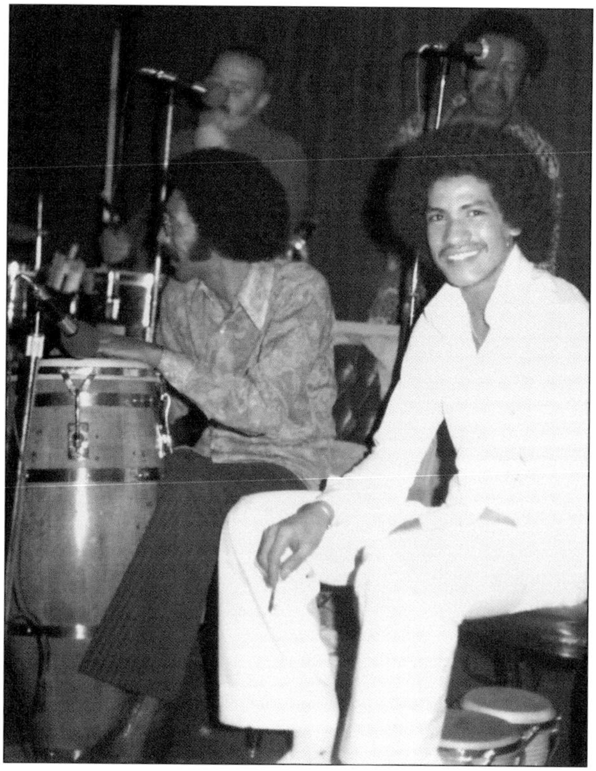

Palomo (left) and Chuckie Lopez are shown here in 1976 about to sit in with Manny Oquendo and Libre at a club in Los Angeles.

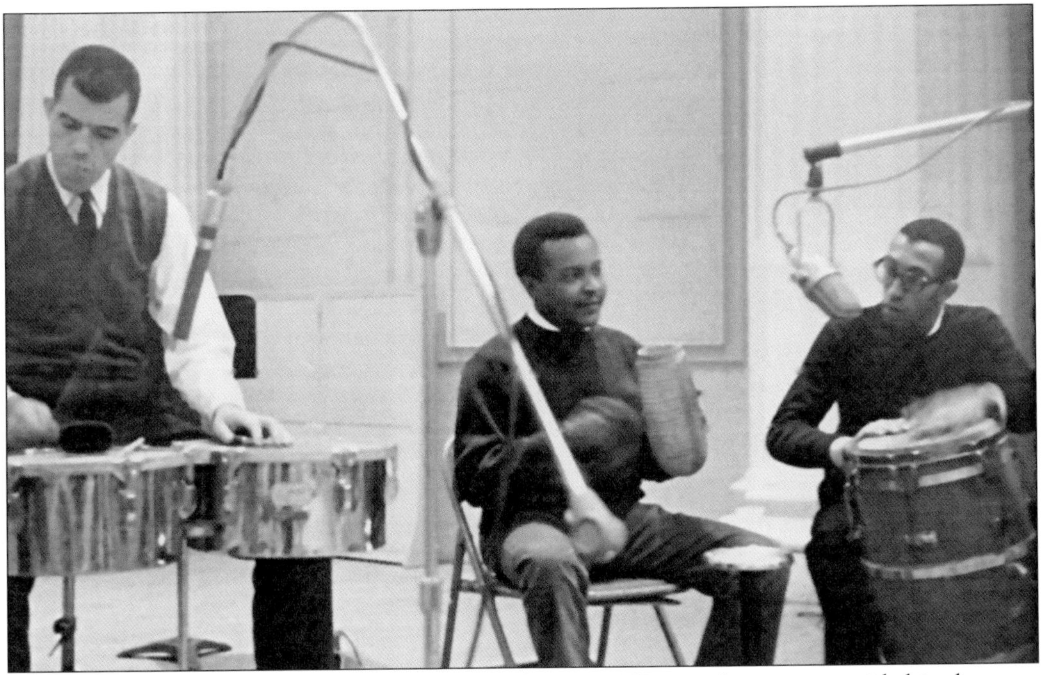

Here is another picture made during Charlie Palmieri's 1958 recording session with his charanga group La Duboney. Pictured from left to right are Joe Rodriguez, Julian Cabrera, and John Palomo.

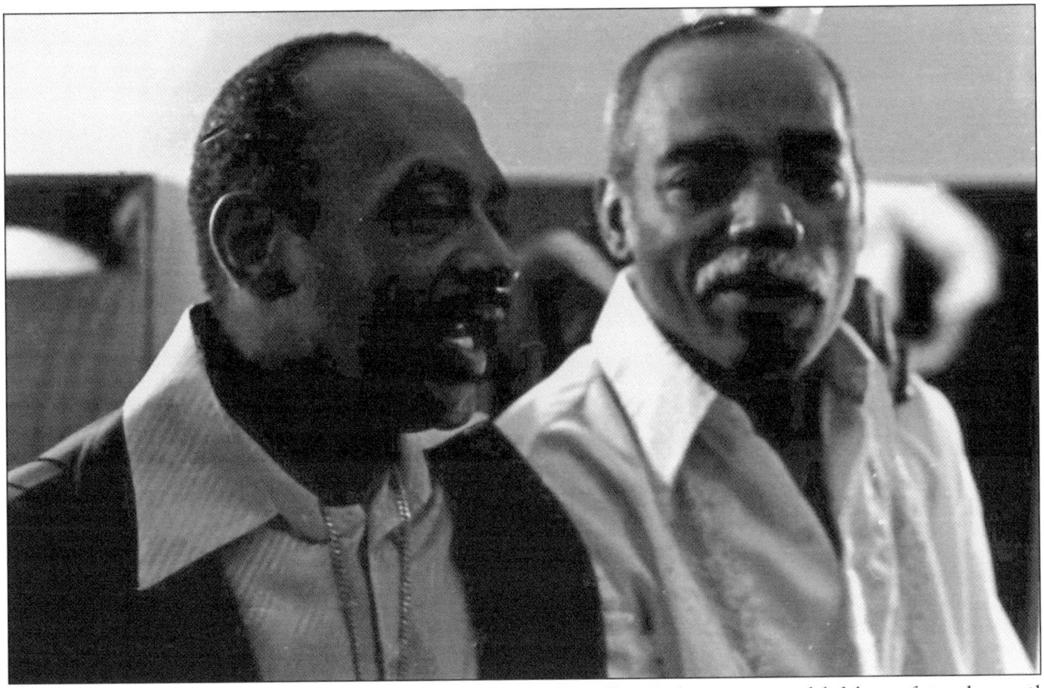

Born in Spanish Harlem, Victor Pantoja (left) and Willie Bobo remained lifelong friends until Bobo's early death in 1983. This 1979 photograph was taken backstage at the Los Angeles Sports Arena just before a performance.

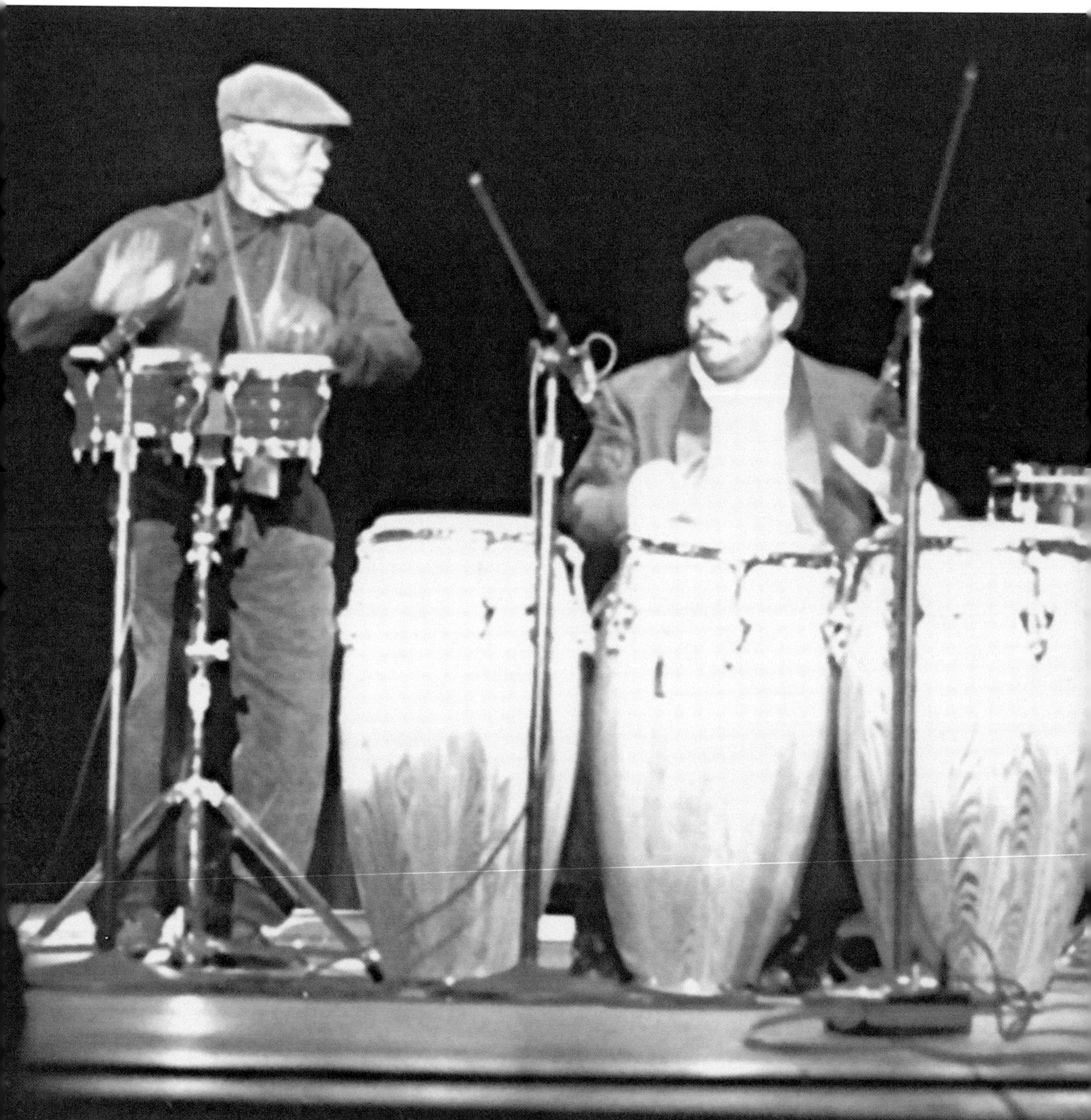

Pictured from left to right at the Los Angeles Greek Theater in 1994 during a performance are

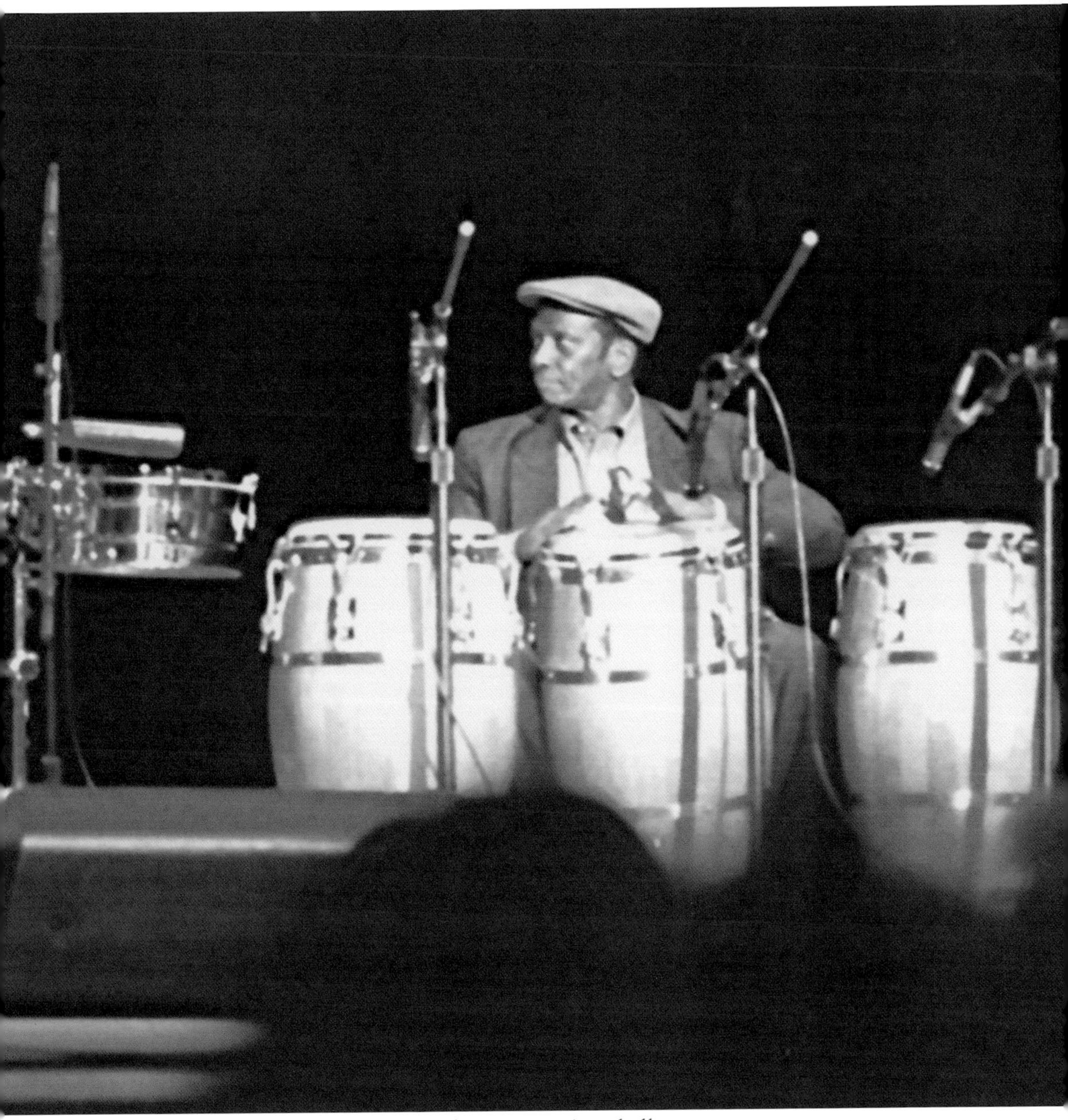

Armando Peraza, Giovanni Hidalgo, and Francisco Aguabella.

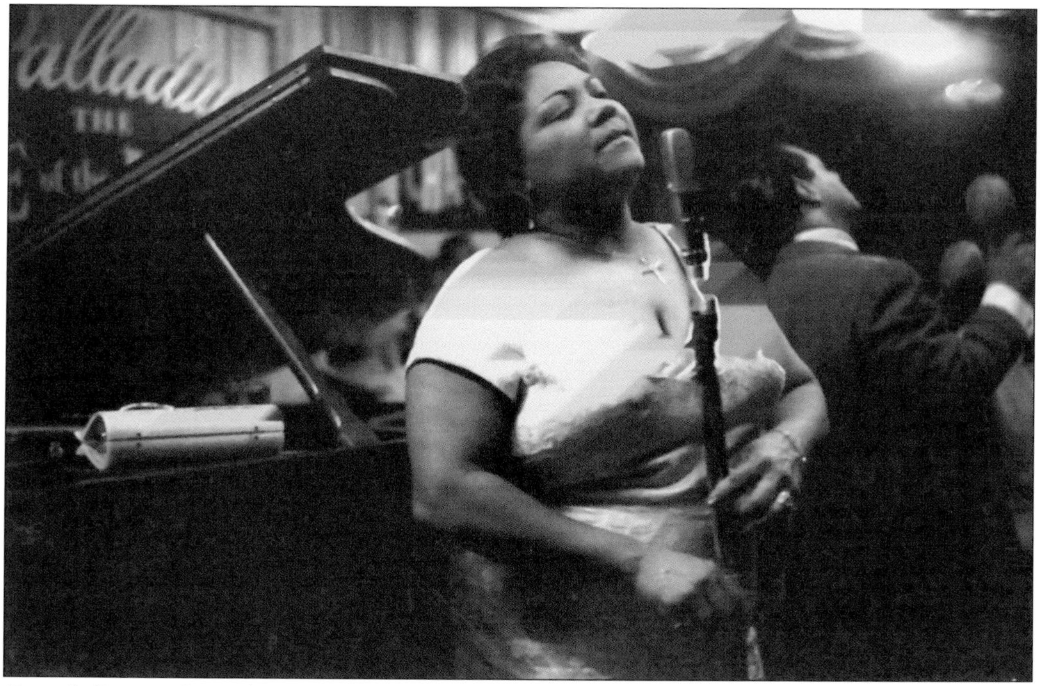

Graciela Perez is shown here in 1958 at the Palladium singing with Machito and His Afro-Cubans.

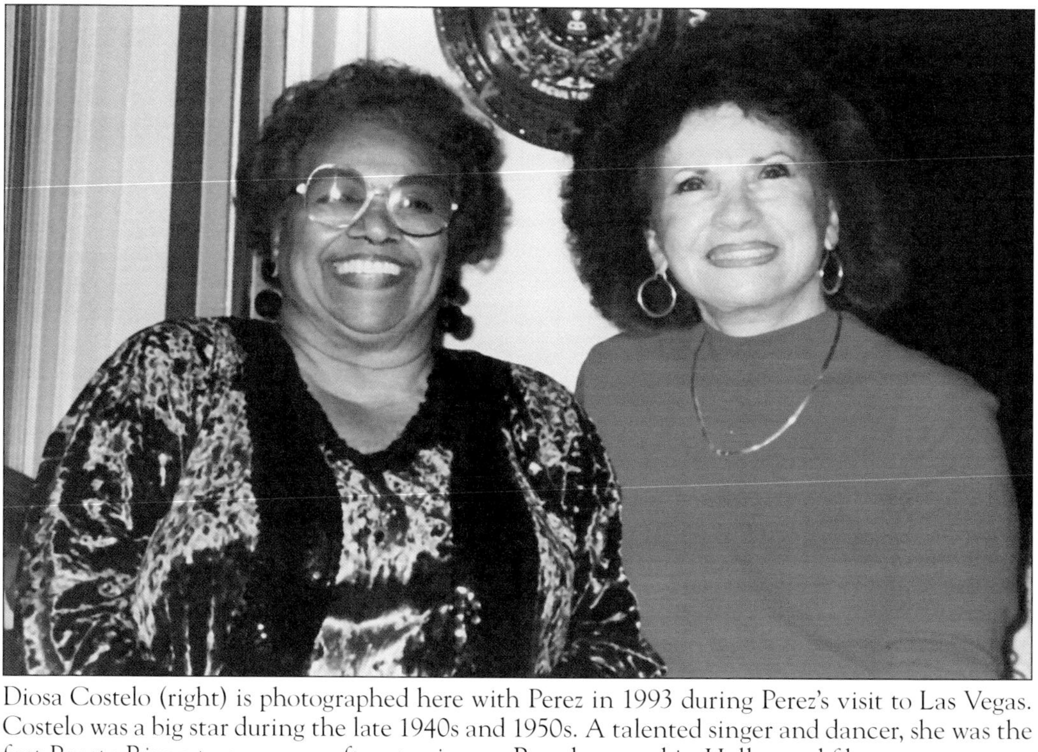

Diosa Costelo (right) is photographed here with Perez in 1993 during Perez's visit to Las Vegas. Costelo was a big star during the late 1940s and 1950s. A talented singer and dancer, she was the first Puerto Rican to crossover after starring on Broadway and in Hollywood films.

Marc Quiñones has been a professional musician for over 20 years. His youthful appearance belies his age and experience. Born in the Bronx, Quiñones's early years were spent learning about drums from family members. When he joined Rafael De Jesus's salsa band, Quiñones was 17 years old. His many jobs have been with groups as diverse as the Allman Brothers Band and Ruben Blades. He was playing with Willie Colon in this 1987 photograph at the Casablanca Ballroom in Los Angeles.

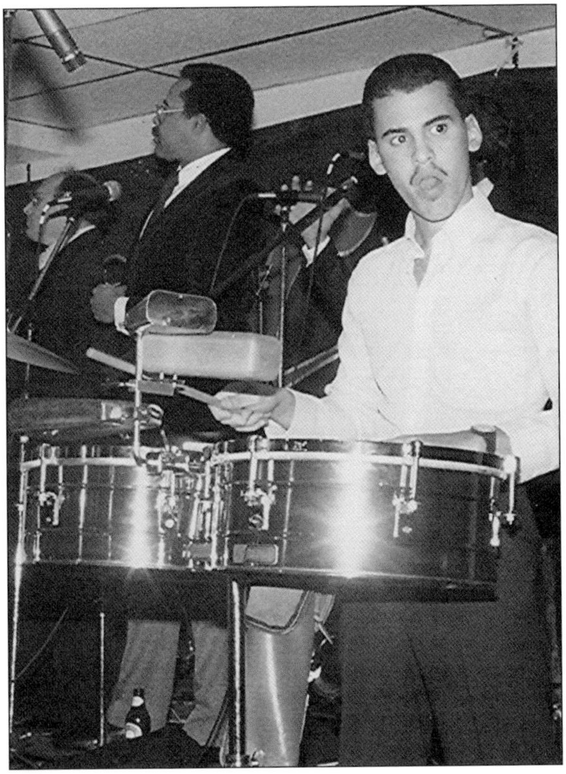

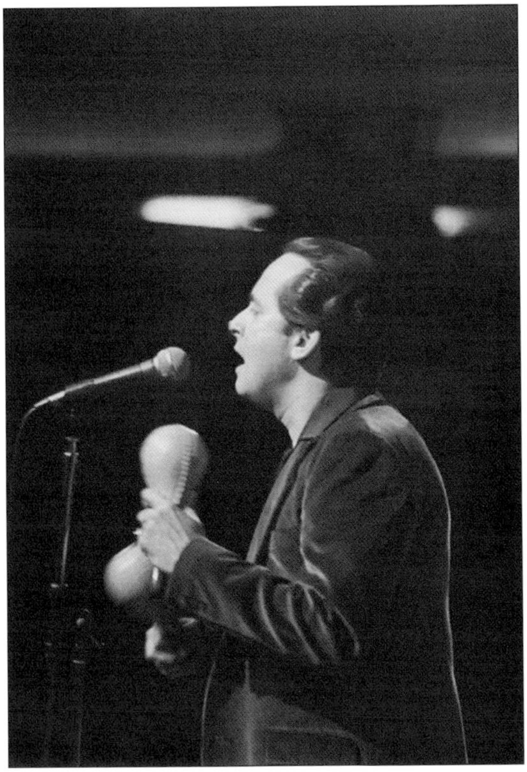

Many consider Ismael Quintana one of the smoothest and coolest soneros in salsa music. A versatile singer able to sing a fast guaracha or a romantic ballad, Quintana spent 10 years with Eddie Palmieri as the lead singer for La Perfecta, Palmieri's first dance band. He left Palmieri in 1972 and was signed by Vaya Records. Quintana traveled worldwide as a member of the Fania All-Stars. He is pictured here in 1983 with Palmieri at the Hollywood Palladium.

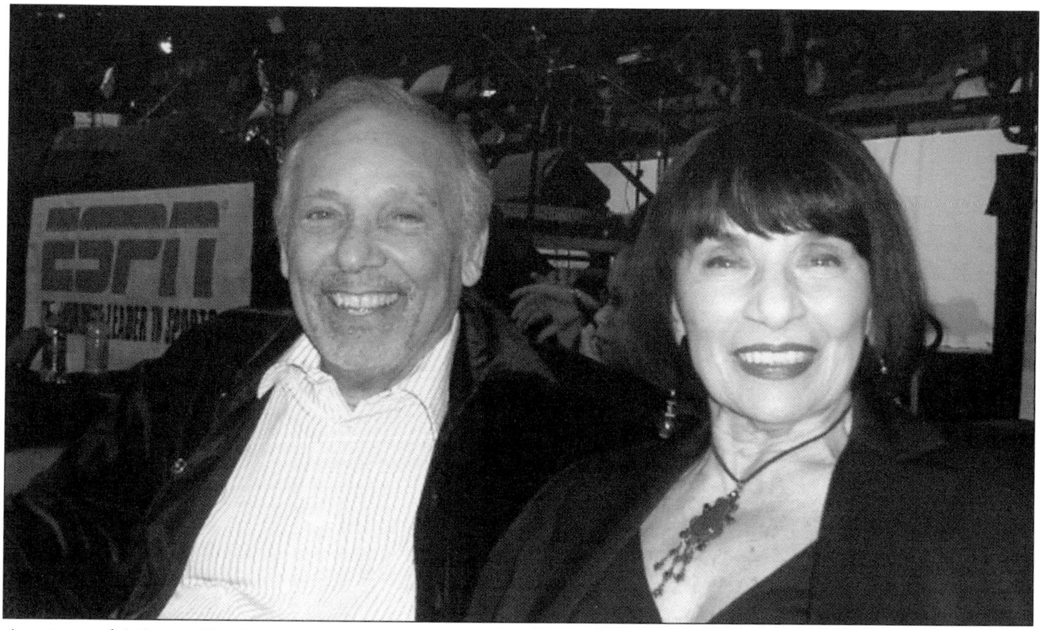

Augie and Margo Rodriguez are pictured here when they attended the 2006 Second Annual World Salsa Dance Championships at the South Coast Hotel and Casino in Las Vegas. They were a popular dance act during the mambo craze at the Palladium during the 1950s and 1960s. They opened shows for Sammy Davis Jr. and Harry Belafonte and traveled worldwide performing their dazzling dance routines.

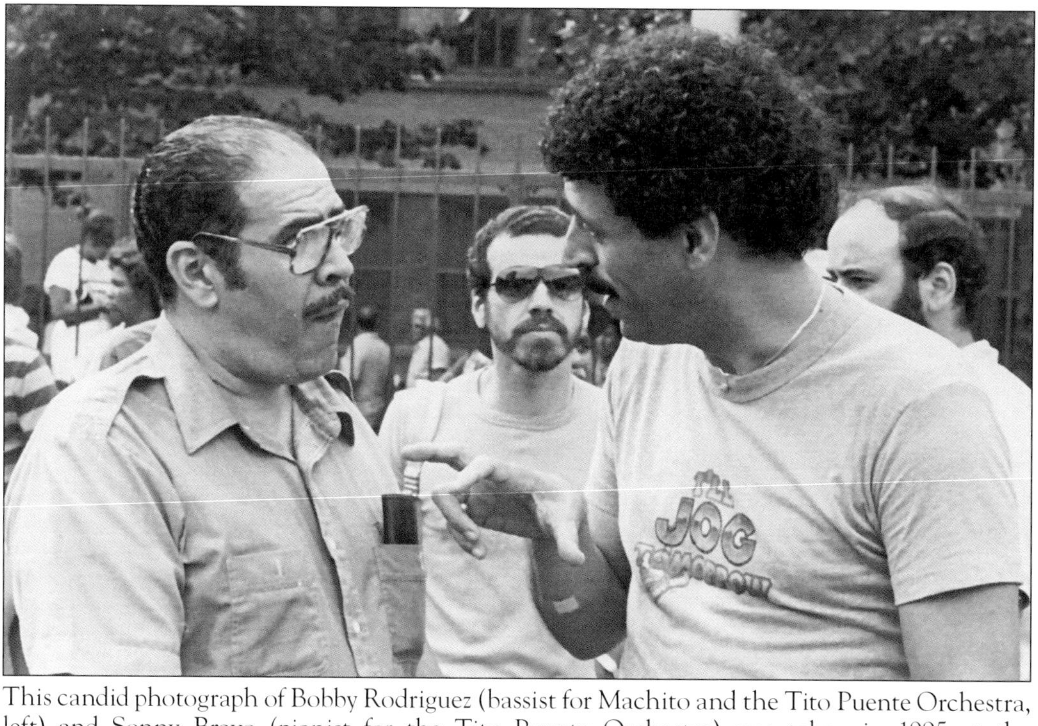

This candid photograph of Bobby Rodriguez (bassist for Machito and the Tito Puente Orchestra, left) and Sonny Bravo (pianist for the Tito Puente Orchestra) was taken in 1995 at the Old-Timers Reunion on 111th Street and Fifth Avenue in Spanish Harlem.

The Mandalay Hotel and Casino in Las Vegas employed the group of Rick Arroyo and his Latin jazz ensemble for several years and served as a meeting place for the growing salsa enthusiast. In 2002, Johnny "Dandy" Rodriguez had just moved to Las Vegas and played regularly with Rick's band.

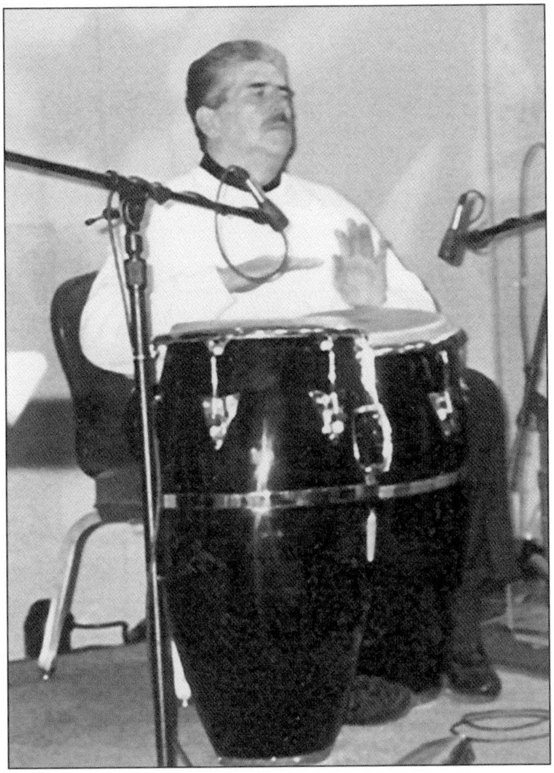

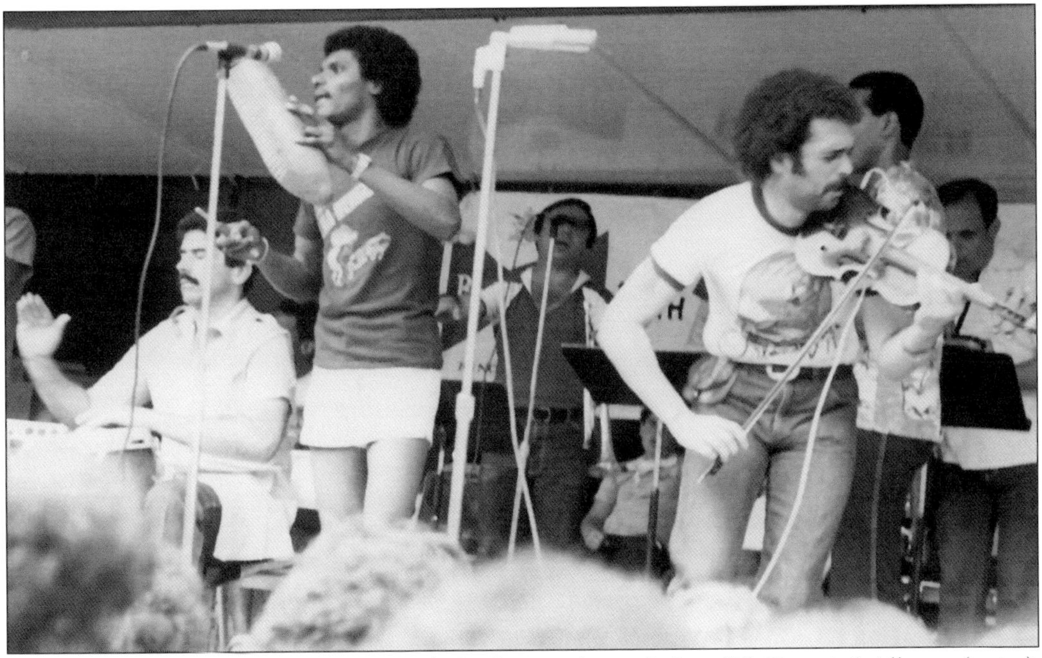

Members of the group Tipica 73, Dandy Rodriguez (conga), Jose "El Canario" Alberto (guiro), and Alfredo De La Fe (violin) are seen on stage at the 1979 Old-Timers Reunion in Spanish Harlem. One of the hottest New York groups during the 1970s and 1980s, Tipica 73 was comprised of the best young talent of that era.

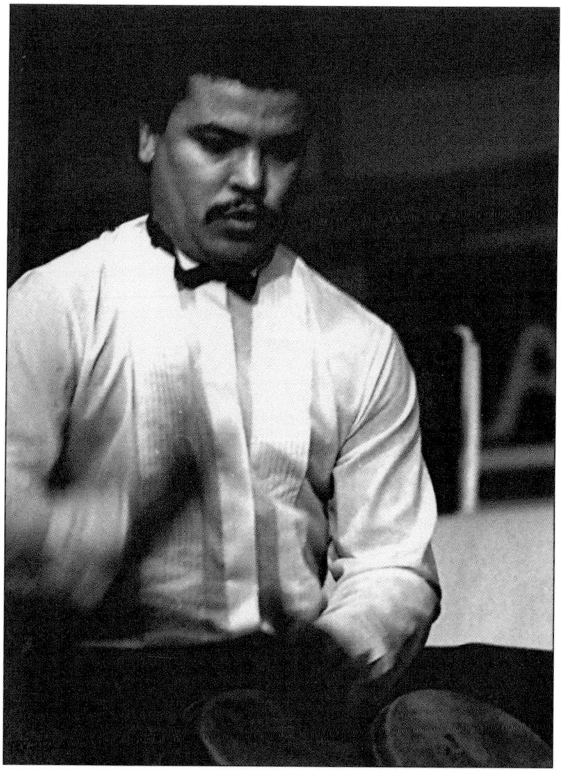

Bronx-born Jose "Papo" Rodriguez grew up in Philadelphia and by the age of 14 was working professionally with his father, Cruz Rodriguez, a conguero. A self-taught musician, Papo developed his skills by listening to master percussionists like Armando Peraza, Jose Mangual Sr., Dandy Rodriguez, and Jack Costanzo.

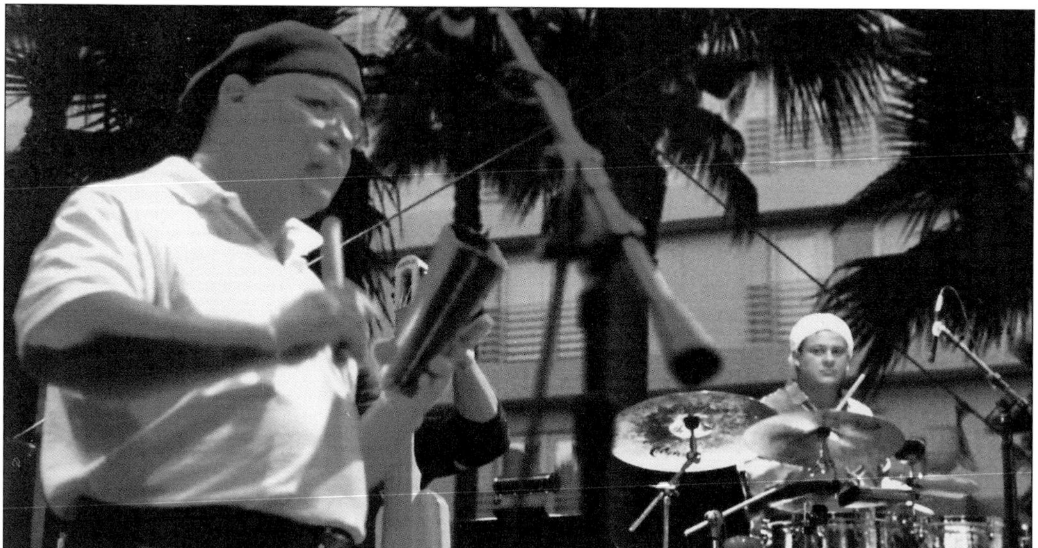

Able to play all the percussion instruments, Papo left the "city of brotherly love" and ventured to New York City where he found work playing bongos with several groups, including Ray Barretto and Rafi Hernandez. In the late 1960s, he relocated to the Los Angeles area and found employment playing with many of the local groups. Poncho Sanchez asked him to join his group, in which Papo stayed for 10 years. He is now freelancing in the Los Angeles area. He is pictured here playing cowbell with Poncho Sanchez at the Hard Rock Hotel and Casino in Las Vegas in 1997. On the right playing timbal is Tiki Pasillas.

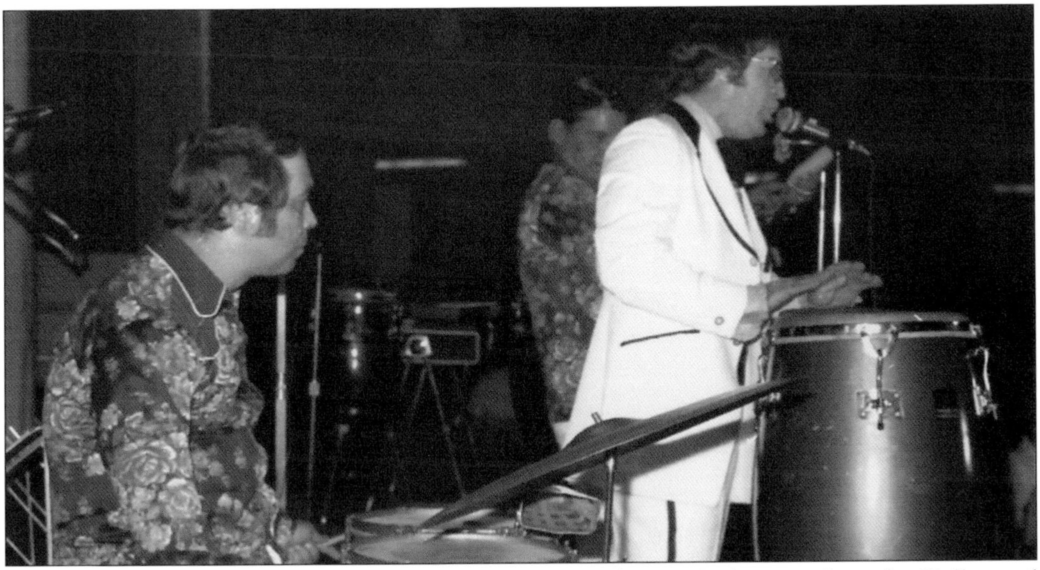

Veteran drummer/timbalero Pat Rodriguez is shown in this 1973 photograph at the Hollywood Palladium with the group led by conguero Orlando "Mazacote "Lopez. While living in New York, Pat went to work for Tito Rodriguez, but after a two year stint Pat left the Tito Rodriguez Orchestra while they were touring in Los Angeles. Out of anger, Tito composed "El Que Se Fue," a song expressing the fact that Pat was no longer needed. Tito always played it as his first number when he followed his rival Tito Puente to the bandstand. For this reason, many fans thought it was a special put down for Puente.

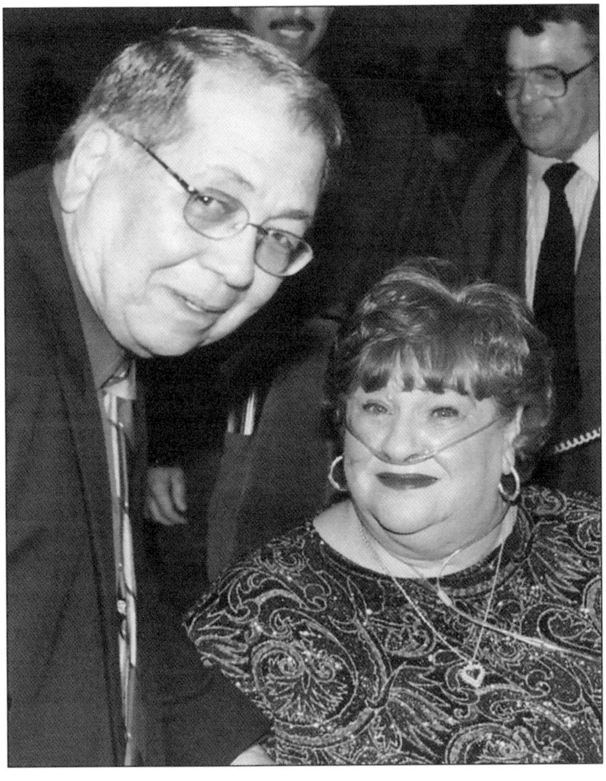

Pat Rodriguez spent many years in the Los Angeles area working as a studio musician and in the local bands of Eddie Cano, Manny Lopez, Miguelito Valdes, Rene Bloch, and Mazacote, the group headed by Orlando Lopez. One of his most memorable jobs was with pianist Al Escobar and the Babalu Revue in Reno, Nevada, that also featured three female dancers, one of which was the legendary dancer Josie Powell. He is pictured here at a 2004 celebration for Rae Arroyo, a popular radio personality on KUNV-FM in Las Vegas. Arroyo was recognized by Las Vegas mayor Oscar Goodman for her work in the Latino community through radio programs and screenings of films dealing with the legacy of Spanish Harlem. Also pictured is Arroyo's husband, Damian. Born in New York City, Rae lived during the golden era of the Palladium. She passed away in 2006.

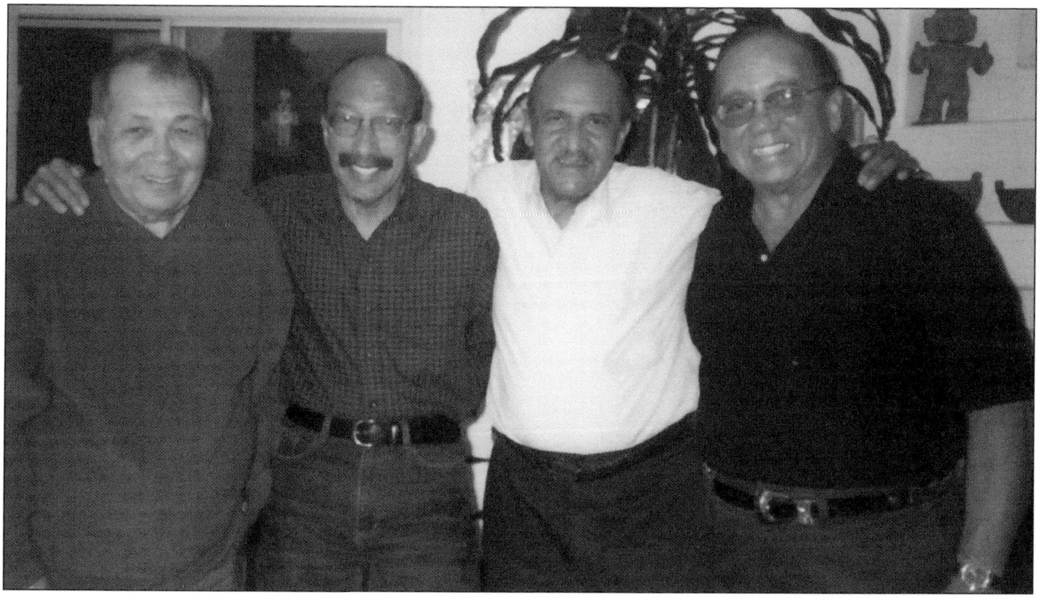

Taken in 2004 when Pat Rodriguez visited his friends living permanently in Las Vegas, this photograph shows, from left to right, Pat Rodriguez, John Palomo, the author, and Luis Miranda.

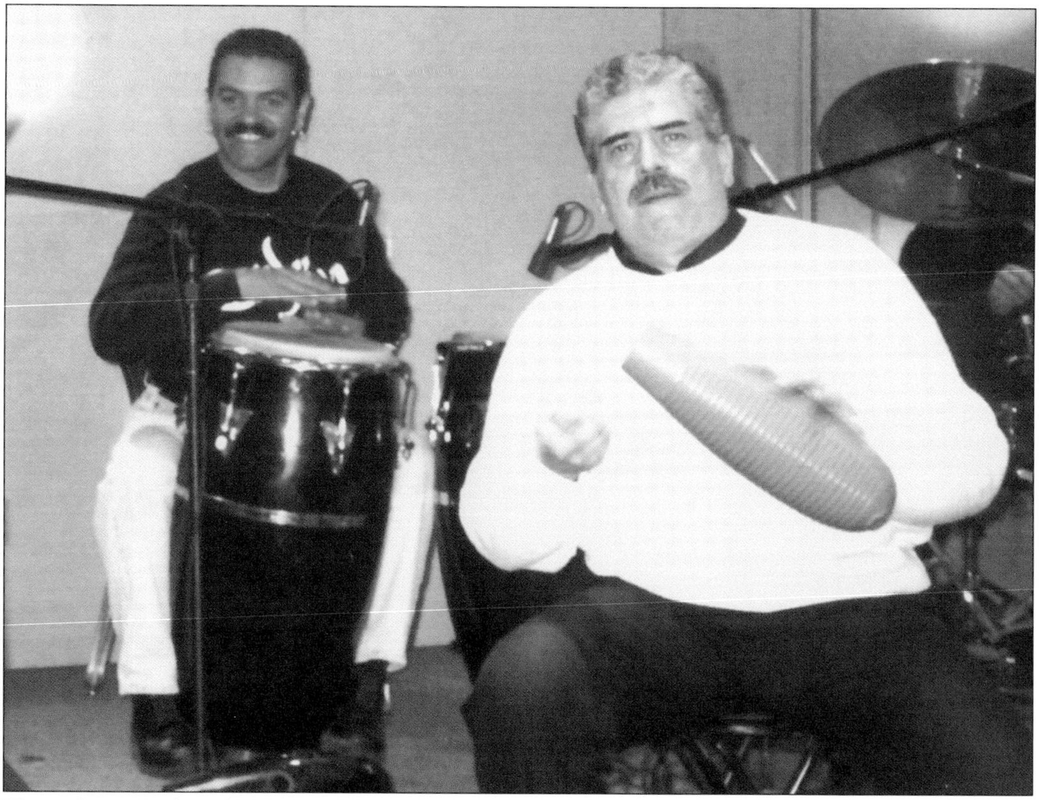

This photograph taken in 2002 is of David Romero playing congas and Johnny "Dandy" Rodriguez playing guiro with the Rick Arroyo Latin Jazz Ensemble at Mandalay Bay Hotel and Casino in Las Vegas. Rick is the son of Rae Arroyo.

Ray "Little Ray" Romero is playing timbales with his lifelong friend Ray Barretto at the Hollywood Palladium in this 1981 photograph. Friends since the mid-1950s, Romero not only played bongos and timbales in many of Barretto's recordings but also the batá drum.

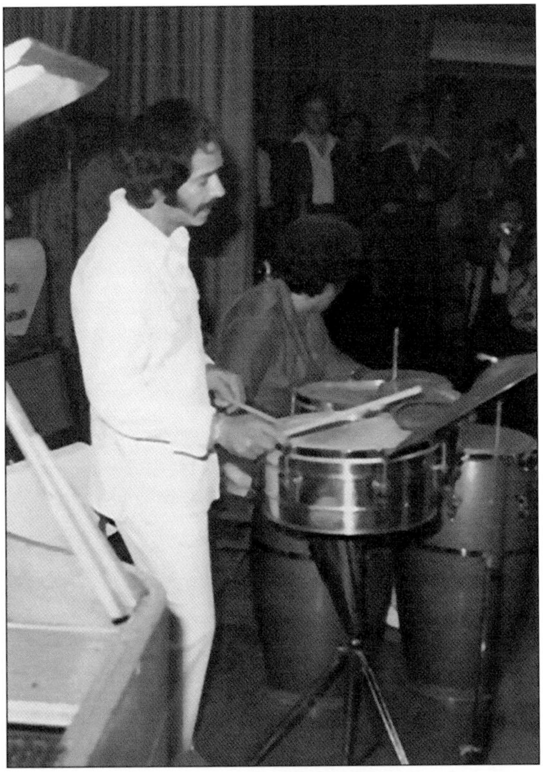

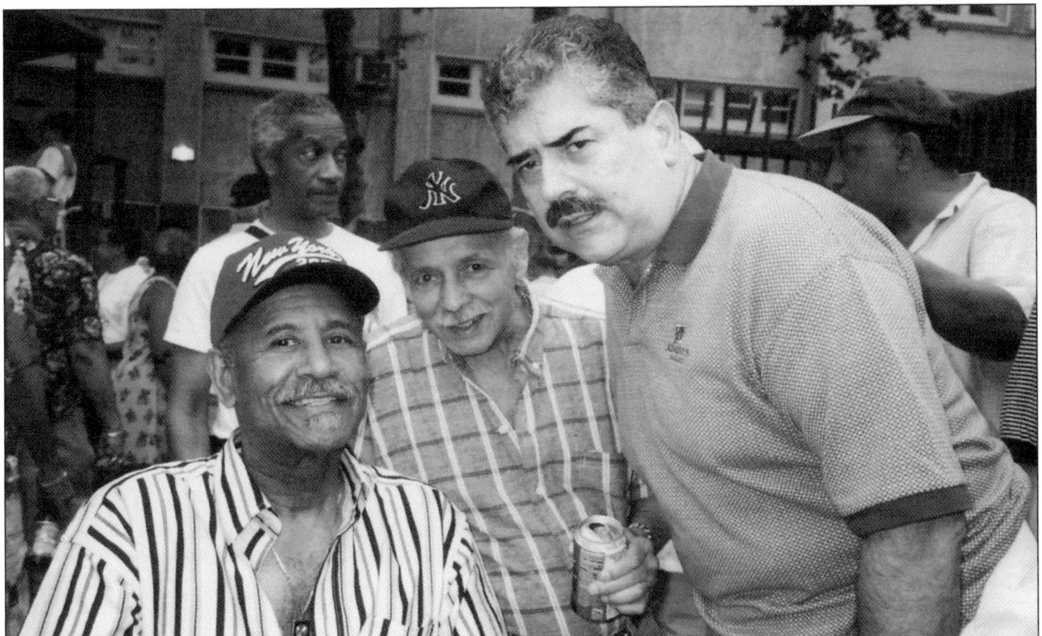

Little Ray Romero (center) is pictured here with Luis Maquina (left), a dance legend from the days of the Palladium. Unfortunately, Romero is now in a wheelchair due to a shooting incident that left him paralyzed from the waist down. This photograph was taken in 2002 at the Old-Timers Reunion in New York City. Also shown is veteran bongocero Dandy Rodriguez.

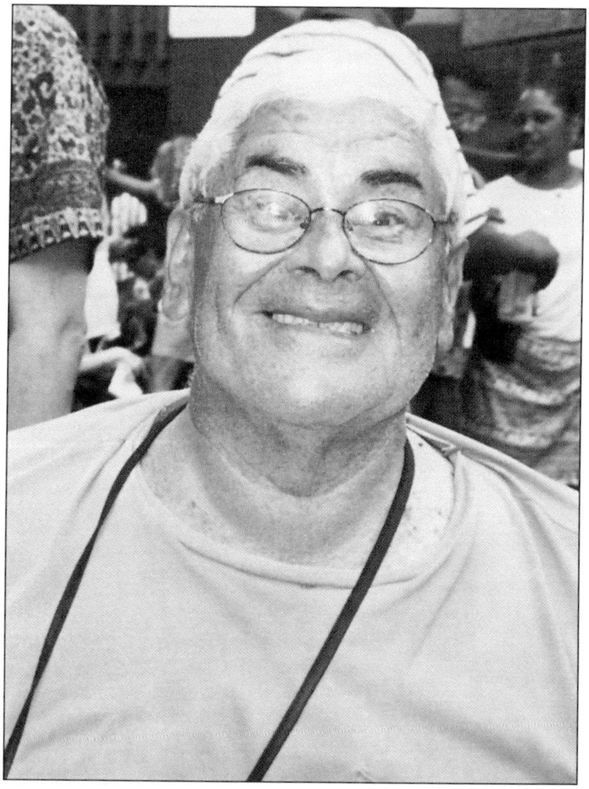

Johnny Rodriguez was dubbed "La Vaca" in 1943, by Machito's trumpeter Mario Bauzá because he was 13 years old, six feet tall, and hefty. He is shown here in 1998 at the Old-Timers Reunion in Spanish Harlem. He is the father of Johnny "Dandy" Rodriguez. At age 15, La Vaca started his professional career as a bongo player for the Noro Morales Orchestra. As a conga or bongo player, he performed or recorded with the orchestras of Xavier Cugat, José Curbelo, Esy Morales, Desi Arnaz, Miguelito Valdés, Pupi Campo, Tito Puente's Picadilly Boys, René Touzet, Alfredito Levy, Chico O'Farrill, Machito, Pete Terrace, Joe Quijano, Louie Ramírez, Lou Pérez, and Orlando Marín. While living a number of years in the Los Angeles area, he played and recorded with the bands of Stan Kenton, Terry Gibbs, Eddie Talamante, Manny López, and Johnny Martínez. John Rodriguez died in the year 2000.

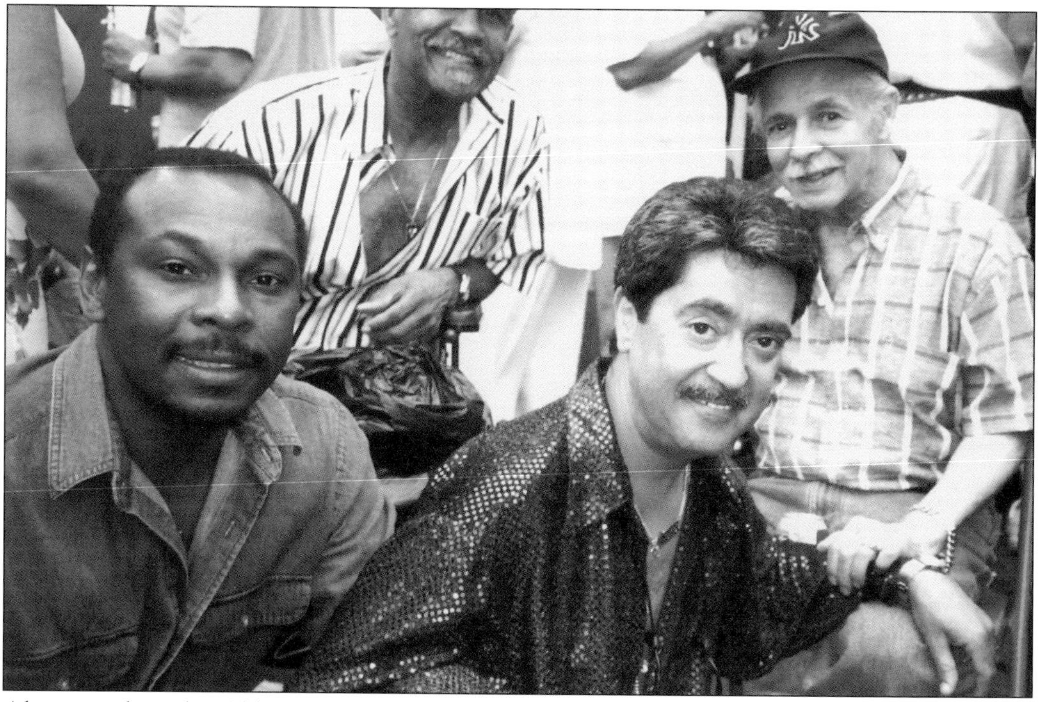

Also attending the Old-Timers Reunion in 2002 are, from left to right, percussionists Jimmy Delgado, partially hidden Luis Maquina (dancer), Nicky Marrero, and Little Ray Romero.

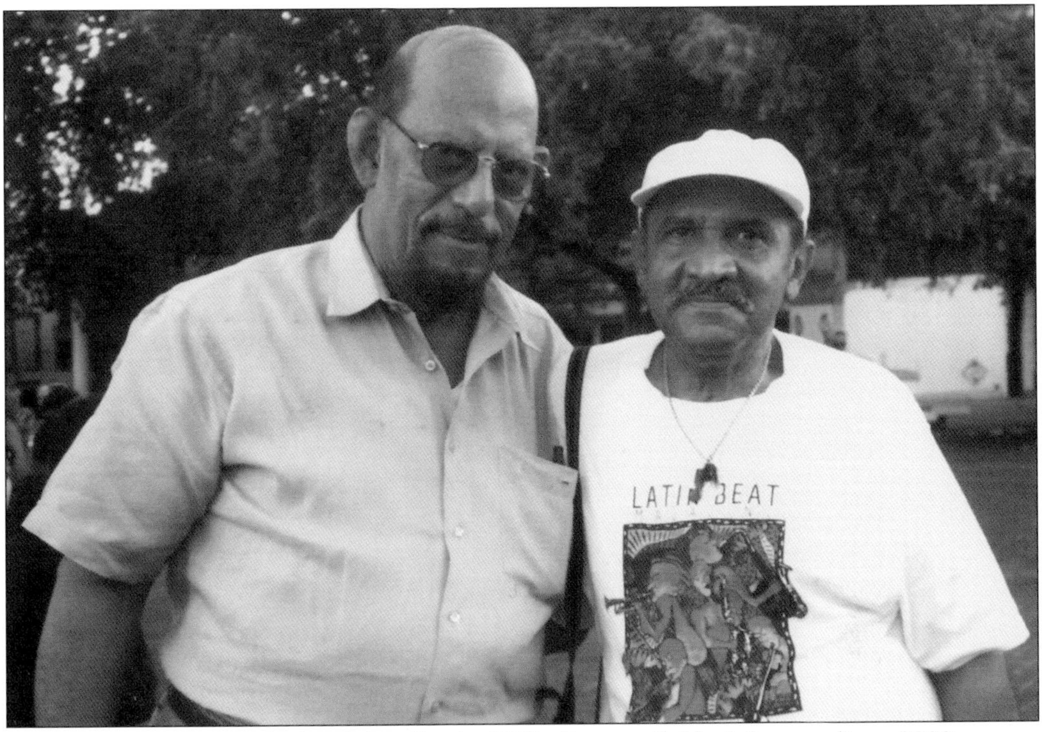

The author is photographed with bandleader Willie Rosario (left) while attending a 2000 concert in Carolina, Puerto Rico, honoring the work of legendary lyricist Tite Curet Alonso.

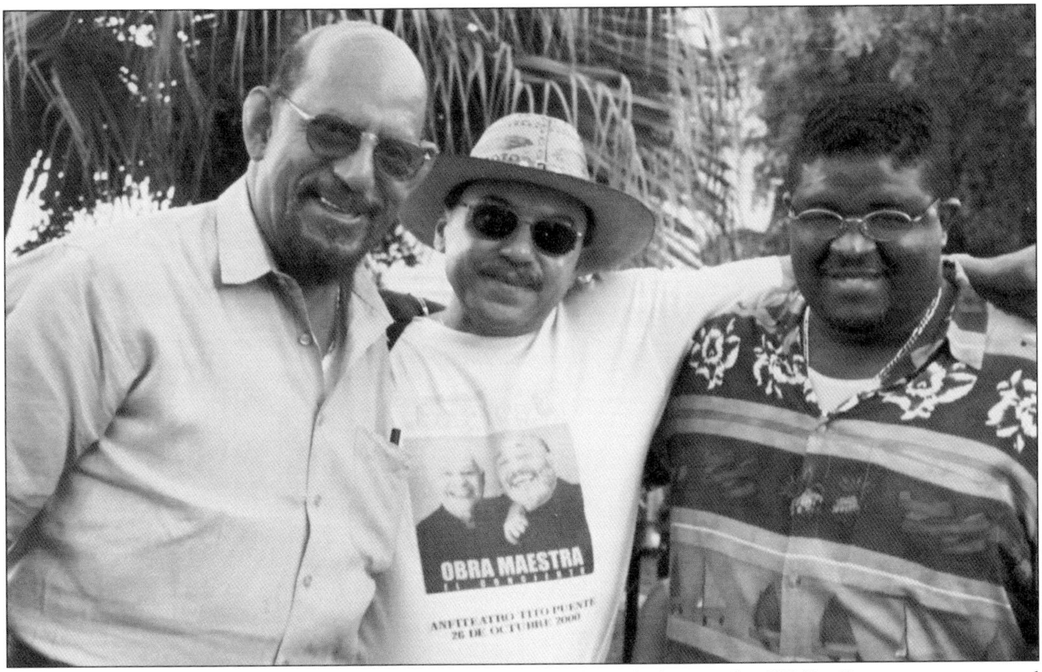

At the same 2000 concert in Carolina, Puerto Rico, from left to right, Willie Rosario is pictured with Orlando "Papo" Amy (aficionado) and popular Puerto Rican bandleader Don Perignon.

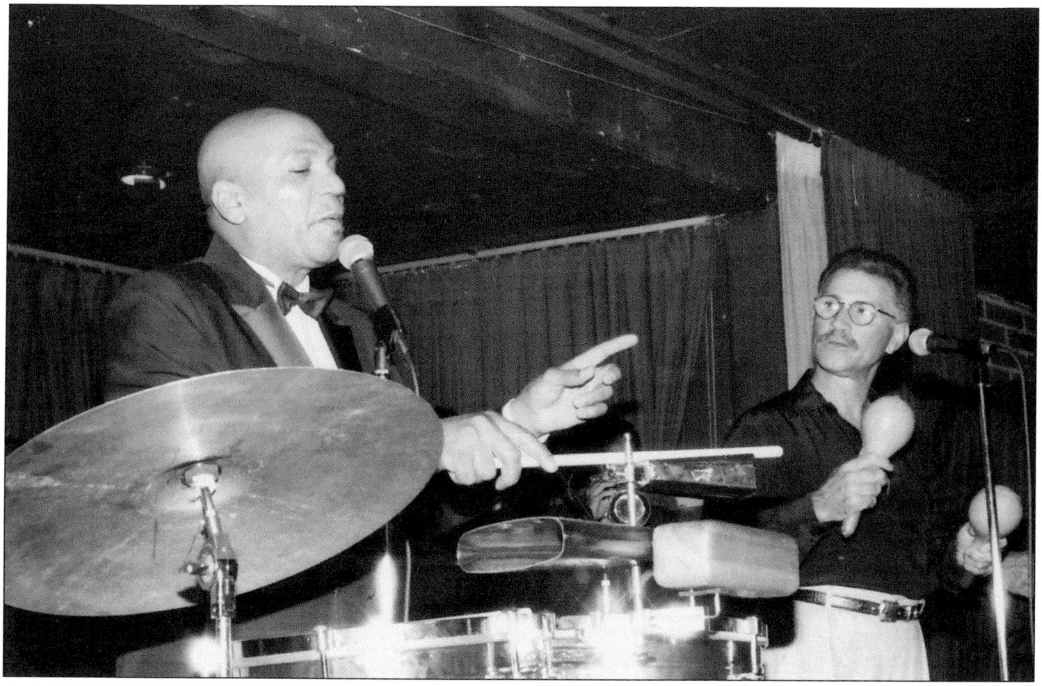

Singer/timbalero Jimmy Sabater (left) and Ralph Garay were working at a club in Los Angeles in 1985 in this image. Both musicians are products of Spanish Harlem and the legacy it embraces. Sabater came to prominence with the Joe Cuba Septet during the mid-1950s.

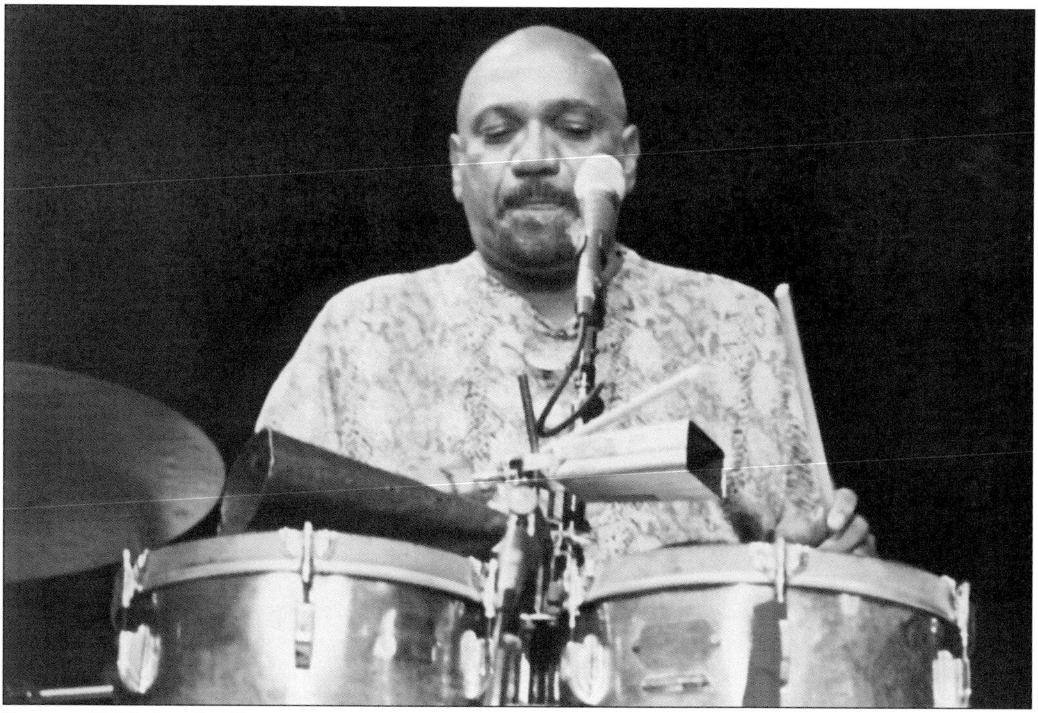

From a 1996 Greek Theater concert in Los Angeles, Sabater is seen here as part of the group Son Boricua.

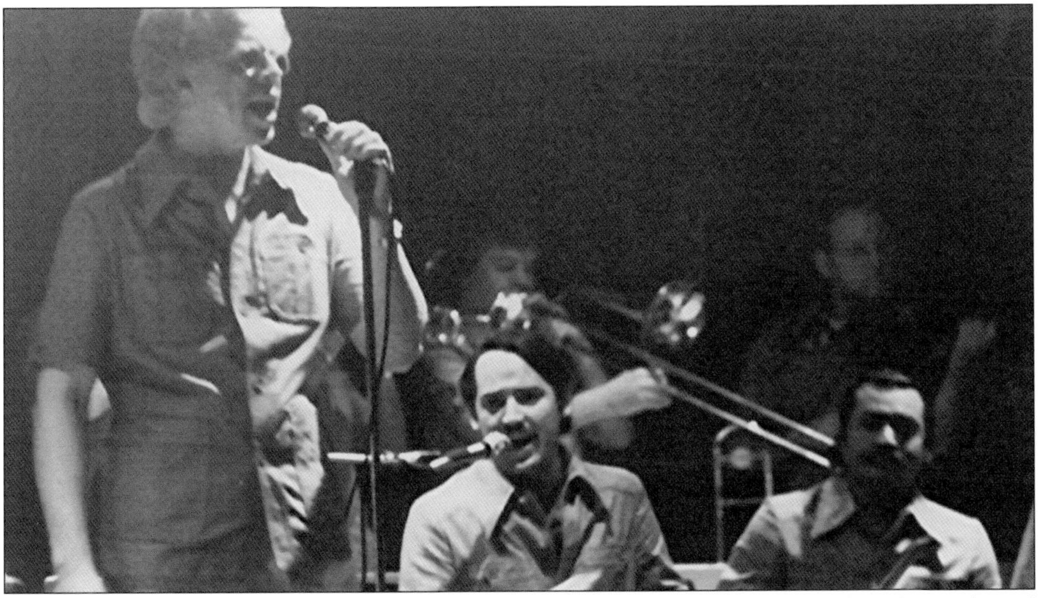

From left to right, this image shows Nestor Sanchez (vocalist), Frankie Rodriguez (congas), and Pablo Rosario (bongo) with the Larry Harlow band in 1976 at the Hollywood Palladium. Sanchez enjoyed some modest popularity during the early 1970s as vocalist with Conjunto Candela and Harlow. Sanchez did a good amount of work singing *coro* (backup) for all the leading bands of the 1960s and 1970s. Rodriguez was one of the leading young percussionists rising during that same era and worked with many of the popular bands. Both Rodriguez and Sanchez are deceased.

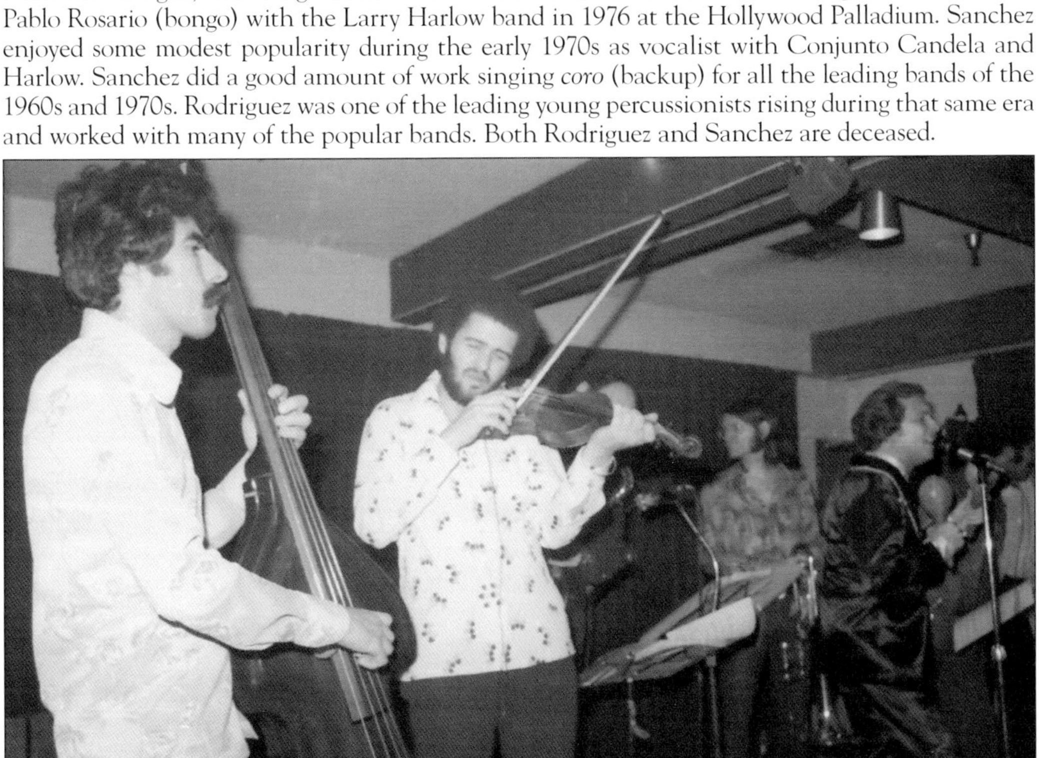

From left to right are Joe Santiago on bass, Alfredo De La Fe playing violin, and Ismael Quintana vocalizing at the Los Angeles Pasta House with the Eddie Palmieri Band in 1976. Santiago has played or recorded with every major musical organization in New York. De La Fe did his early work with Tipica 73 before relocating to South America. Since returning several years ago, he continues to do studio work as well as club dates in the New York area.

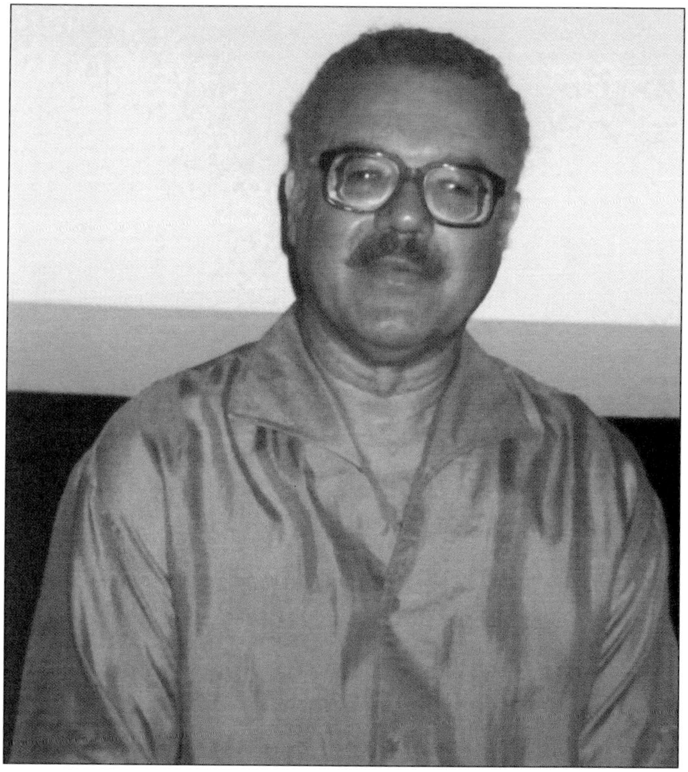

Pictured here is veteran arranger Joe Santos while on the set of the movie *The Mambo Kings*. The author spent several days in 1991 hanging out with Pedro "Cuban Pete" Aguilar and Santos, who were hired as consultants for the movie. Aguilar worked with the choreography department and Santos did special musical material for the score. Santos arranged music and saxophone for Tito Puente, Tito Rodriguez, and Machito during the 1950s and 1960s.

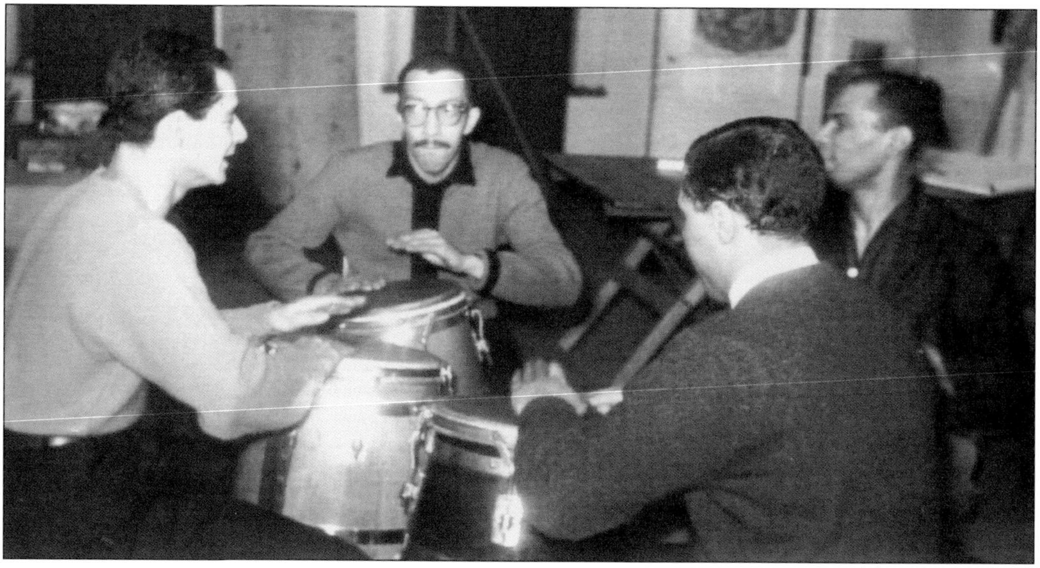

This image and the next three images were taken in 1958 in an artist's loft on 19th Street and Sixth Avenue, now known as Avenue of the Americas. Little Ray Romero and John Palomo organized a group of working percussionists to meet every Monday evening for jam sessions. Pictured from left to right are Romero, Palomo, Papi Paganni, and Tommy Lopez.

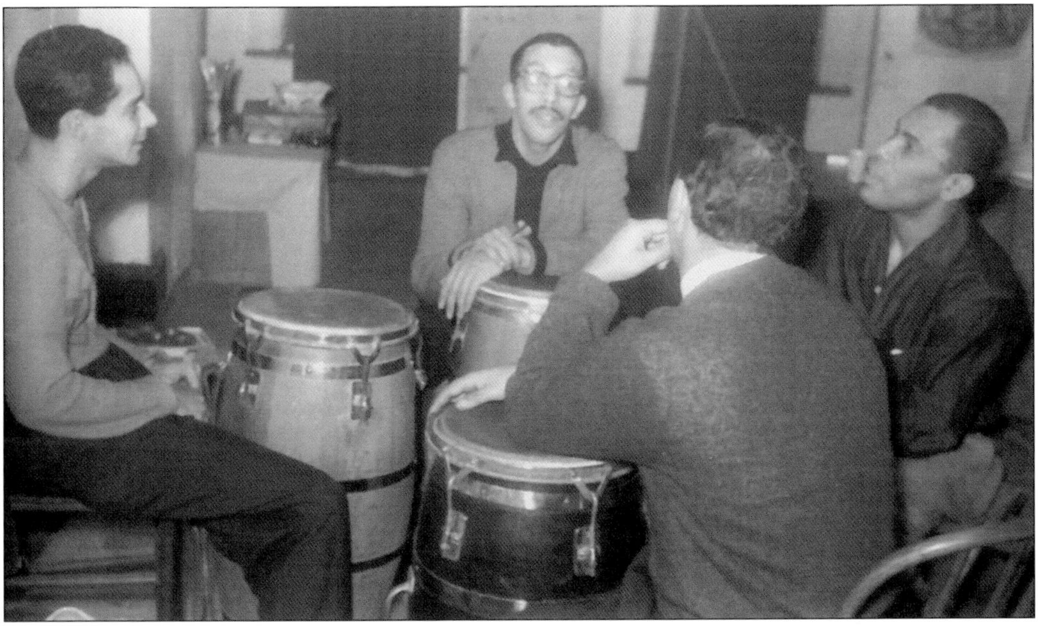

Pictured here taking a break, from left to right, are Romero, Palomo, Paganni, and Lopez.

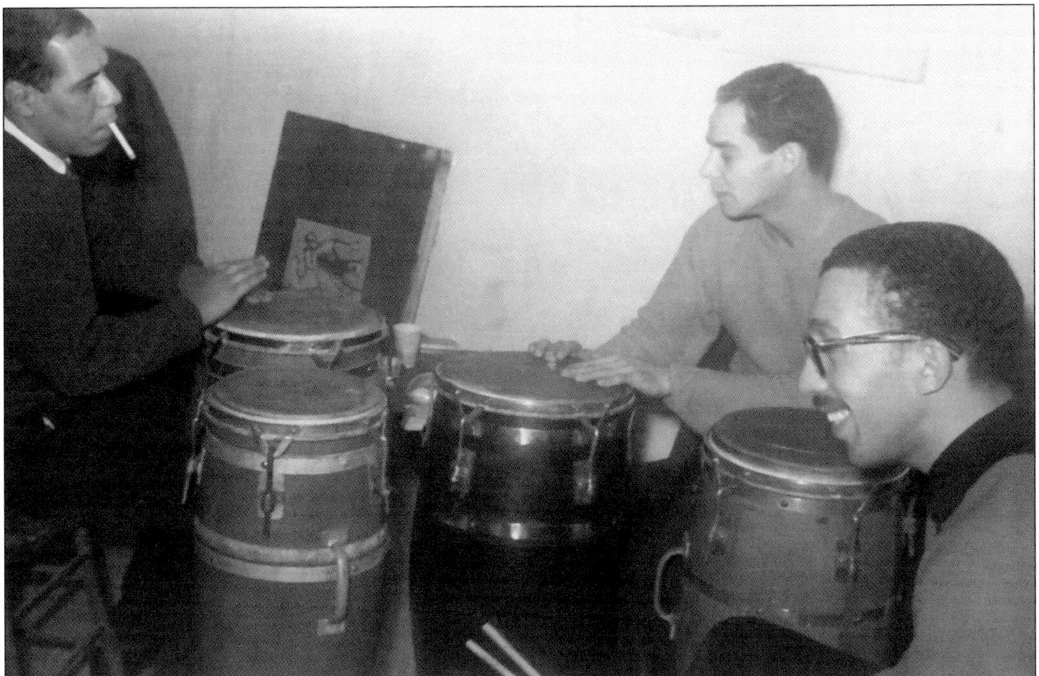

Shown here, from left to right, are Paganni, Romero, and Palomo.

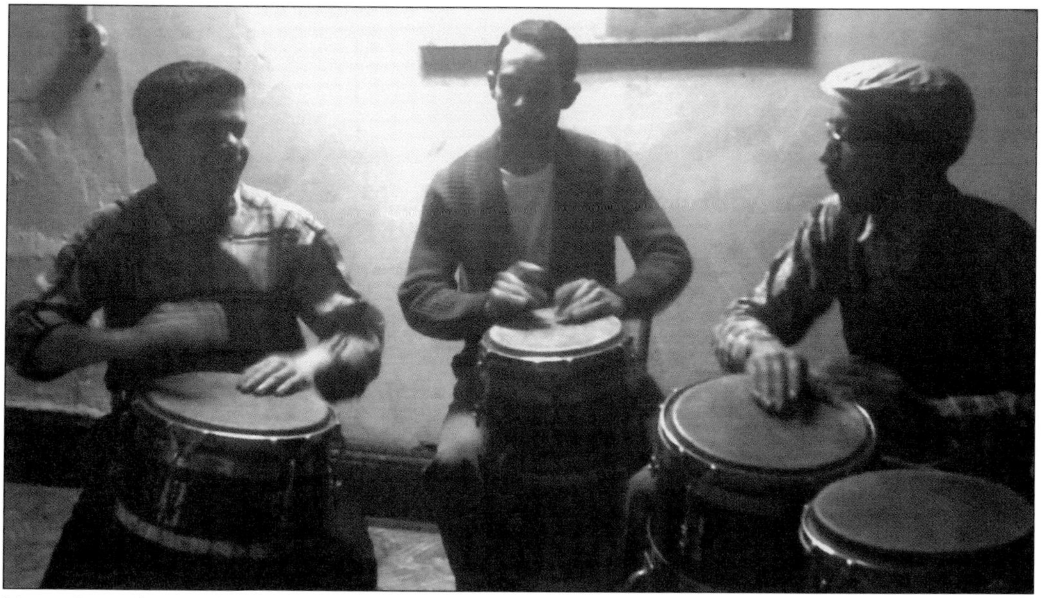

Vitin Gonzalez, Little Ray Romero, and John Palomo are pictured from left to right.

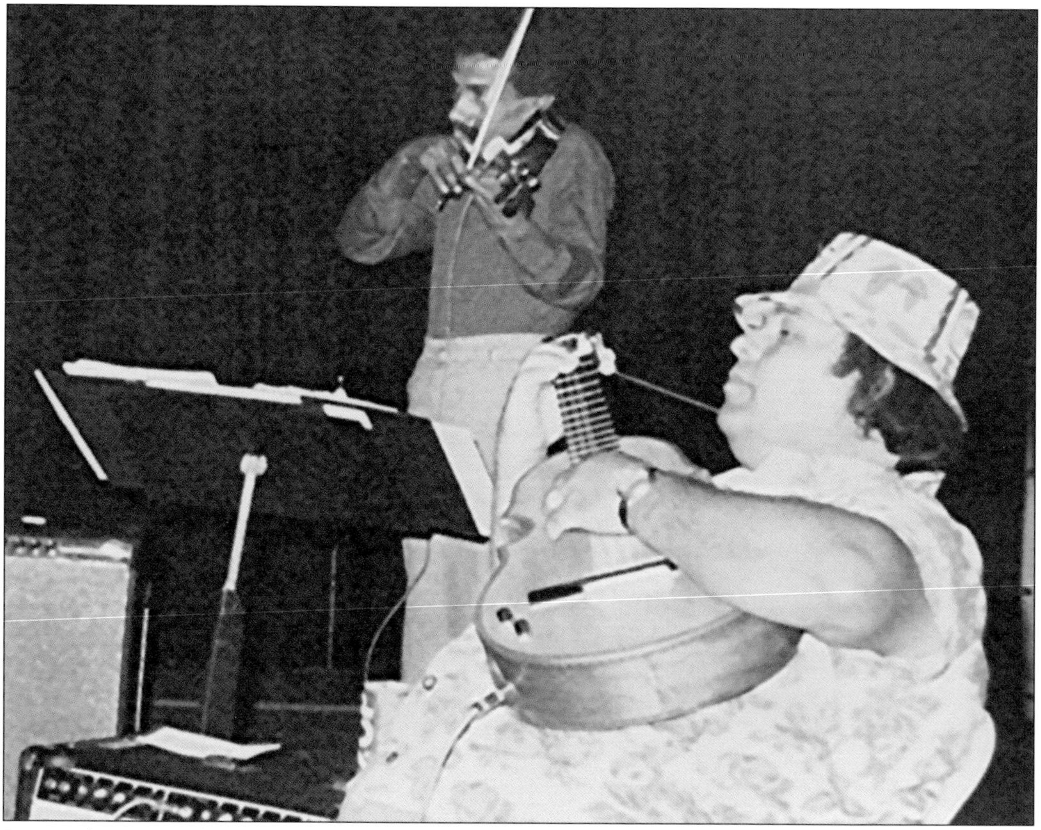

Pictured in 1983 during rehearsal for the Fani All-Stars show at the Hollywood Palladium are Felix "Pupi" Legarreta on violin and Yomo Toro on tres.

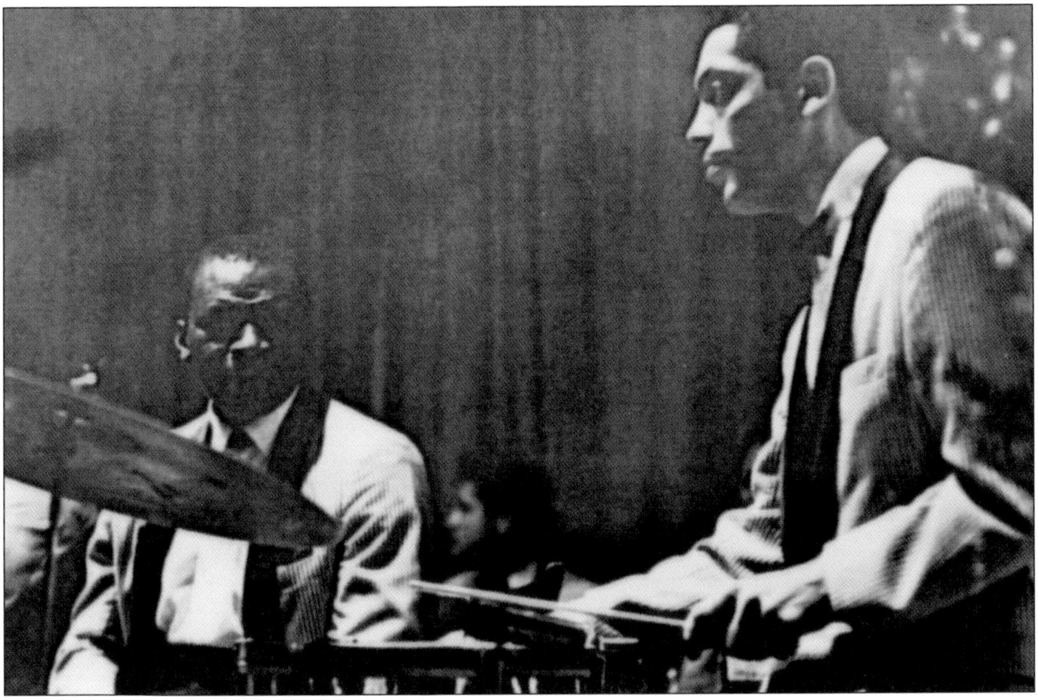

Joe Torres, on the right playing timbale, is shown here as a member of Arsenio Rodriguez's group in 1958 in New York City. With him playing bongo is Raul Rodriguez, Arsenio's brother.

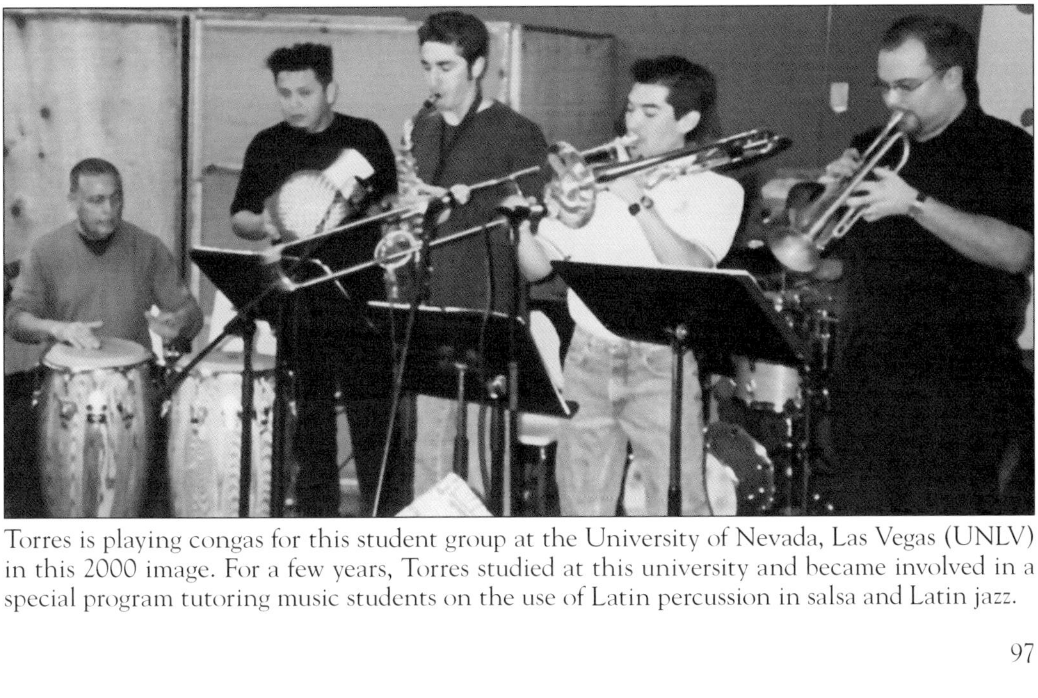

Torres is playing congas for this student group at the University of Nevada, Las Vegas (UNLV) in this 2000 image. For a few years, Torres studied at this university and became involved in a special program tutoring music students on the use of Latin percussion in salsa and Latin jazz.

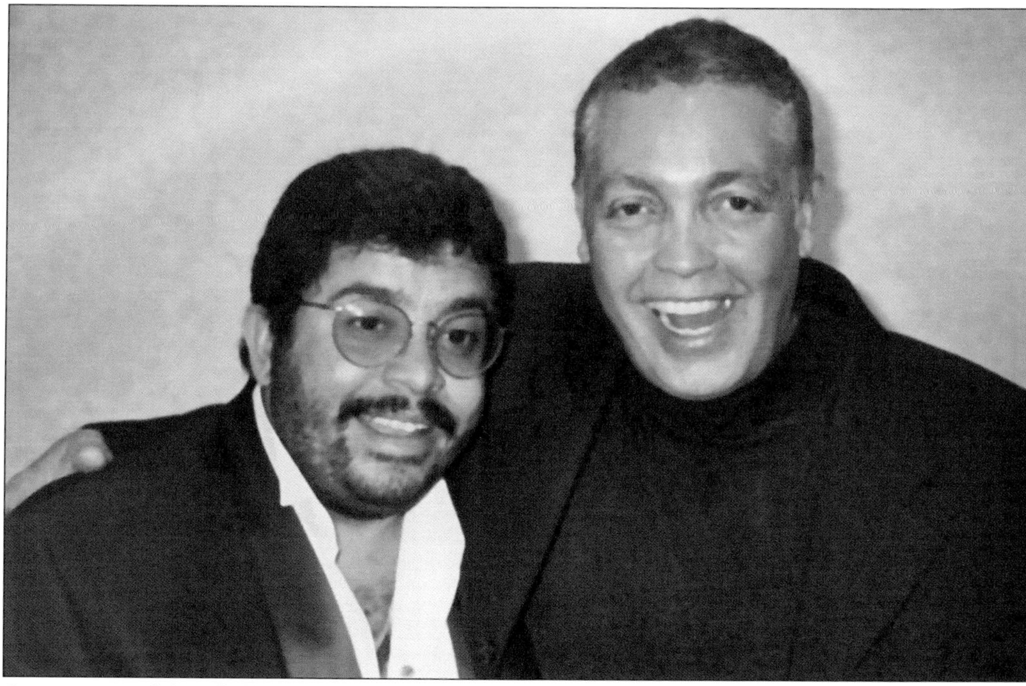

Giovanni Hidalgo (left) and Joe Torres are back stage at the Greek Theater of Los Angeles in 1996.

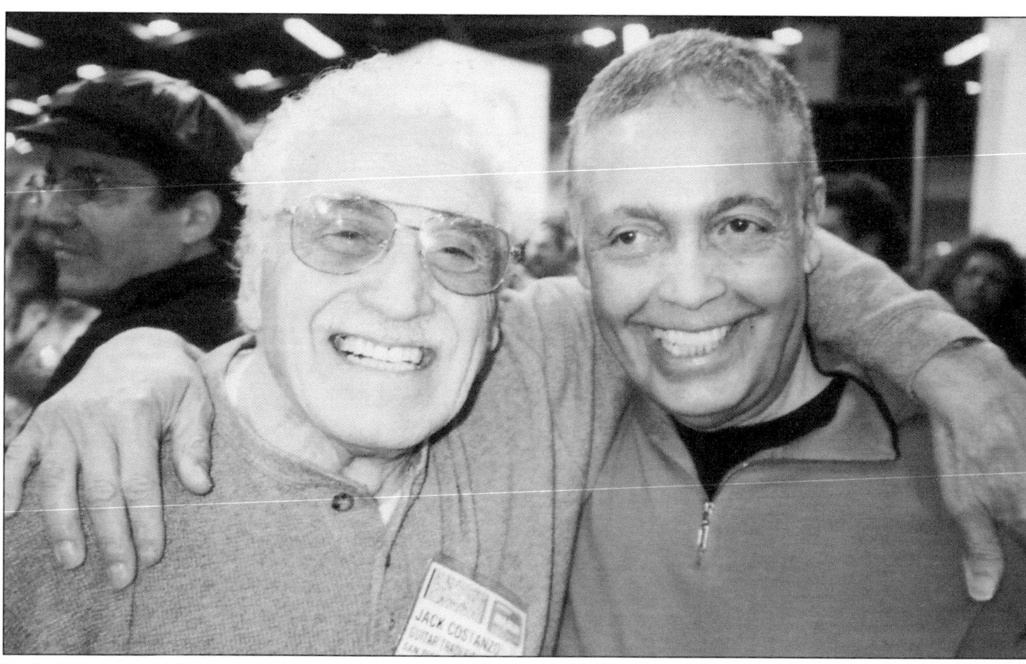

Jack Costanzo (left) and Torres are at the NAMM Show in Anaheim, California, in 2001. Costanzo gained popularity when he joined the Stan Kenton band in the 1950s. He helped introduce the bongo instrument into American music with the big hit recordings of "The Peanut Vendor," "Bongo Riff," and "Cuban Carnival."

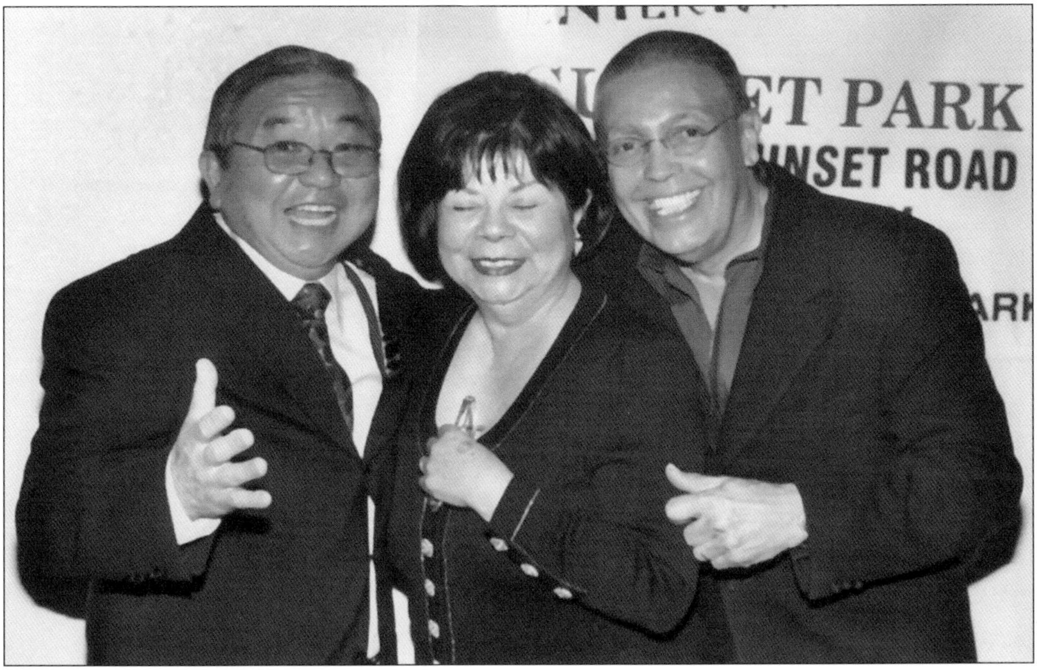

Pictured here in 2004 with Tommy and Gloria Saito is Torres at Rae Arroyo's fund-raiser celebrated at the UNLV campus. Tommy was shown in a previous image playing conga with the Tito Rodriguez Orchestra.

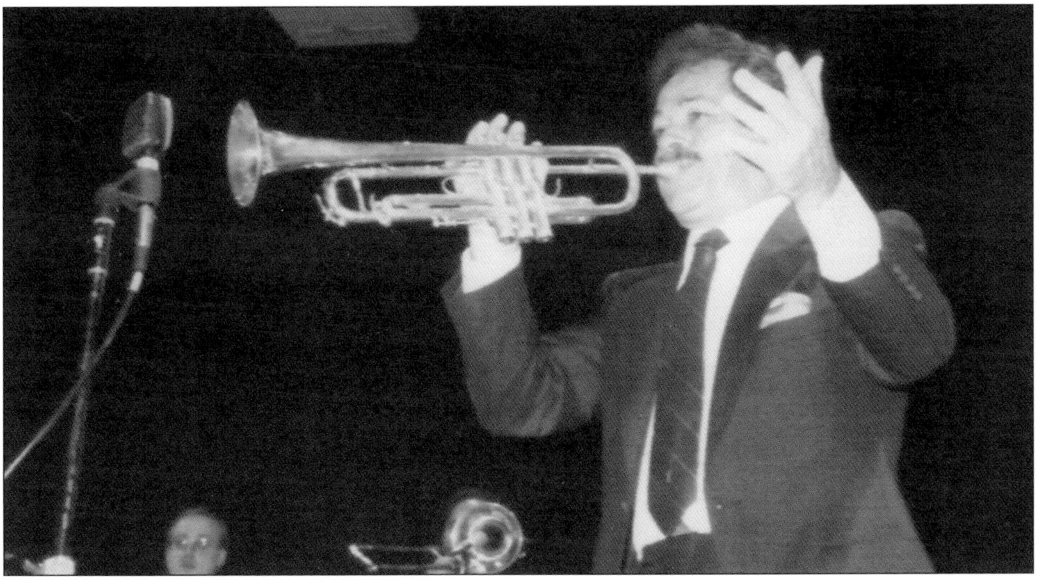

Juancito Torres was every bandleader's dream. He was not only exceptional in the trumpet section but took delightful solos as well. Commencing in his native Puerto Rico in the early 1950s, he played with the orchestras of Rafael Muñoz, Cesar Concepción, and Miguelito Miranda. By the end of the decade, he moved to New York and obtained jobs with Tito Rodríguez, Noro Morales, Joe Quijano, La Plata Sextet, and Charlie and Eddie Palmieri. For a brief period in the 1970s he joined Herb Alpert and the Tijuana Brass. He is shown here in 1994 at a dance in Los Angeles with the Eddie Palmieri Band. Juancito died in 2003.

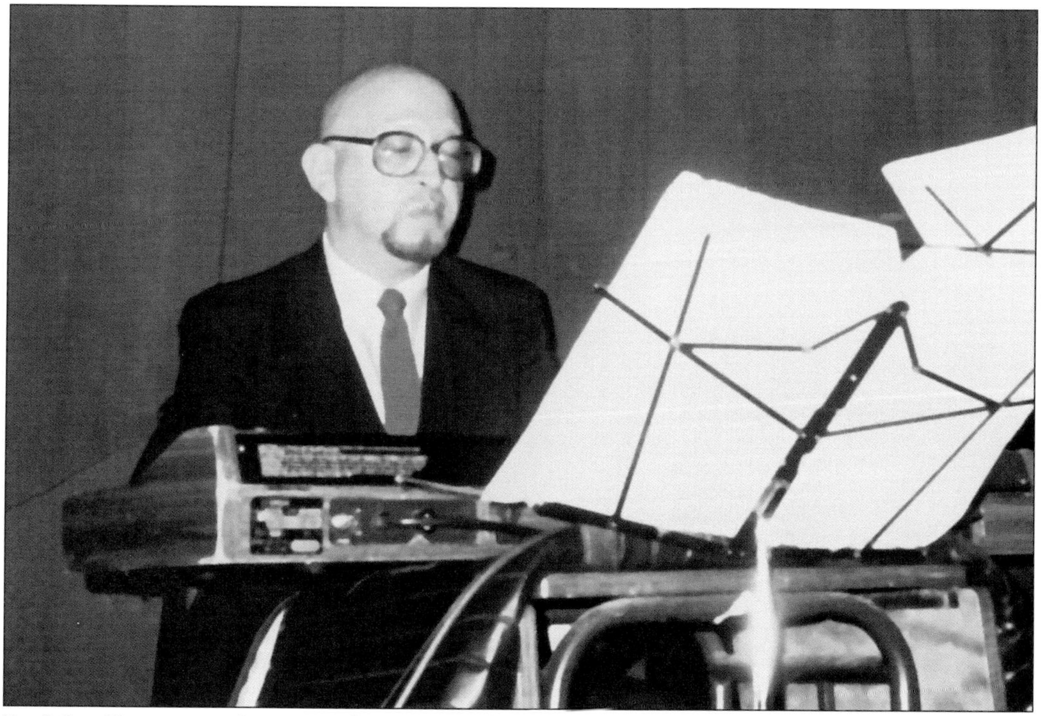

Prof. Joe Torres was the original pianist with the groups of Willie Colon, Hector Lavoe, and Orquesta Novel. He is pictured here with Lavoe's group at the Hollywood Palladium in 1979.

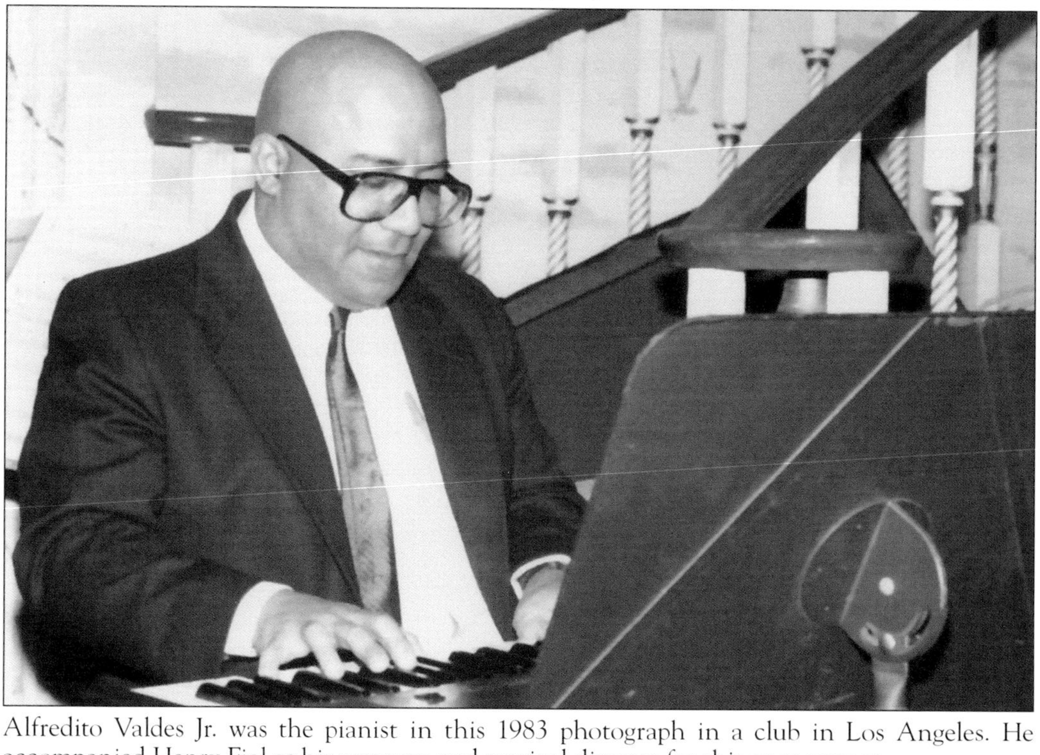

Alfredito Valdes Jr. was the pianist in this 1983 photograph in a club in Los Angeles. He accompanied Henry Fiol as his arranger and musical director for this engagement.

Carlos "Patato" Valdez is shown relaxing at the Old-Timers Reunion in New York City in 1998. An early transplant from his native Cuba, Patato came to the United States in 1954, and throughout his long career has worked with every well-known group from Machito and His Afro-Cubans to Herbie Mann.

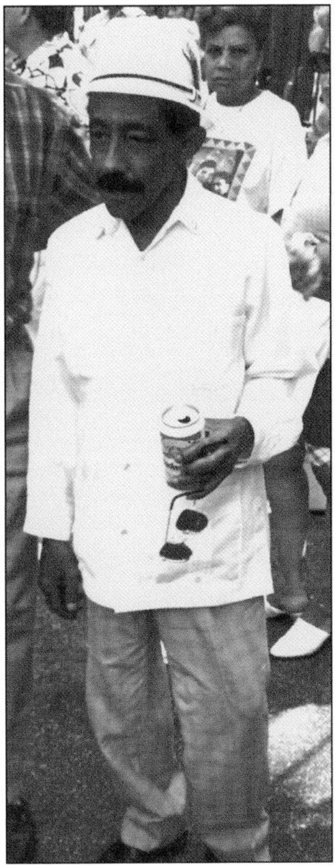

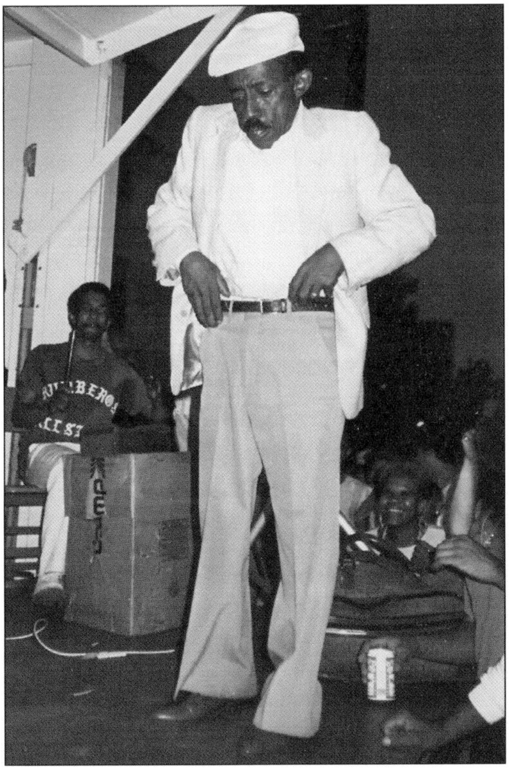

Known for his funny antics, Patato is seen at the 1999 Old-Timers Reunion in New York City preparing to show the audience how to dance a guaguanco.

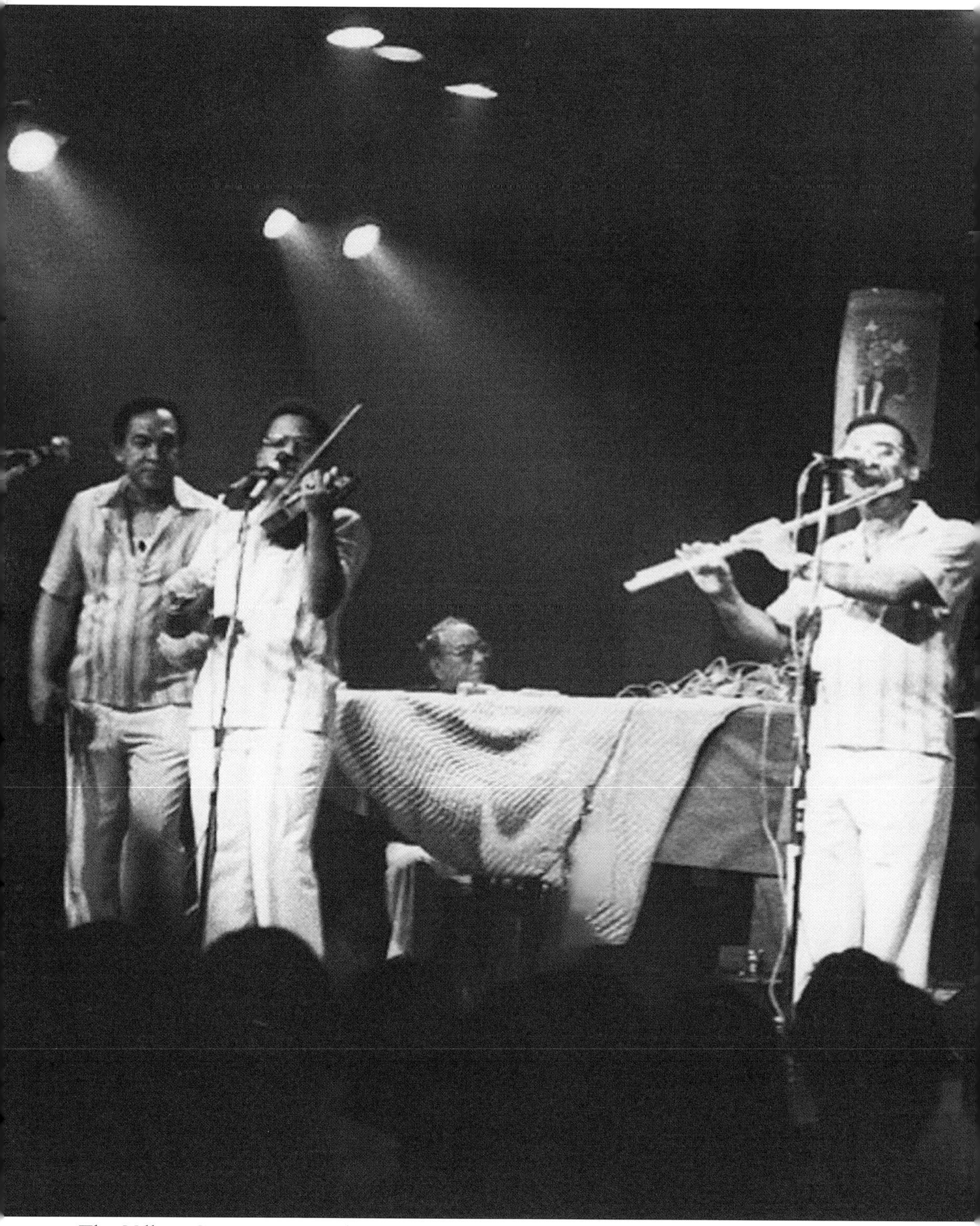

The Village Gate in New York City is the scene for this 1979 image. Orquesta Aragon came from Cuba for several appearances. The concert was almost cancelled due to a telephone bomb

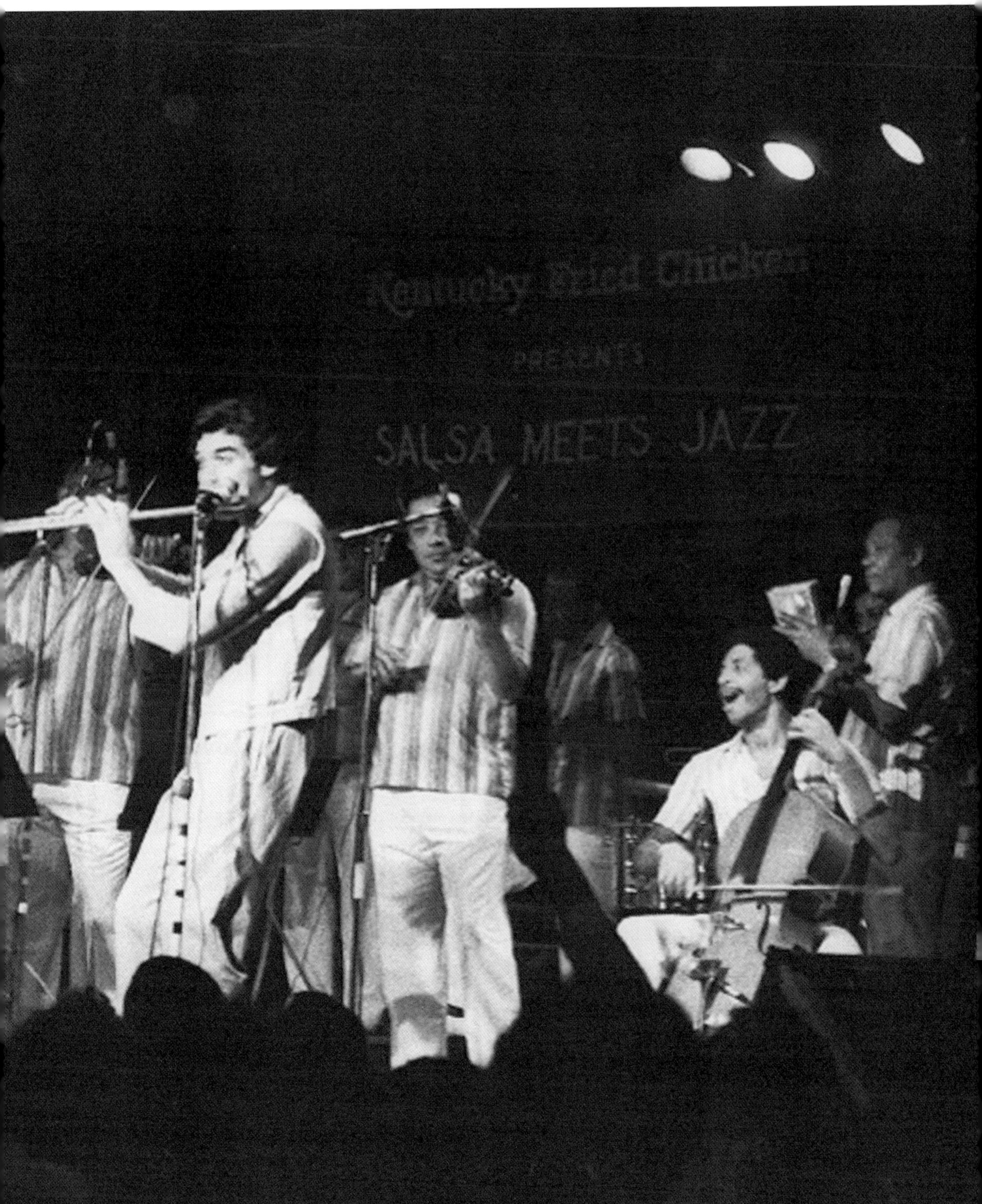

threat, but the fans came and filled the club. On stage with flutist Richard Egues is flutist Dave Valentin on the right.

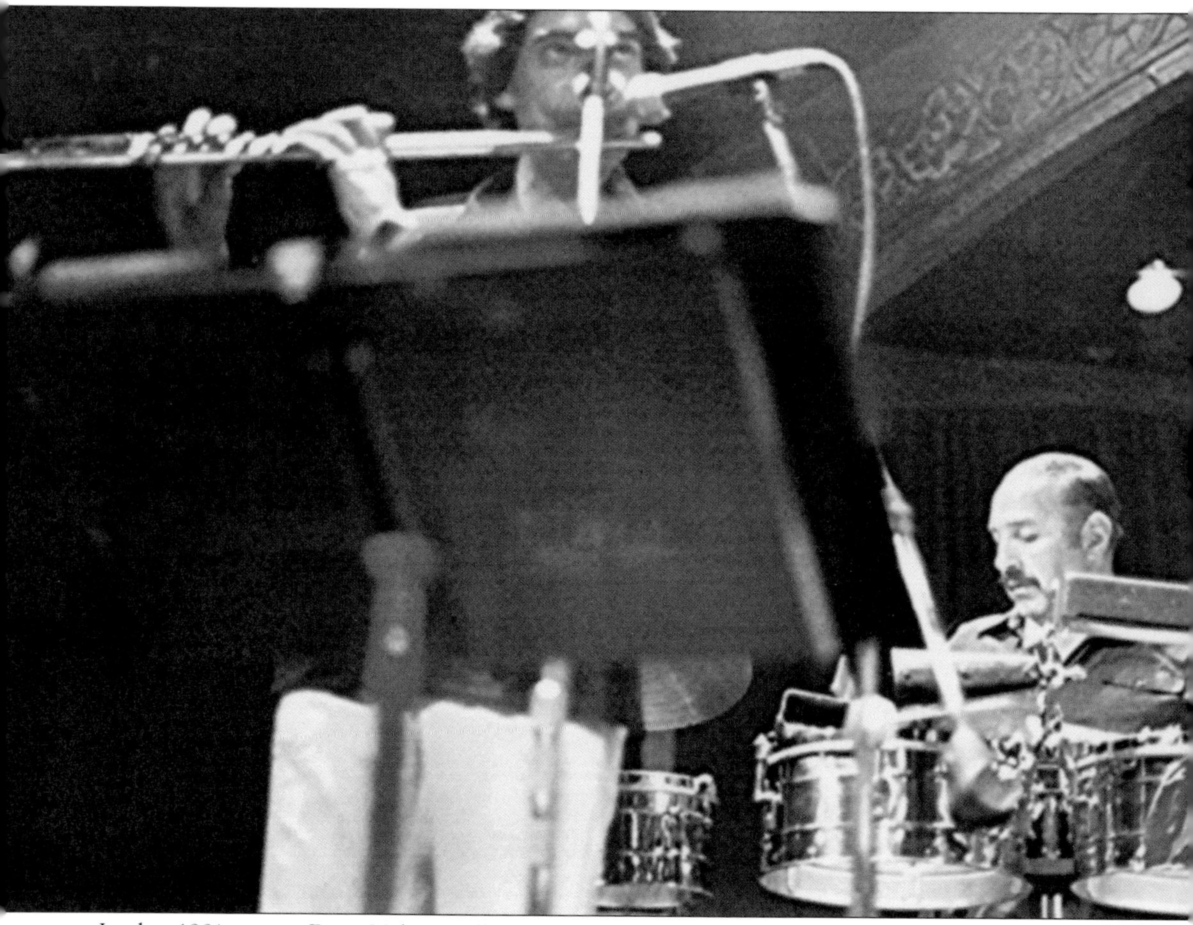

In this 1991 image, Dave Valentin (left) is with Manny Oquendo and Libre at the Maganette in New York City. Valentin picked up the flute for the first time at the late age of 16 and received lessons from jazz flutist Hubert Laws. He spent several years as a schoolteacher instructing inner-city students on Latin and jazz music.

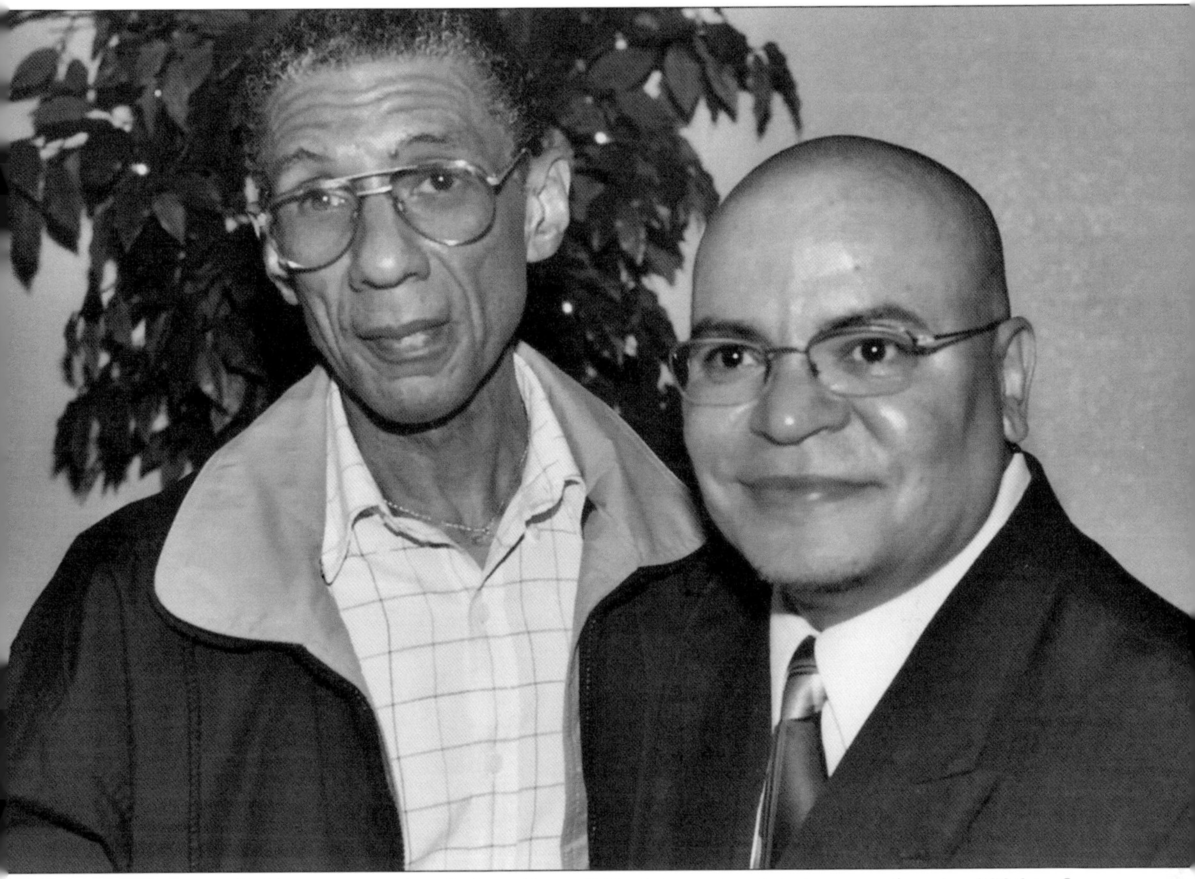

Javier Vasquez (left) is pictured with Jose "Papo" Rodriguez in this image taken in 2006 in Las Vegas, where Vasquez now resides. A talented pianist, arranger, and producer, Vasquez worked during the 1950s and 1960s in New York City and Puerto Rico with artists such as Ismael Rivera, Daniel Santos, and Candido.

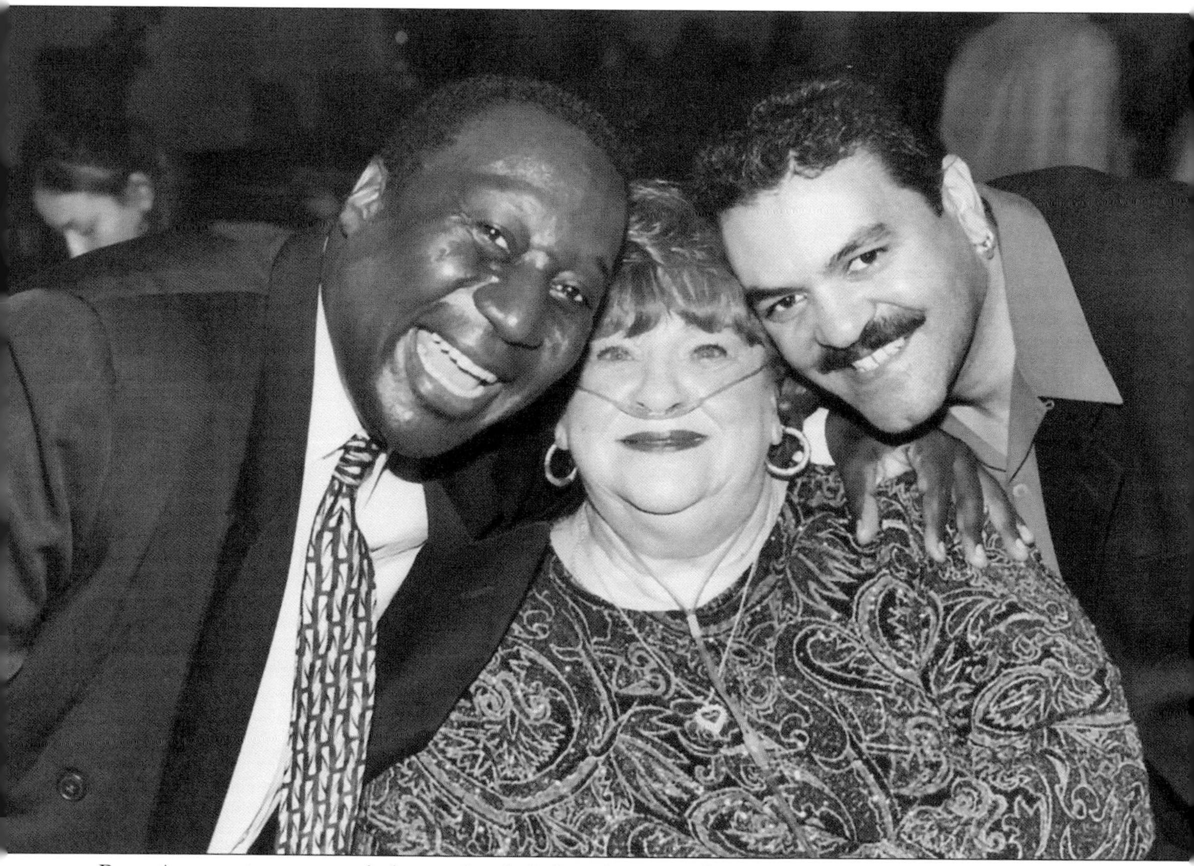

Rae Arroyo is surrounded on the left by Artie Web, currently the flutist with the Los Angeles–based Johnny Polanco group Amistad. Web spent many years in New York City playing with several charanga bands and the orchestra of Ray Barretto. Also pictured is Wayne Newton's percussionist, David Romero, in this 2004 image taken on the campus of UNLV in Las Vegas.

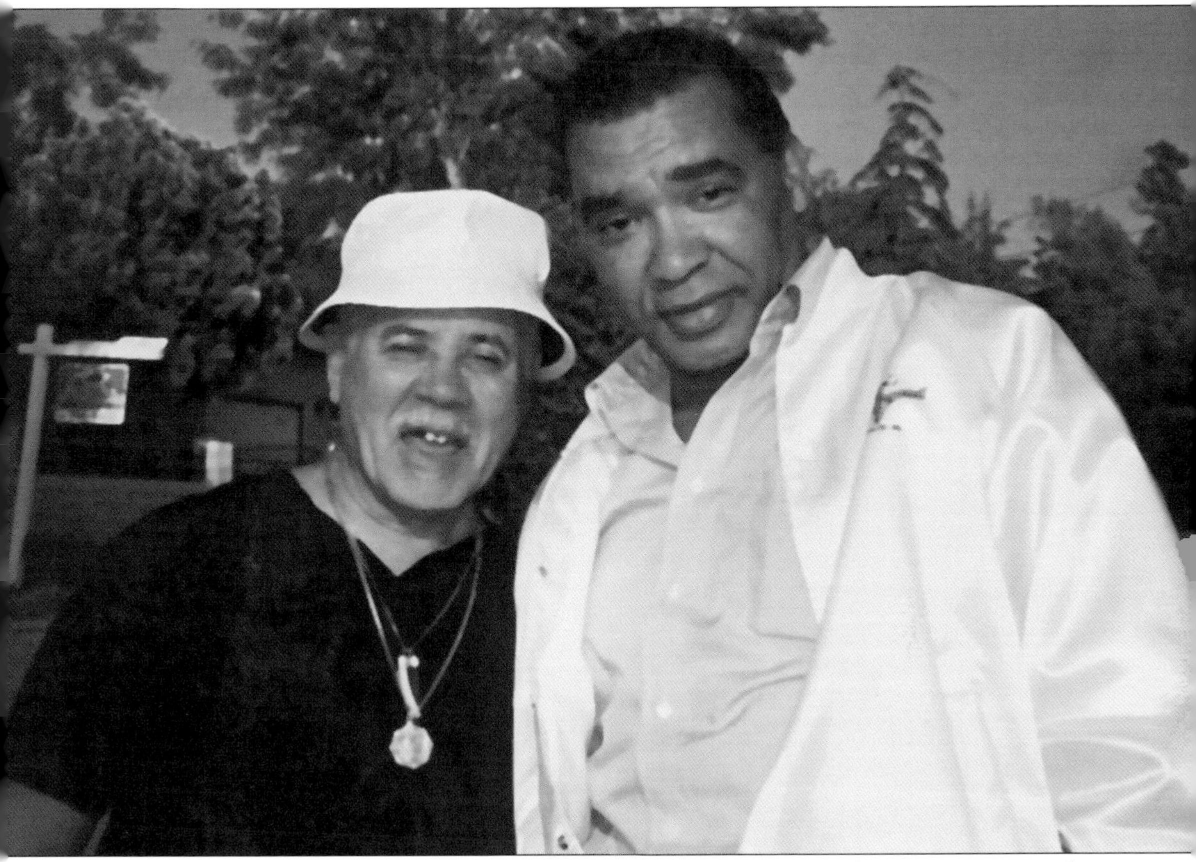

Legendary New York Palladium dancer Pedro Aguilar, also known as Cuban Pete, is pictured in this 1996 candid image with lifelong friend and fellow Spanish Harlem alumni Ralph Vila.

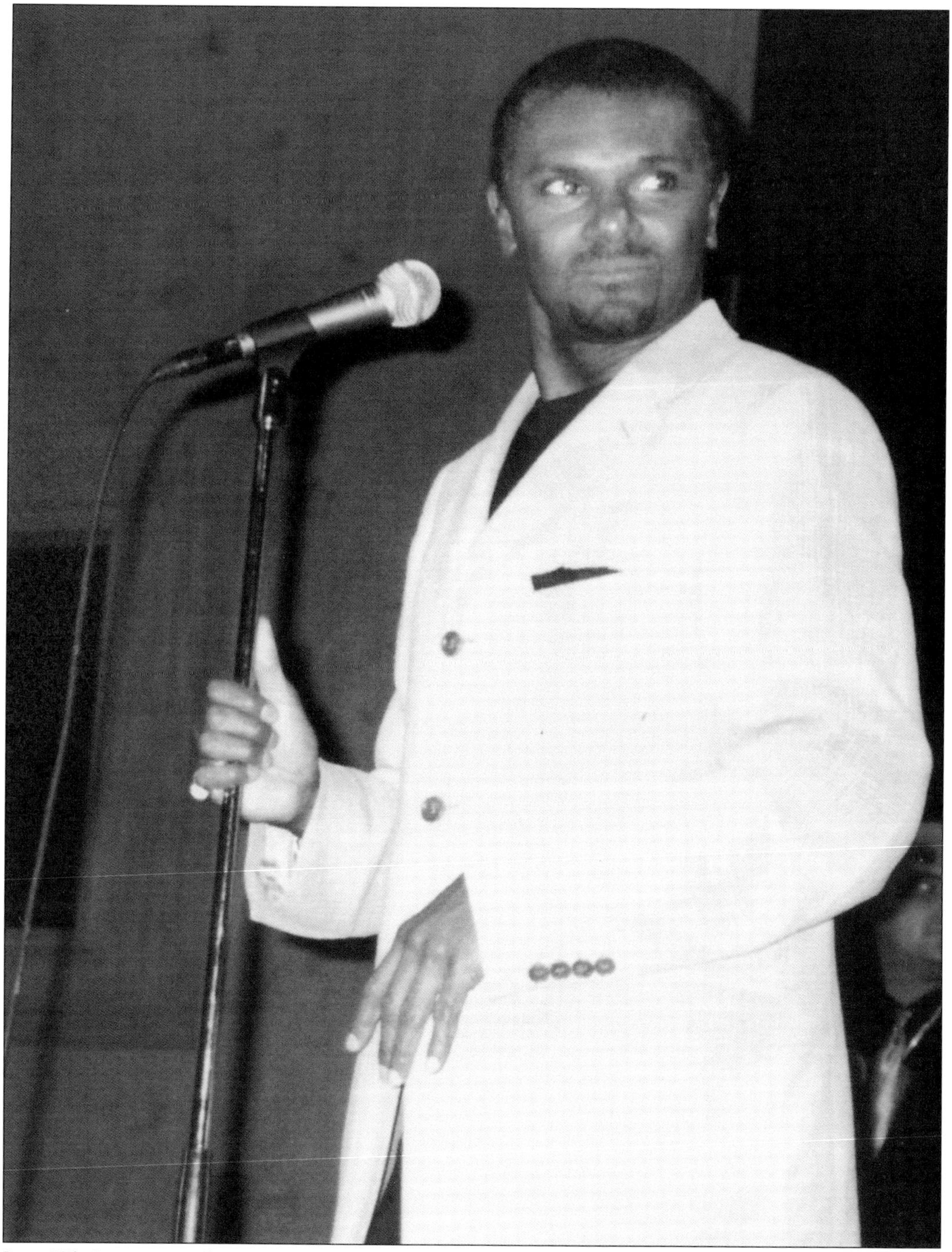

Jose "El Canario" Alberto is seen here in 2004 at an outdoor concert in Dorado, Puerto Rico. During festival time, major cities compete for the services of top musical groups.

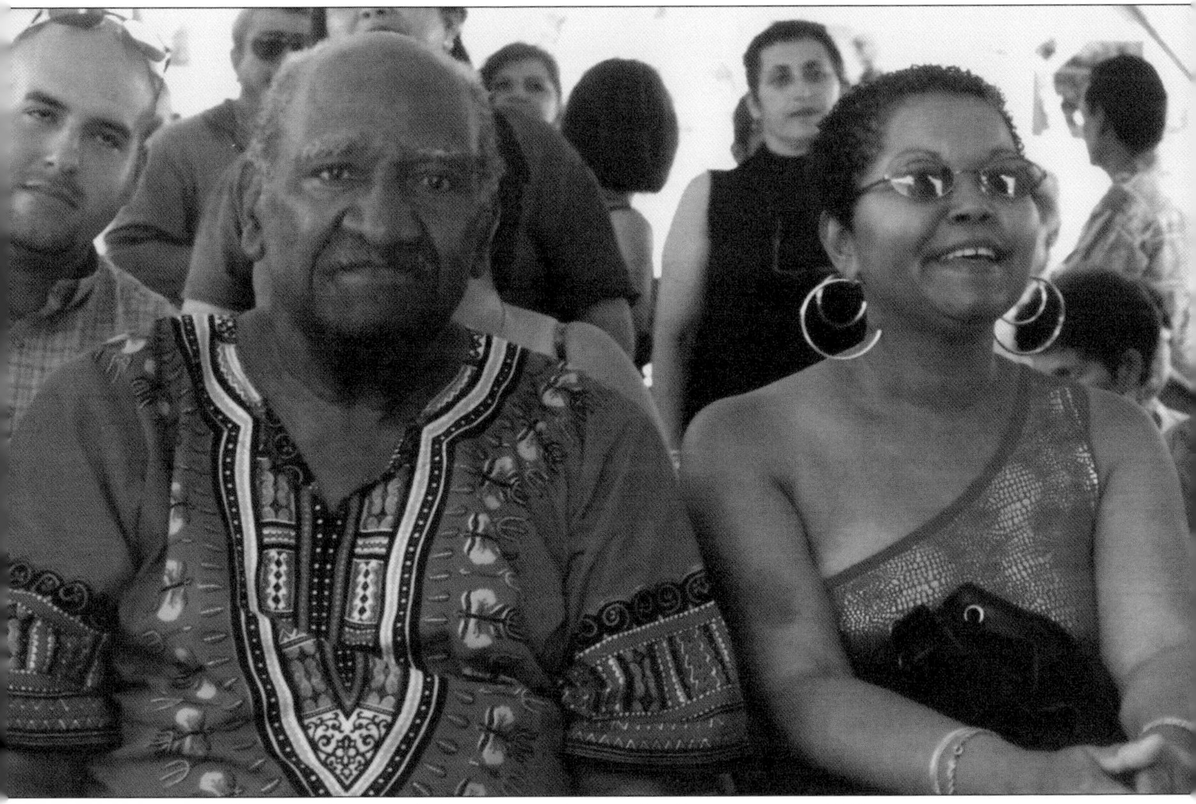

Catalino "Tite" Curet Alonso (left) is seated with Fe Cortijo at a 2000 concert in Carolina, Puerto Rico, honoring his work. Fe is the niece of famed musician Rafael Cortijo. Present also was Cheo Feliciano as guest artist. One of Puerto Rico's prolific and loved composers, Alonso dedicated his life to creating meaningful lyrics depicting the Afro Caribbean culture. Alonso died in 2003.

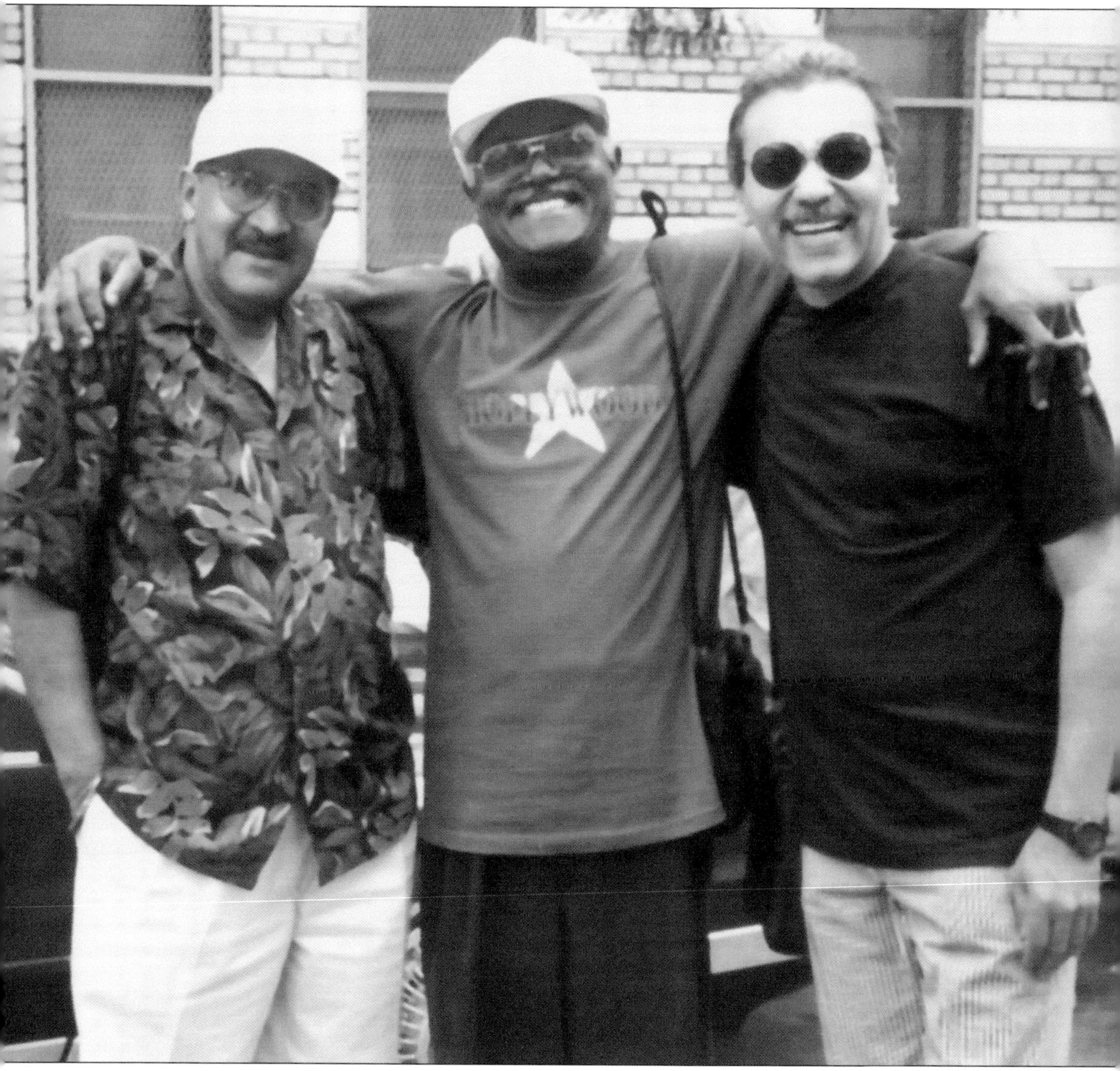

Standing on either side of trumpet master Alfredo "Chocolate" Armenteros are the author and Eddie Lopez on the right. This photograph was taken at the 1996 Old-Timers Reunion in Spanish Harlem.

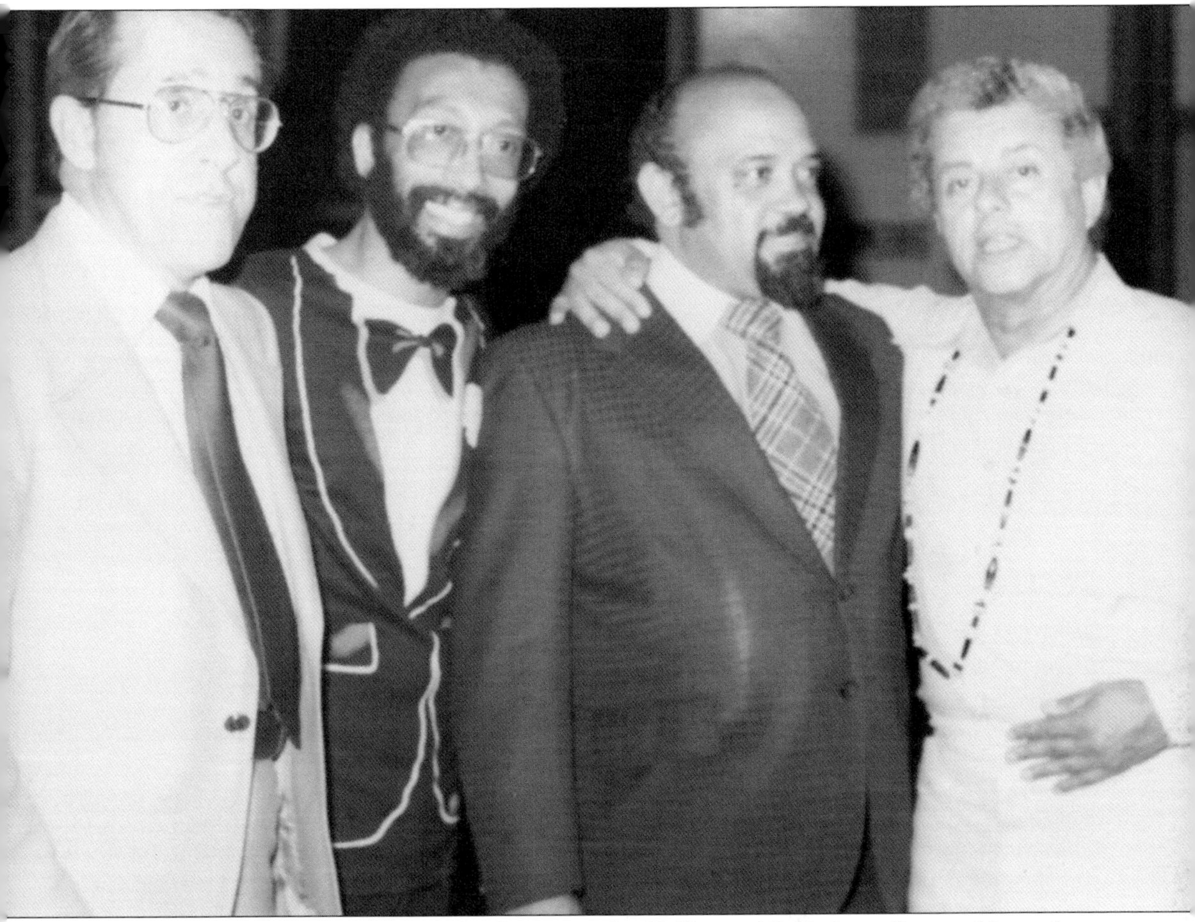

This photograph was taken in 1981 backstage at the Hollywood Palladium. Pictured here, from left to right, are Jose Curbelo (bandleader/booking agent), John Palomo (percussionist), Rudy Calzado (singer/composer), and the late Tito Puente. Calzado died in 2002.

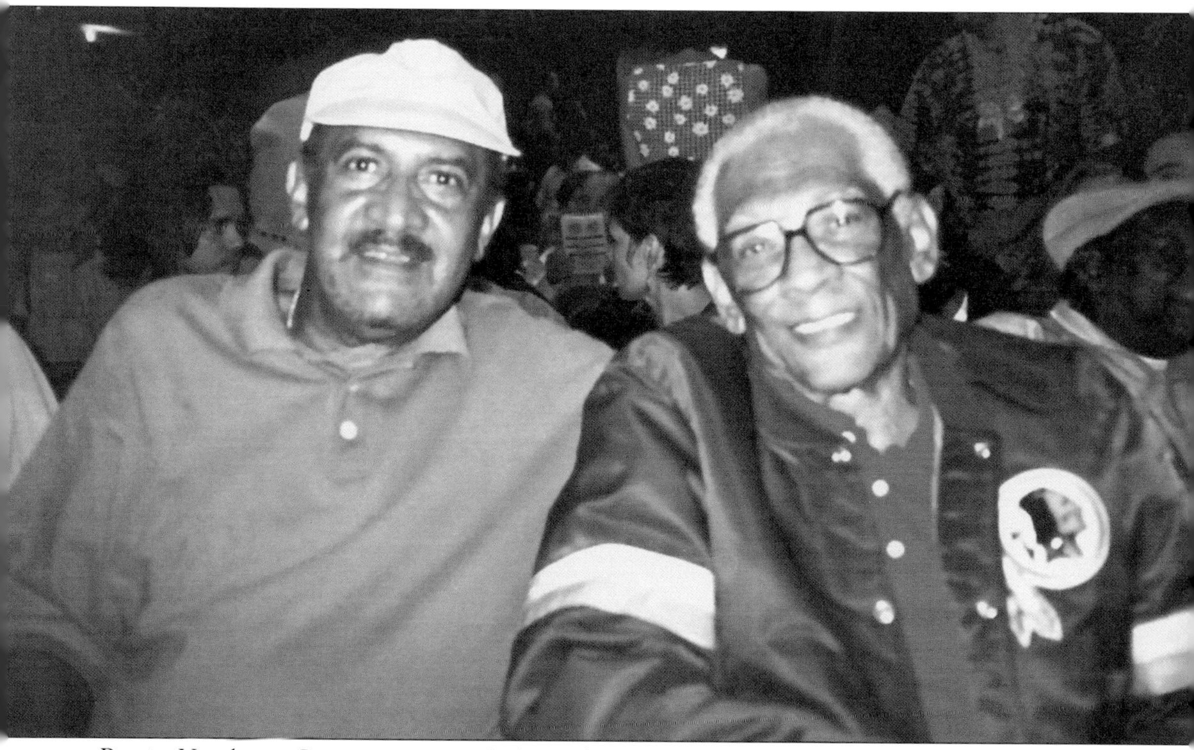

Bassist Humberto Cané is sitting with the author in 1994 at a concert in Los Angeles. A resident of Los Angeles since 1958, Humberto is the son of Valentine Cané, the founder of La Sonora Mantancera of Cuba. A tresero at first, he formed his own group and traveled to Mexico. Out of necessity he learned to play the bass. He said, "I had to eat!" In 1947, he accompanied Beny Moré in his first recording. Humberto worked in Mexico City at the height of its movie-making history, both in clubs and providing music for sound tracks. While living in California, he worked with all the popular bands from the 1960s through the 1980s. Humberto died in the year 2000.

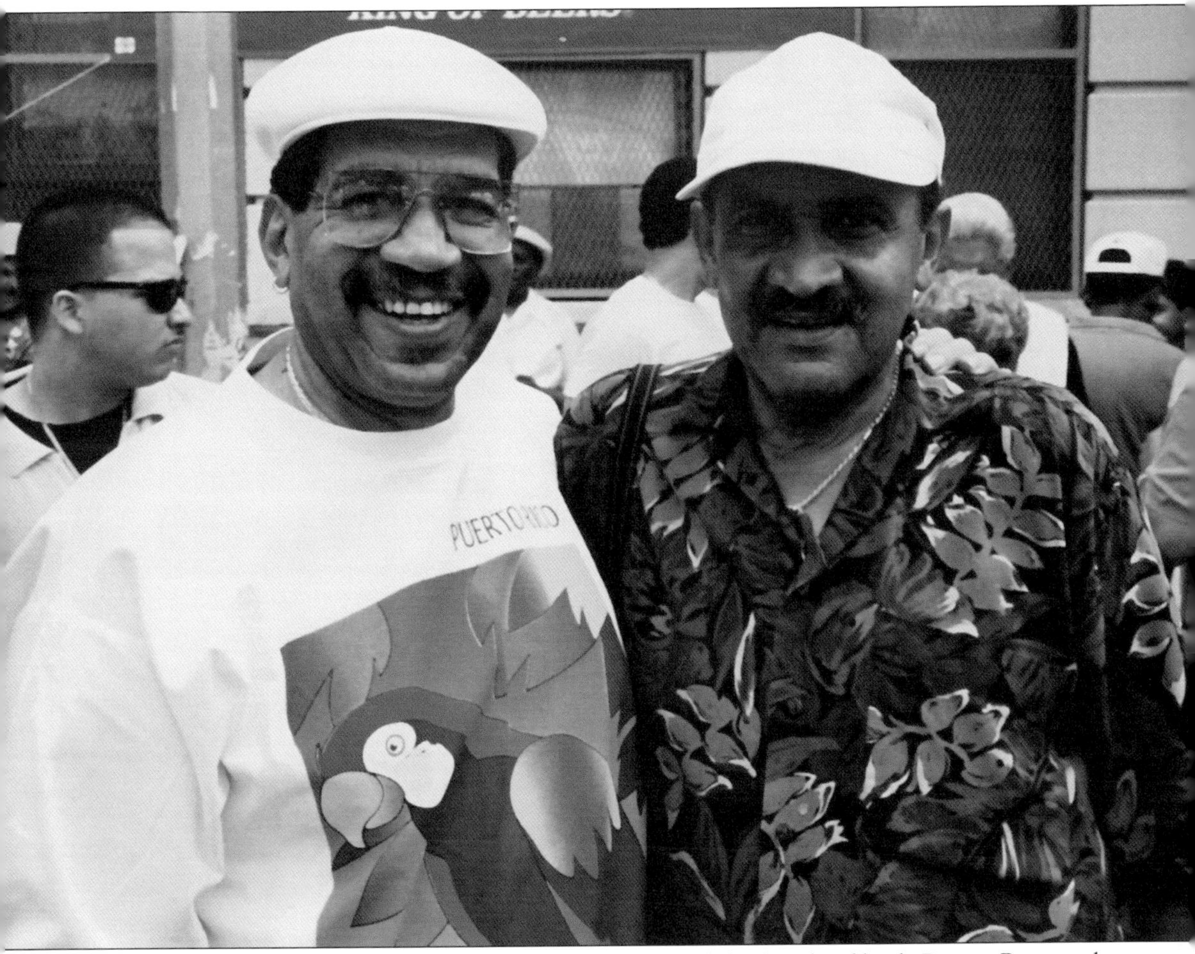

Madamo Diaz (left) has played and recorded with many of the bands of both Puerto Rico and New York City. A versatile percussionist able to play conga, bongo, or timbale, Diaz has been a professional musician for over 25 years. He played conga on Tito Puente's 1972 album *Para Los Rumberos* and the 1973 album *Tito Puente and His Concert Orchestra*. He is shown here with the author attending the 2002 Old-Timers Reunion in Spanish Harlem.

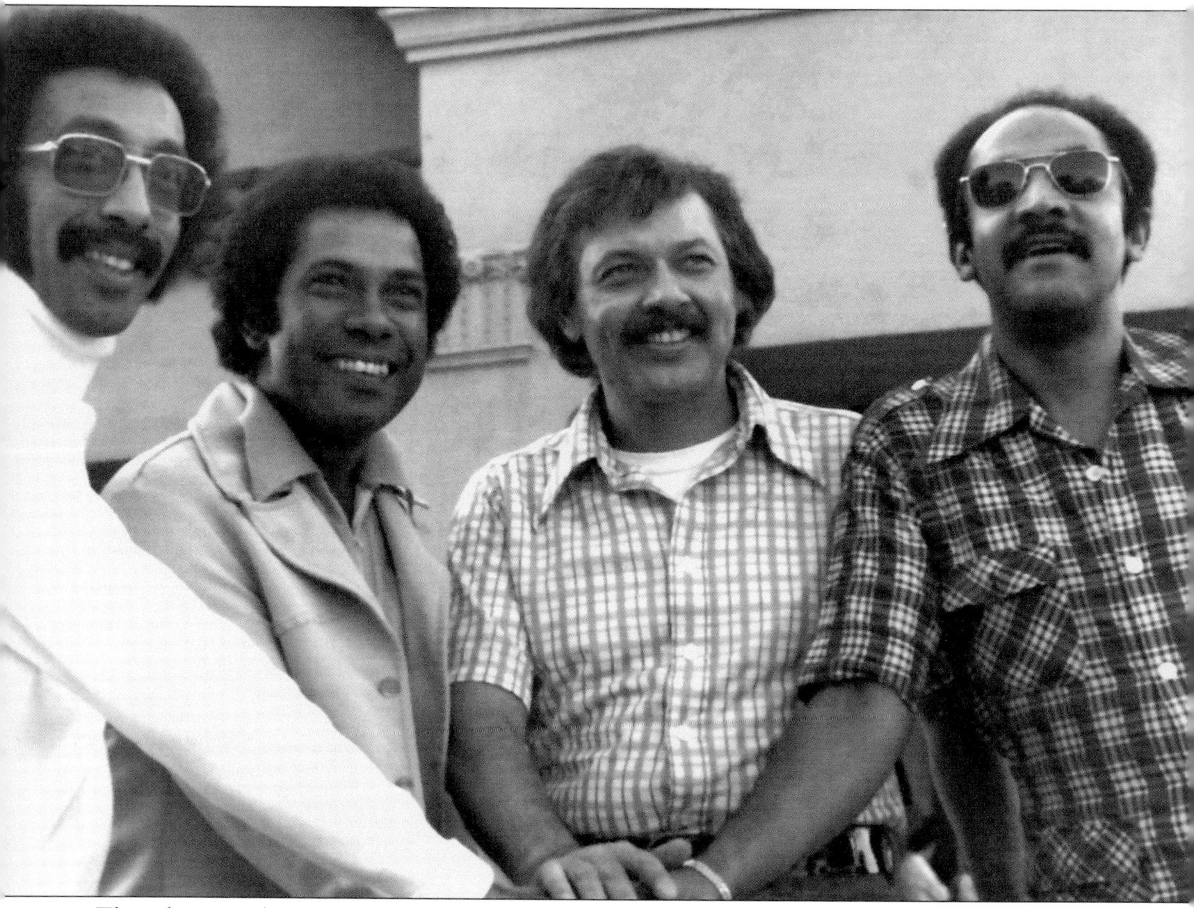

This photograph was taken when Cheo Feliciano came to Los Angeles in 1979 for a club date and took time to spend with some close Spanish Harlem friends. Pictured here, from left to right, are John Palomo, Cheo Feliciano, Louis Gomez, and the author.

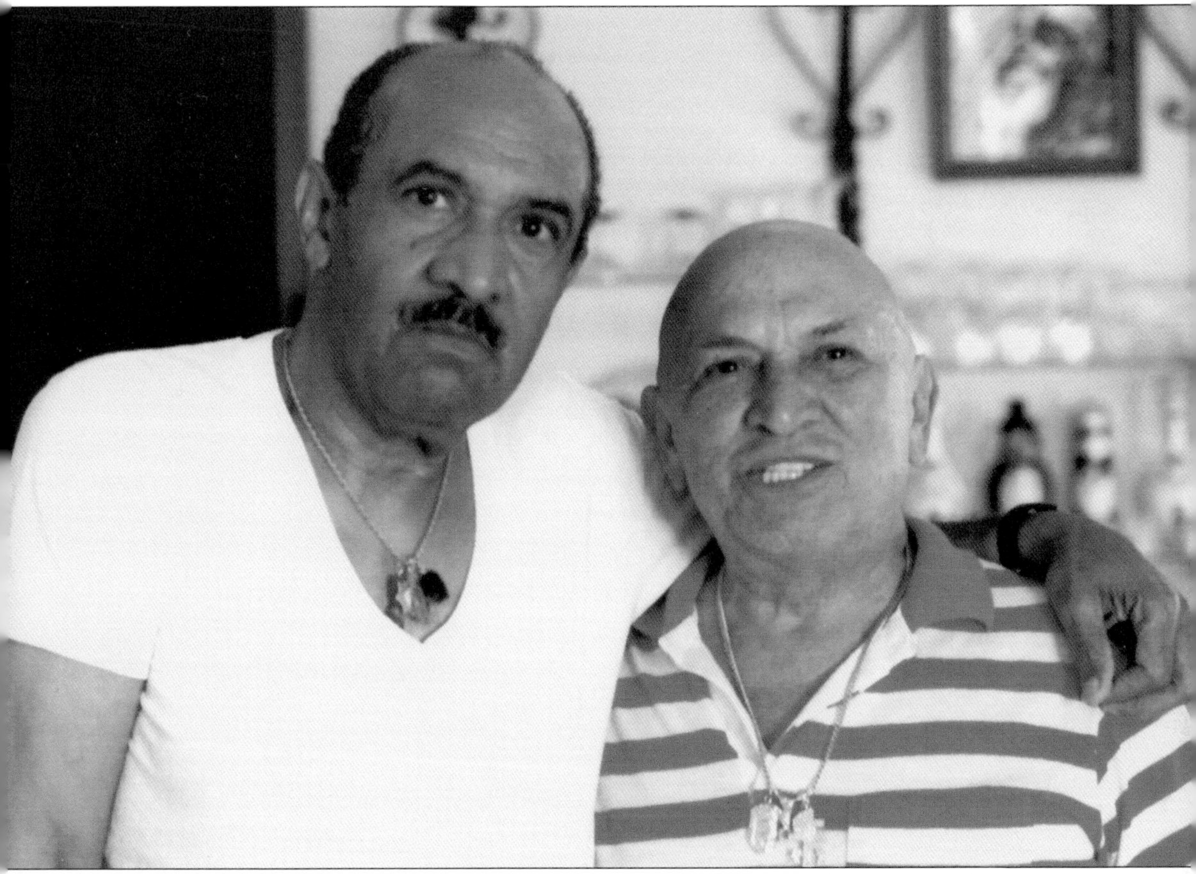

When Tito Puente, Machito, and Tito Rodriguez were sidemen working with other bands, a Panamanian by the name of Luis Kant, also known as "Puntillita," arrived in New York City to begin his career. The nickname was given to him by the noted New York promoter Federico Pagani. Puntillita is pictured here on the right with the author in his home in Las Vegas in 1997. A native of the barrio Chorrillo, which was also the home of the pugilist Roberto Duran and Ruben Blades Sr. (the father of Ruben Blades), Kant sharpened his singing and percussion skills on the road. He traveled to Cuba, Mexico, and Central America with Myrta Silva, the popular Puerto Rican singer. He has played or recorded with groups such as Alberto Iznaga in New York City and Judy Garland in Las Vegas. His home was decorated with dozens of 8-by-10-inch photographs of the stars he had worked with all over the world. Kant died in the year 2006 in Las Vegas.

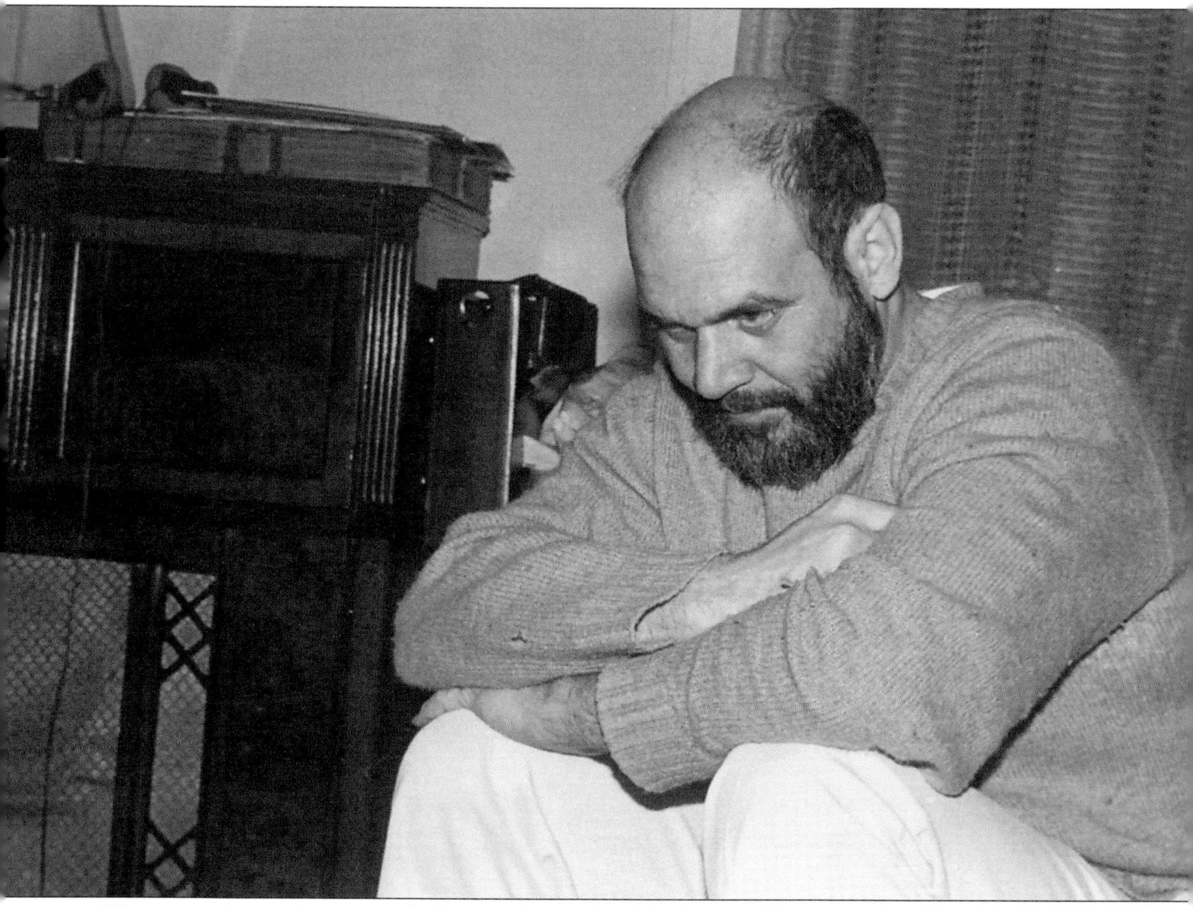

Whenever the author visited New York City, one visit had to be with Rene Lopez. A noted musicologist and producer, Lopez has amassed a large collection of Cuban music. A blank 90-minute cassette tape was a necessity in order to take home a copy of the gems that he played. During this 1984 visit, he sat mesmerized listening to a rare Arsenio Rodriguez tune, or perhaps it was something special by Las Estrellas De Chocolate. Major figures in the New York City salsa scene spent many hours in his home looking for material to record on future record dates.

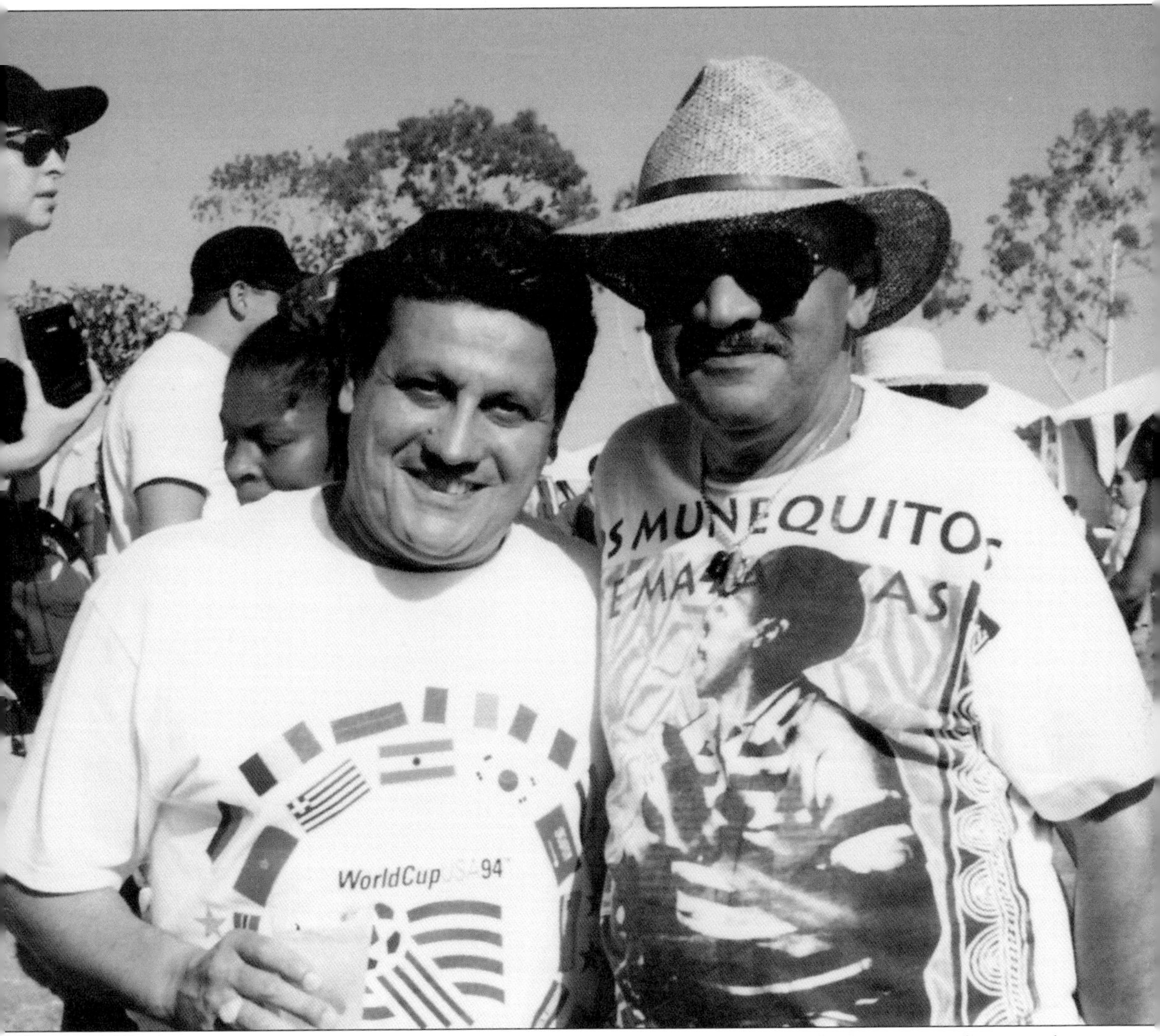

Early one afternoon this author received a telephone call from a friend who was working with the promoter bringing a group of musicians from New York City. She had a problem with her vehicle and asked if he could go to the airport and pick up Ray Barretto, Yomo Toro, and Ismael Miranda. Miranda, the gentleman in this photograph, and all the others were delightful company all the way to the concert. This was taken just prior to the outdoor concert commencing in Long Beach, California, in 1994.

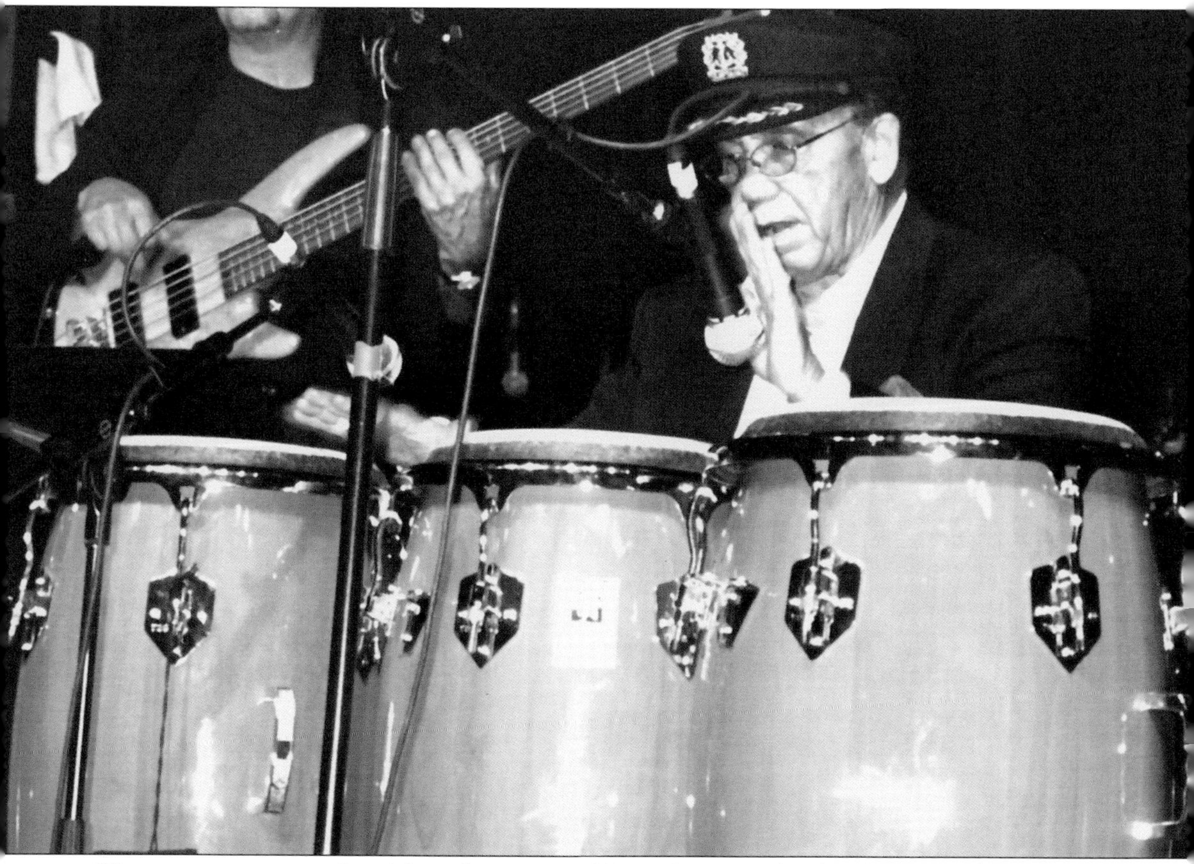

The veteran conguero Luis Miranda is pictured here playing with a band organized by Joe Torres at the author's 50th wedding anniversary celebration in Henderson, Nevada, in the year 2003. From Machito and His Afro-Cubans to Cal Tjader, his rock steady playing, often referred to as "marcha" (march), enhanced any band he played with. Now retired in the Las Vegas area, he is regarded by many as the exemplary big band conguero.

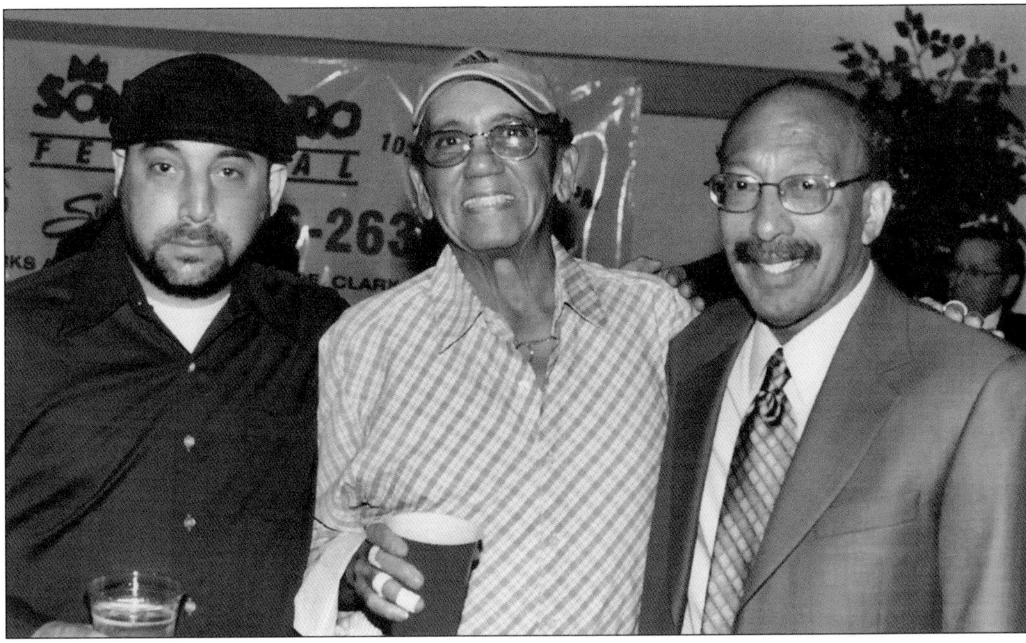

Seen here with Miranda are Miles Perlich on the left and John Palomo at the celebration given for Rae Arroyo in Las Vegas at the University of Nevada, Las Vegas in 2004. Miles is a disc jockey, musicologist, and producer from the Los Angeles area and a lover of Afro Caribbean music.

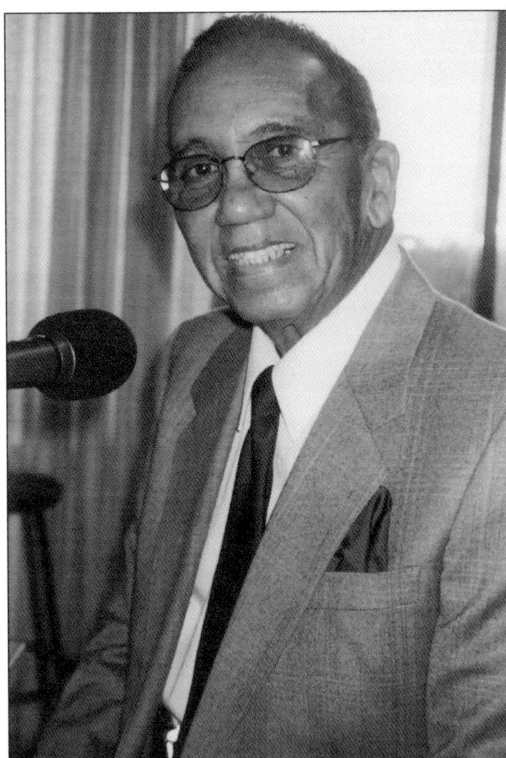

Miranda is all spruced up for an interview in 2004 on Arroyo's radio show over KULV 91.5 FM, Las Vegas's only salsa program.

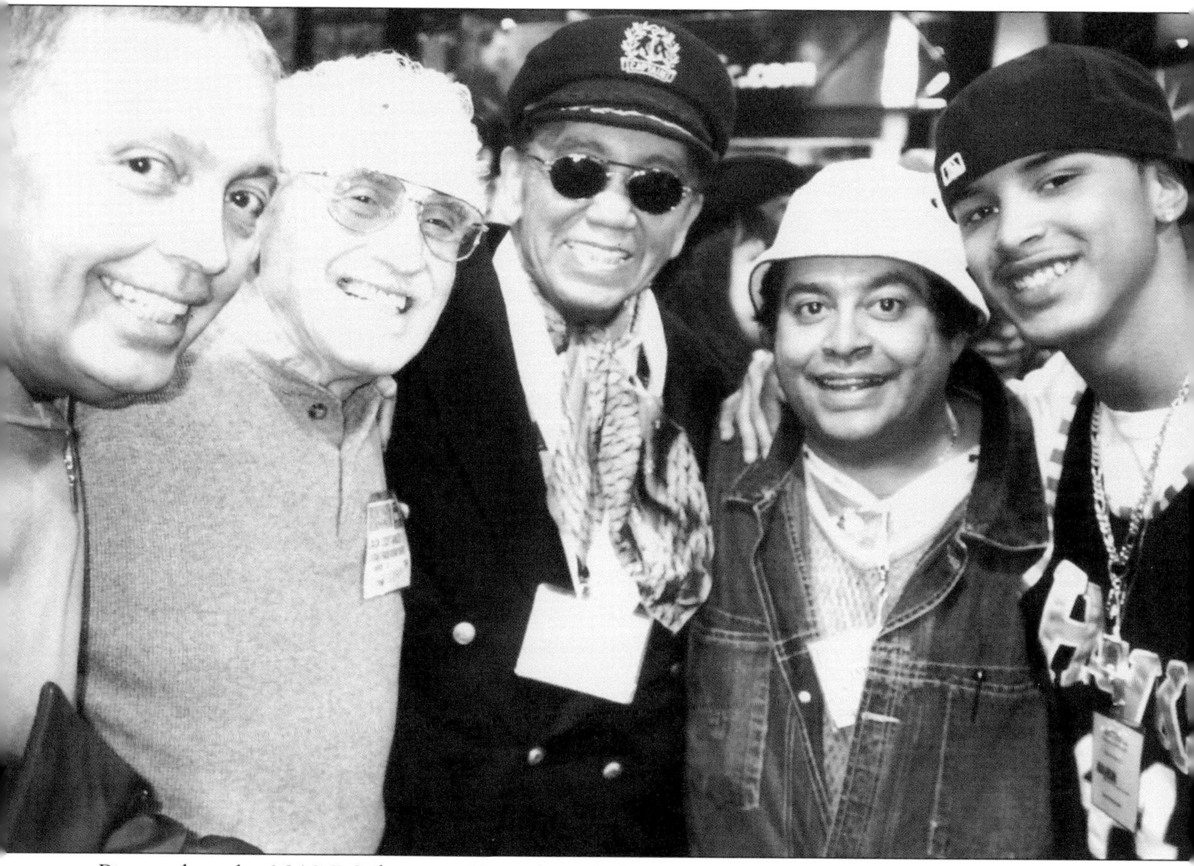

Pictured at the NAMM show in 2004, from left to right, are Joe Torres, Jack Costanzo, Luis Miranda, Giovanni Hidalgo, and Hidalgo's son Ianmanuel.

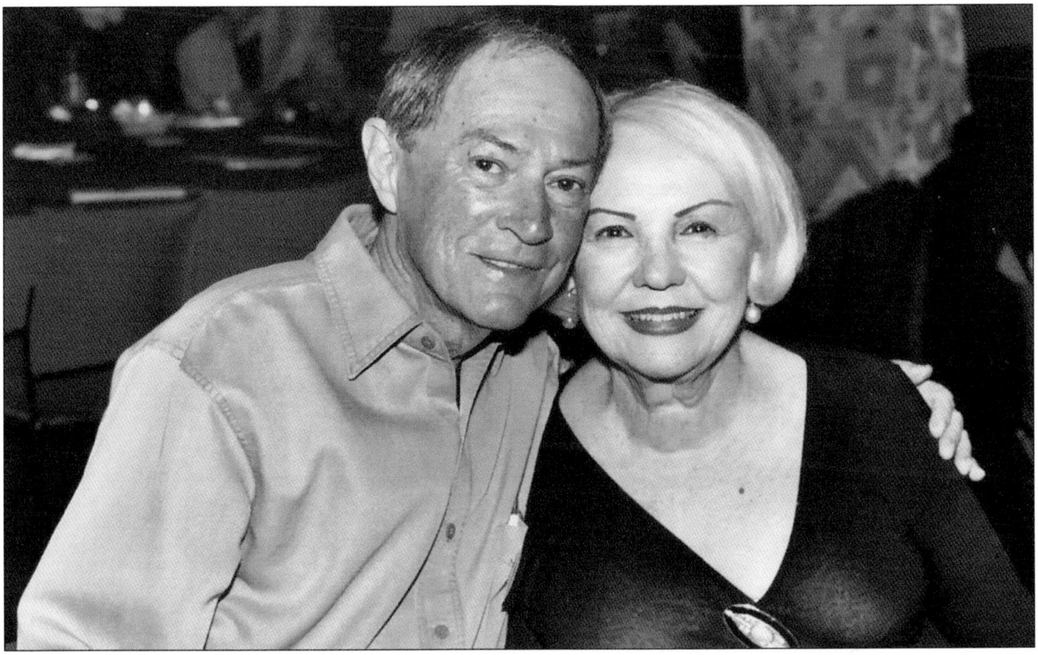

Tata Palau and his wife, Cookie, are pictured in 2004 at Rae Arroyo's celebration given at the University of Nevada, Las Vegas campus. A member of an important musical family in Cuba, Palau played saxophone and flute with Tito Puente and Tito Rodriguez in the 1950s and with Israel Cachao Lopez and other groups in the Miami area, where he has lived for many years.

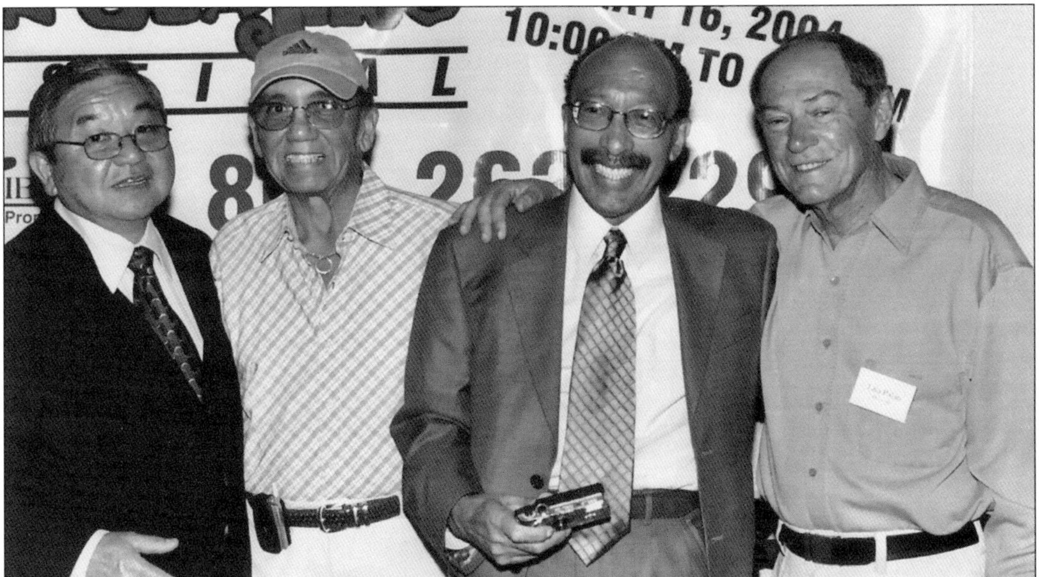

Also taken in 2004 at Rae Arroyo's celebration at University of Nevada, Las Vegas, this photograph shows, from left to right, Tommy Saito, Luis Miranda, John Palomo, and Palau.

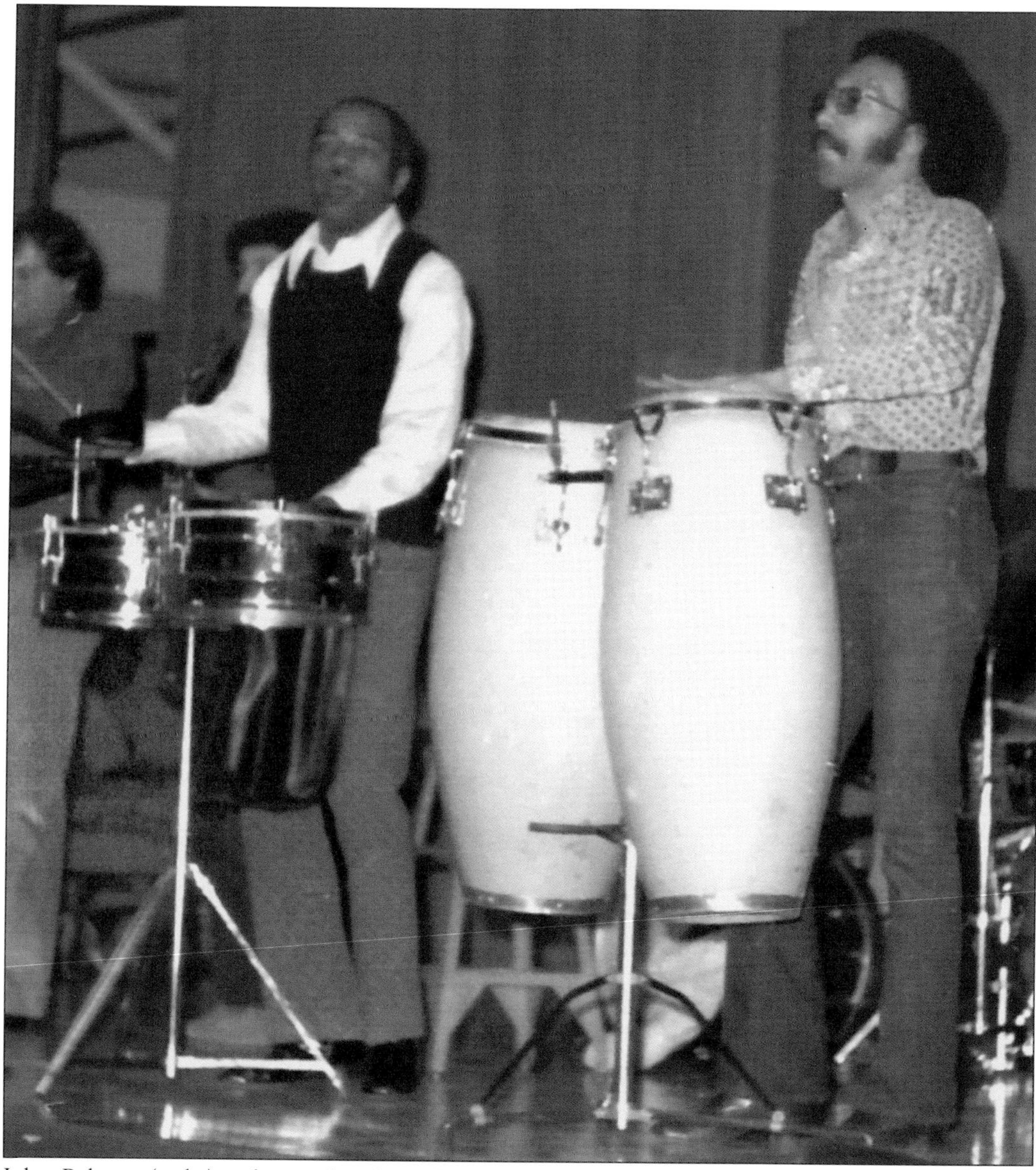

John Palomo (right) is featured with Willie Bobo's group in 1978 at Concerts by the Sea in Los Angeles. Bobo is seen on the left.

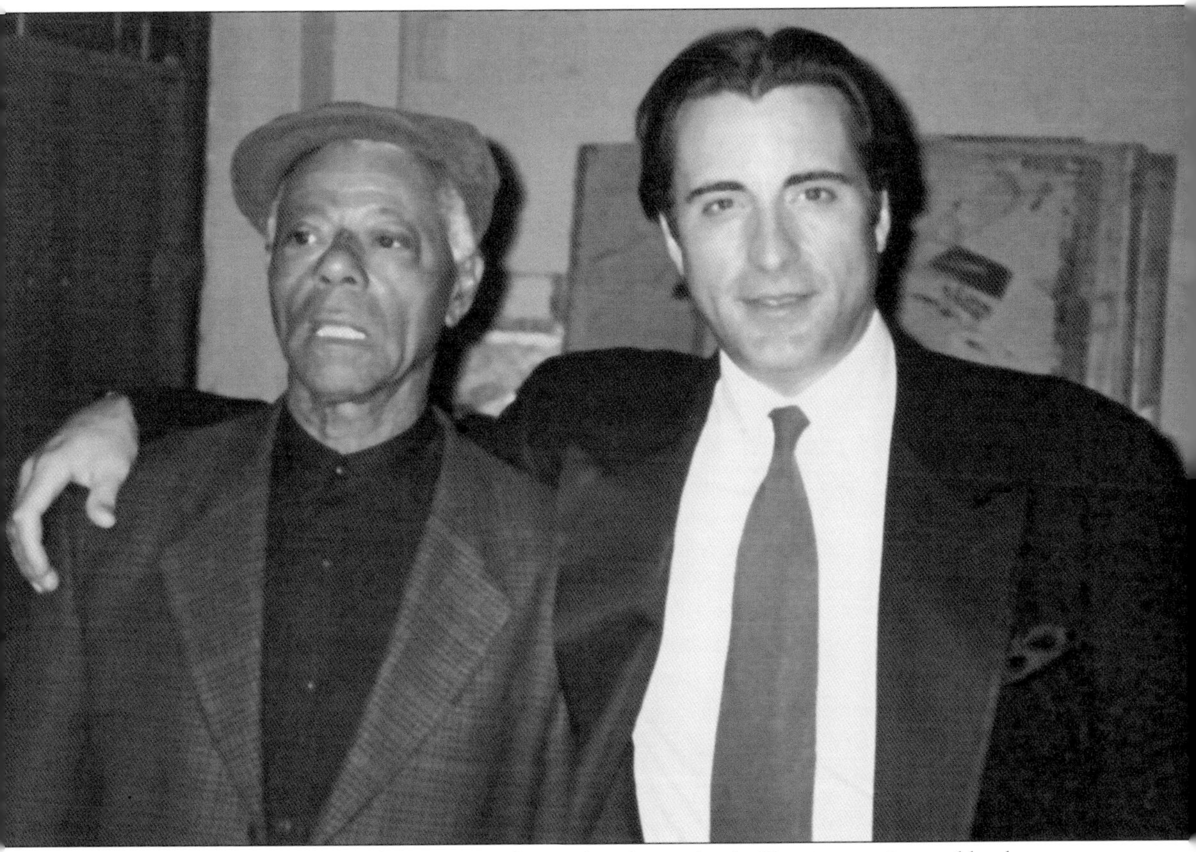

Master percussionist Armando Peraza and actor/producer Andy Garcia are pictured backstage at the Greek Theater in Los Angeles in 1996.

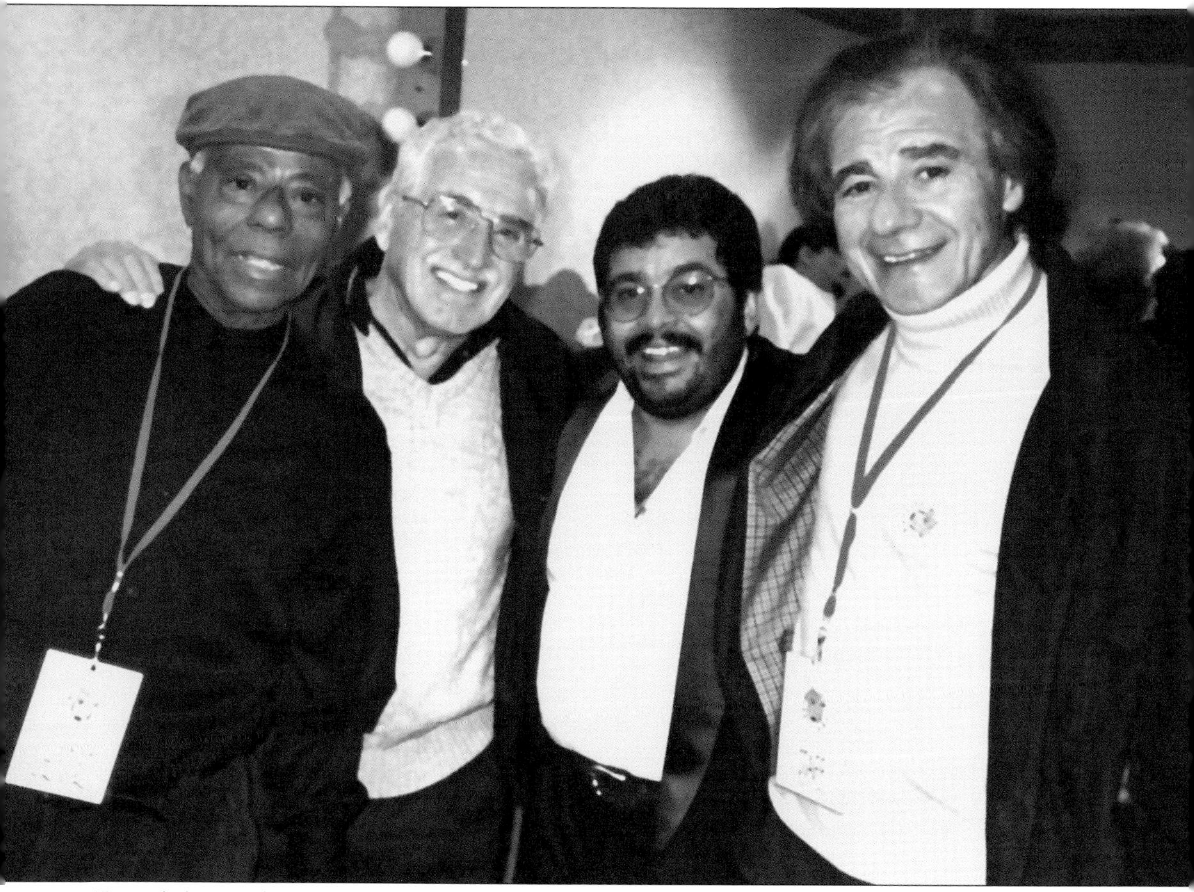

From left to right, Armando Peraza, Jack Costanzo, Giovanni Hidalgo, and composer/arranger Lalo Schifrin are pictured backstage at the Greek Theater in Los Angeles in 1994.

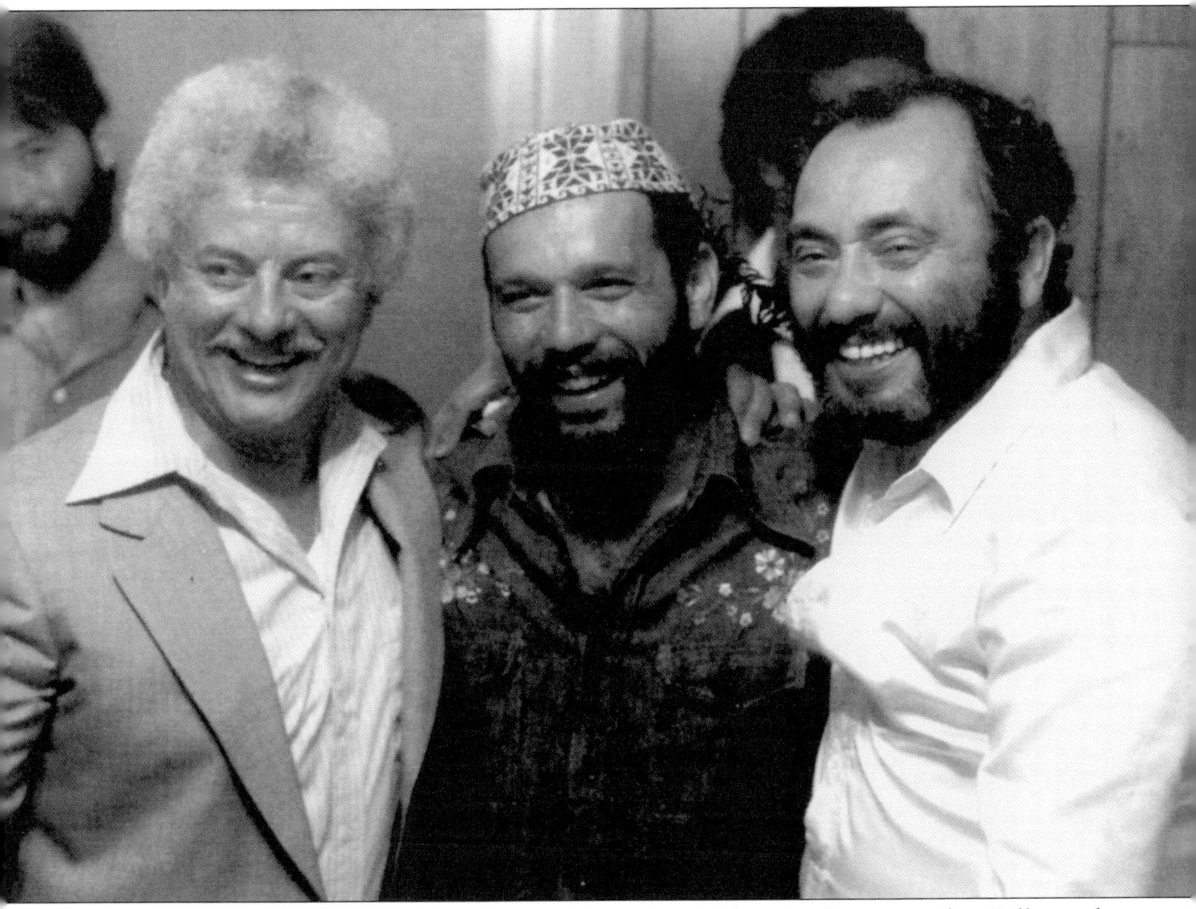

Tito Puente (left) and Eddie Palmieri (right) are pictured here backstage at the Hollywood Palladium in 1984 with Miguel Piñero (center), Puerto Rican playwright, actor, poet, and cofounder of the Nuyorican Poets Café. Before Piñero had reached his 20th birthday, he was a drug addict with a long criminal record. Incarcerated in Sing Sing Prison at the age of 25, Piñero wrote a play called *Short Eyes*, which won much acclaim and the attention of producer Joseph Papp, who put it on Broadway. Nominated for six Tony awards, it went on to win the New York Critics Circle Award and an Obie Award for the "best play of the year." Piñero died from cirrhosis on June 16, 1988.

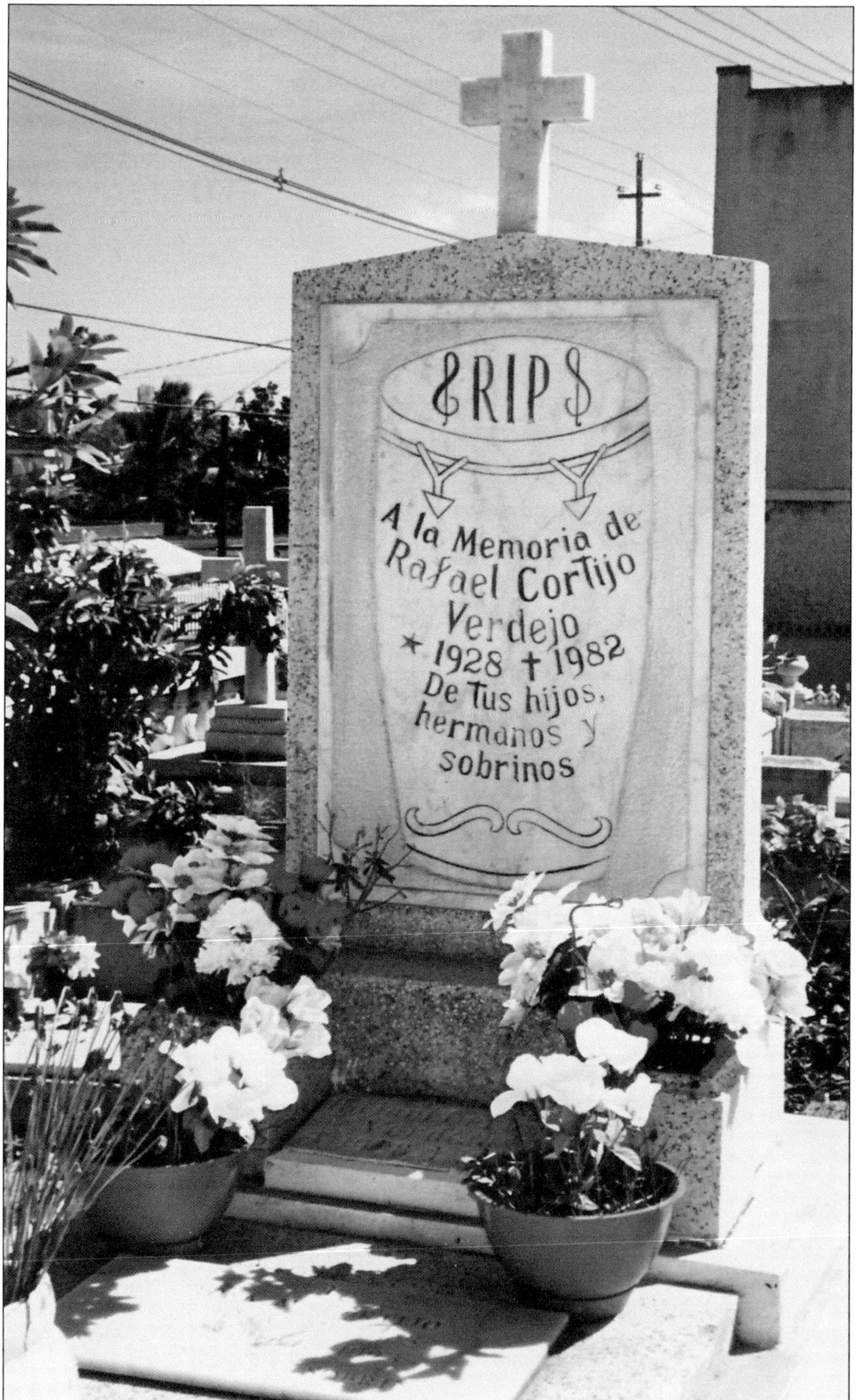

The next two images are the grave sites of Ismael Rivera, who died on May 13, 1987, and Rafael Cortijo, who died on October 3, 1982. These photographs were taken in the year 2000 in the Villa Palmeras Cemetery of Santurce, Puerto Rico.

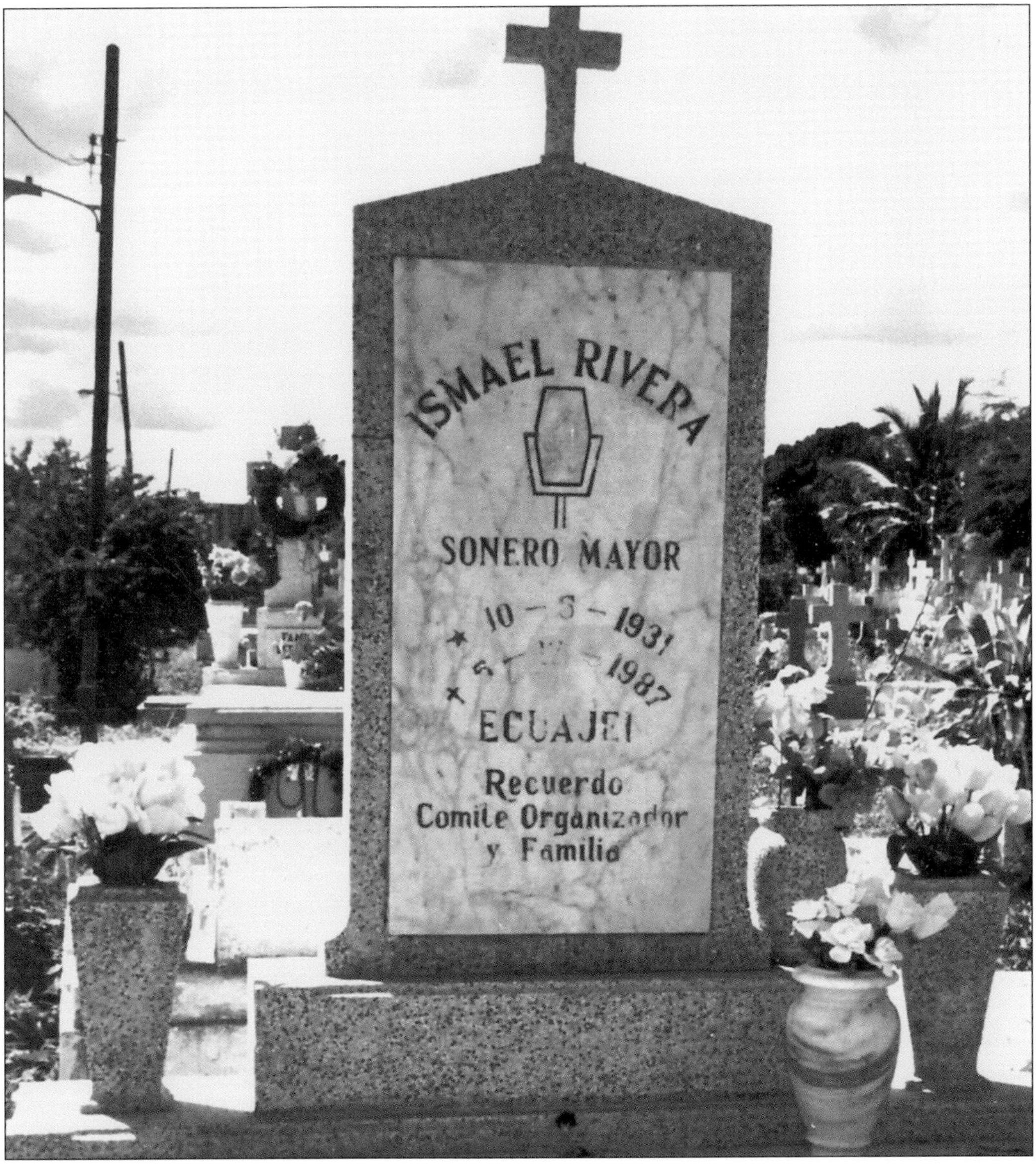

Two of the island's most celebrated musicians, Ismael Rivera and his good friend Rafael Cortijo, left a large Afro Caribbean musical legacy.

Discover Thousands of Local History Books Featuring Millions of Vintage Images

Arcadia Publishing, the leading local history publisher in the United States, is committed to making history accessible and meaningful through publishing books that celebrate and preserve the heritage of America's people and places.

Find more books like this at
www.arcadiapublishing.com

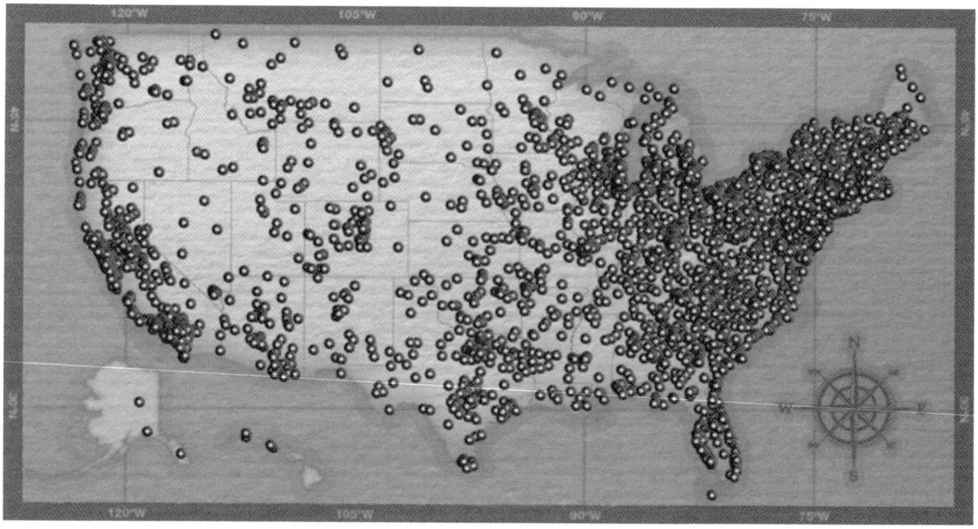

Search for your hometown history, your old stomping grounds, and even your favorite sports team.

Consistent with our mission to preserve history on a local level, this book was printed in South Carolina on American-made paper and manufactured entirely in the United States. Products carrying the accredited Forest Stewardship Council (FSC) label are printed on 100 percent FSC-certified paper.

MADE IN THE USA